Now They Call Me Infidel

Now They Call Me
Infidel

Why I Renounced Jihad
for America, Israel, and
the War on Terror

Nonie Darwish

Sentinel

SENTINEL
Published by the Penguin Group
Penguin Group (USA) Inc., 375 Hudson Street,
New York, New York 10014, U.S.A.
Penguin Group (Canada), 90 Eglinton Avenue East, Suite 700,
Toronto, Ontario, Canada M4P 2Y3
(a division of Pearson Penguin Canada Inc.)
Penguin Books Ltd, 80 Strand, London WC2R 0RL, England
Penguin Ireland, 25 St. Stephen's Green, Dublin 2, Ireland
(a division of Penguin Books Ltd)
Penguin Books Australia Ltd, 250 Camberwell Road, Camberwell,
Victoria 3124, Australia
(a division of Pearson Australia Group Pty Ltd)
Penguin Books India Pvt Ltd, 11 Community Centre, Panchsheel Park,
New Delhi – 110 017, India
Penguin Group (NZ), Cnr Airborne and Rosedale Roads, Albany,
Auckland 1310, New Zealand
(a division of Pearson New Zealand Ltd)
Penguin Books (South Africa) (Pty) Ltd, 24 Sturdee Avenue,
Rosebank, Johannesburg 2196, South Africa

Penguin Books Ltd, Registered Offices:
80 Strand, London WC2R 0RL, England

First published in 2006 by Sentinel,
a member of Penguin Group (USA) Inc.

10   9   8   7   6   5   4   3   2   1

LIBRARY OF CONGRESS CATALOGING IN PUBLICATION DATA

Darwish, Nonie.
   Now they call me infidel : why I renounced jihad for America, Israel, and the war on
terror / Nonie Darwish.
   p.   cm.
   ISBN 1-59523-031-9
   1. Darwish, Nonie.   2. Egyptian American women—Biography.   3. Jihad.   4. Islamic
fundamentalism.   5. War on terrorism, 2001–   6. United States—Politics and govenment—
2001–   I. Title.

   E184.E38D37 2006
   973'.04927620092—dc22
   [B]   2006044360

Printed in the United States of America
Set in Janson Text
Designed by Spring Hoteling

To the memory of my father, Mustafa,
and to my mother, Dureya

Acknowledgments

I want to thank the many people who enriched my life and helped make this book a reality. I thank my husband, Howard, for his help, support, and encouragement; he was the first one to say, "You have a story to tell" at a time when I wanted to block out my past. I am grateful for my children's love and patience with my long hours of work and many days of travel. Thank you, Laura, Shirene, and Omar. Thank you to Pastor Dudley Rutherford, whose inspiring words elevated my spirit. I thank Uncle Abbas Hafez for being there at a time of need. To my dear friends Selma Alpert and Jacqueline Streiter, I appreciate your friendship, guidance, and encouragement. I also wish to thank the staff of Stand With Us and its national director, Roz Rothstein; the staff of the Israel Project and its president, Jennifer Laszlo; and Minnesotans Against Terrorism and its director, Ilan Sharon.

Thanks to Elizabeth Black for her talent and hard work. She guided the project from start to finish, editing and polishing my words. I also very much appreciate the dedication, tireless efforts, and high standards of Lynne Rabinoff, my literary agent, without whom this book would not have seen fruition. I am indebted to my editor, Bernadette Malone, for her belief in and enthusiasm for my project, as well as to the whole team at Sentinel for their expertise.

And finally, I thank all the people who have written to me over the years; their kind words, encouragement, support, and hope have helped sustain me, and are central to the message of this book.

Contents

Now They Call Me Infidel

One | In the Eye of the Storm

When I hear a train whistle, I need only to close my eyes to transport myself to a special time and place—to the mid-1950s in the Sinai desert just outside Gaza.

I am eight years old. I am running through a train in complete, unabashed excitement, making those daring leaps between cars while the train rushes across the desert. We are on our way from Gaza to Cairo to see my grandparents. On the train I can be who I am. I don't have to be so careful. My father is an important man, a military officer in the Egyptian army. We have a special compartment all to ourselves, and the conductor and other staff on the train give us special attention. When I finally settle down to sit and look out the window, all I see is sand and more sand. My sisters and I spot, here and there, familiar groupings of dark Bedouin tents, stark against the white sand, and then we look for the small flocks of sheep and goats tended by Bedouin children and women. Sometimes they turn their backs to us. Other times, they stop to stare as the train passes.

One time our suitcases were all packed and we were ready to leave for the train station in Gaza when we were told the tracks had been bombed, so we had to delay our trip. But this time all is well. We are on our way to Cairo. I love the wonderful, rhythmic choo-choo sound the steam-engine train makes as it chugs across the Sinai. Soon we will cross the Suez Canal and we'll know we are not far away. My excitement builds as I anticipate arriving in the middle of Cairo, a busy, bustling city with its exciting marketplaces, movie theaters, and cafés. And, of course, the best part is knowing how excited my grandparents will be to see us. They will shower us with gifts and attention nonstop—until the moment we have to say good-bye to return to Gaza. And then my grandmother will cry and so will my mother.

My childhood memories of our trips between Gaza and Cairo remain with me today. In the 1950s it was unusual for Egyptians, even middle-class ones, to travel. So our trips took on an air of in-dulgent excursion. It was often joked that many Egyptians—even Cairo residents—live and die without ever seeing the pyramids in Giza, which sit on the outskirts of the city.

While in Cairo, life would be a cascade of family outings, end-less dinners with extended family—uncles, aunts, cousins—and shopping, lots of shopping. We would start with a trip to a large downtown department store to buy fabric to make our clothes—ready-made clothing was not available in Egypt at that time. Then we'd go to the ancient, narrow, connecting streets of Cairo's fa-mous bazaar, called Khan el-Khalili, with its many open-air mar-kets selling spices and perfumes, jewelry, hand-painted pottery, exotic fabrics, and sweet, sticky baklava. There my mother would stock up on her favorite spices. And then we'd have the best shish kebab in all of Cairo at our favorite restaurant, El Dahhan—which still exists today—nestled off an alleyway in the Khan el-Khalili.

The train trips back to Gaza were always less exciting. I remember wishing we could stay in Cairo; I felt so safe there. Even though we were returning to the only home I knew at the time, I was dogged by the feeling that we were going back to a place that was not safe. But, looking on the brighter side, we always returned home with treasures—toys, clothing, and tasty treats that could not be found in Gaza. On one trip, I brought home a wonderful doll imported from Europe that said "Mama" and "Papa." I was thrilled.

On our last train trip back to Gaza—when I was eight years old—the treasure I carried back was a very special birthday gift from my father and mother, a gold necklace and bracelet inscribed with verses from the Koran and blue beads to protect against the "evil eye." As on all the other trips, my mother lectured us about how we must not show off our gifts to other children in Gaza or brag about our trips to Cairo. Any show of pride might provoke envy. My mother and grandmother continually reminded us what the Koran says about *hasad*, which is envy. The evil eye from others, we were told, can take away the good things in life that God gives us. I often saw the old men squatting in the marketplace fingering their blue beads. And now I had the blue beads to protect me as well.

The two things we feared most were the evil eye and Jews. As a child, I was not sure what a Jew was. I had never seen one. All I knew was they were monsters. They wanted to kill Arab children, some said, to drink their blood. I was told never, ever, take candy or fruit from a stranger. It could be a Jew trying to poison me.

My father, Colonel Mustafa Hafez, was a high-ranking intelligence officer in the Egyptian army. I was five years old when President Abdel Nasser assigned him to Gaza and our family moved there. Looking back, I find it hard to believe that Nasser would have put our young, growing family on the frontier of a war zone—or that my mother would have tolerated such a move. But as an obedient Egyptian wife, she knew it was her duty to go with her husband. As did everyone in our culture, she subscribed to the fatalistic view that all was in Allah's hands. At the time, I was the second-oldest among four children—three girls and one boy. Another sister was born while we lived in Gaza, bringing our family to five children. When we arrived in Gaza, we were driven in military vehicles to our home, a lovely villa with a large balcony, trees, and a garden. The house was surrounded by soldiers and security personnel— armed men who often played with us and drove us to school in jeeps and trucks. I fondly remember trips to the beach with all of us children piled into the back of a truck, riding in the open air. Our favorite soldier, Abdel Halim, who often helped with chores around the house, was clowning around for our amusement and fell off the moving truckbed. We had to knock hard on the window of the truck cab to alert the driver we'd lost one passenger in the dust along the road.

My father worked in a building close to our home. As a child, I could tell that despite his being an Egyptian authority figure, he was truly loved, trusted, and respected by the Palestinians. I am told that he treated all people similarly, regardless of rank or social standing.

My father came from a large middle-class Egyptian family. Born in 1920, he fought against the new state of Israel in the War of 1948 when the Jewish state was first established. His father was of Turkish ancestry and his mother's family was rooted in the Egyptian delta. They had a home on a huge lot in the agricultural outskirts of Cairo. I remember many chicken, ducks, and rabbits running around.

In 1952 the Egyptian king Farouk was deposed in a relatively bloodless coup led by a young army officer, Gamal Abdel Nasser, who then became Egypt's president. The charismatic Nasser in-spired Arabs everywhere to dream of the unification of all Arab countries under one government to bring back the "old lost glory" of the Arabs. Nasser's vision, which was firmly linked to hatred of Western imperialism and Zionism, rallied the Arab world into a warlike frenzy. Many people gathered in cafés to listen on the ra-dio to his passionate speeches, heroic defiance of the West, and promises to restore Arab glory. The national anthem of Egypt at the time was *"Wallah Zaman Ya Selahi, Eshtaetelak Fi Kefahi,"* which translates to "I miss and long for my weapons in my struggle and resistance." This cry, along with similar songs on the radio, glorified war and jihad, and expressed love and adoration for the new Arab savior, Nasser. His face was visible everywhere—on posters, in all the newspapers, and in schoolbooks.

Nasser's overriding passion was to destroy Israel and throw her Jewish population into the sea, thereby restoring Arab dignity. He saw Gaza, situated between Egypt and the new State of Israel, as the staging ground for accomplishing this goal. And that is why he sent my father, one of his most trusted officers, to this place.

When we arrived, the relatively small area of the Gaza Strip had begun to explode with population, poverty, and unemployment. The problems were compounded by an Egyptian military administration that did little for the infrastructure of Gaza. Arab politics got in the way of making life easier for the Palestinian refugees. The Arab world wanted to see the Palestinians live in intolerable conditions, pushed against Israel with no place to go, not even allowed to visit other Arab countries without a visa. The thinking was that the worse off the Palestinians were, the more pressure the world would bring to bear on Israel. Furthermore, Egypt discouraged and rejected the relocation of the Gaza refugees into the huge and relatively empty Sinai desert, which might have solved the problems of overcrowding.

I remember my parents taking me along to the Jabalia refugee camp in Gaza. I think we were going there to buy Sham El Nessim eggs, an Arab spring tradition similar to Christian's Easter eggs. These were intricate creations that Palestinian women decorated with colored wax. The Palestinian women also did beautiful needlework, and my mother would buy the lovely table linens they produced. (Today I still have some of these beautiful tablecloths and napkins.) As we walked through the refugee camp, I saw that families were living in makeshift tents. Children were running around with very little clothing and no shoes. I saw women cooking over fires outside the tents. I remember feeling very sad for them, and wondering what they did in the rain. My mother noticed that despite their poverty, Palestinian women were very clean and kept their children cleaner than many of the poor Egyptian peasants.

I recently saw a television newscaster reporting from the Jabalia refugee camp, which still exists today, and was saddened to see it didn't look much better than I remember it as a child—this nearly fifty years later.

My father had been sent into a complicated hotbed of political turmoil. When, in 1948, the United Nations partitioned the British mandate of Palestine into two areas—one a Jewish homeland, the other a Palestinian entity—the Jews declared a state. The Palestinians did not. Instead, Arab countries from all sides invaded Israel to "drive it into the sea." That did not happen. During that war, Egypt took Gaza, and Jordan took the West Bank. But instead of helping Palestinians create a nation, Arab governments chose to keep Palestinians as refugees and use their areas as staging grounds for continuing the attacks and terror against Israel.

The Egyptian regime in Gaza—with support from the whole Arab world—shamed, blamed, bribed, bullied, and abused Palestinians into resisting and fighting Israel. Palestinians were made to feel that they needed to prove they were worthy of the respect of the rest of the Arab world. I once heard Egyptian visitors in our home criticize the Palestinians as being traitors to the Arab cause for having sold out to Israel because they did not show *enough* resistance. They said, "Palestinians went right back to work after Israel became a state like nothing happened. We Egyptians have to get them out of their fields and businesses and start their resistance."

Indeed, Gaza Palestinians were accustomed to visiting relatives, trading and selling goods, even taking jobs in Jaffa or other Arab areas in what was now Israel. And some were quite willing to sneak across the cease-fire line to continue doing what they had always done. Some even crossed the border to terrorize, rob, and loot Israelis. But now the Arabs of Gaza were forbidden by Egypt from crossing into and out of Israel, and those who did so were accused of violating what was called the *hudna* line, a temporary cease-fire line. Those who were caught crossing were accused of being traitors or spies. Some were killed on the spot. Others were arrested by the Egyptian military authorities and jailed for five to ten years. Their crimes were called violating the *hudna* border line.

Furthermore, within Gaza society, political subcurrents made it difficult for the Egyptian leadership in Gaza. At that time, Gaza had two dominant political ideologies that were at odds with each other (they would eventually work hand in hand)—the Muslim Brotherhood, which was legal, and the Communist Party, which was not. The Muslim Brotherhood, a radical Islamic group, which originated in Egypt and was headquartered in Cairo, attempted to assassinate Nasser in 1955 because he was deemed too secular. That resulted in retaliatory arrests, jailings, and the murder of many Muslim Brotherhood members all over Egypt. Muslim Brotherhood members in Gaza were also brutally treated, arrested, and jailed by the Egyptian authorities.

In addition to being unable to cross the border into Israeli areas, Gaza residents were also prohibited from crossing into Egypt, even though at the time Gaza was technically part of Egypt. Trapped in this narrow strip under Nasser's oppressive military regime, the people in Gaza revolted. The resulting violent confrontation with the Egyptian authorities in 1955 was called an intifada. Slogans were shouted and posted against Nasser and his Egyptian military dictatorship. Both the Communists and Muslim Brotherhood now became totally illegal, and both groups began working together in underground cooperation against their common enemy. They demanded that the Egyptian military governor, Brigadier Abdallah Refaat, allow more freedoms and end the arrests of members from both groups. They also demanded more border patrols to protect Palestinian civilians from getting caught in the middle as casualties of Egypt's military operations against Israel. Egypt, at that time, was employing its own military forces against Israel. But Palestinian civilians bore the brunt of the casualties whenever Israel hit back. To quell the rebellion, the Egyptian governor promised the Palestinians more freedoms and greater protection.

However, arrests and jailing of the political opposition in Gaza continued. And many Palestinians felt betrayed when the Egyptian governor did not keep his promises. Finally, seeking to improve his image in Gaza, Nasser formed a "Palestinian army" composed of local Arabs. The Egyptian administration said if they don't like our attacks on Israel, then let them—the Gaza citizens—do it.

In 1955 President Nasser visited Gaza to launch the Palestinian fedayeen ("freedom") movement under the direction of the young head of his intelligence operations in Gaza, Mustafa Hafez, my father. My father, loved, trusted, and respected by the Arabs of Gaza, was the right choice for Nasser. He was given a mission by Nasser to mobilize the first fedayeen unit, made up of fifty-two men, specially hand-picked Gaza Arabs, to conduct both overt and covert guerrilla-style operations inside Israeli territory to cause as much death and destruction as possible.

At the same time, to support my father's activities, working from the Egyptian embassy in Jordan, another figure was chosen to organize fedayeen raids into Israel from its eastern border. His name was Salah Mustafa. Over the next two years, Israel's security would be seriously threatened by the fedayeen activities of both my father and Salah Mustafa.

My father convinced the Egyptian war minister Abdel Hakim Amer to allow him to draw from the prison population of Palestinians as a way of showing compassion and quelling unrest in Gaza. And so my father built the ranks of the fedayeen by freeing young Palestinians who had been jailed for crossing into Israel. All fifty-two of the first unit came from jail. (It is likely that solved another problem—a shortage of volunteers.) Needless to say, his freeing of jailed young men endeared my father to many Palestinian families. I remember Palestinian women coming to our home to plead with my mother to use her influence with my father to have their sons freed as well. While my mother had deep sympathy for these women, she had to explain that she had no control over who my father picked for his fedayeen ranks.

Attempting to fully integrate into Gaza society, my siblings and I were sent to elementary schools in Gaza. The other children liked my Egyptian accent and treated me as though I had descended from heaven—I suppose they thought that coming from Cairo was impressive—though I often wondered if they would still feel that way if they knew of Cairo's rampant poverty and misery. I secretly liked the attention, this feeling of being "special"; however, I struggled not to show it, ever mindful of the evil eye. The hatred of Israel and our obligation to pursue jihad was somehow worked into every subject we discussed in school. In fact, clearly, the main goal of our education was to instill a commitment to destroy Israel. Peace was never discussed as an option, and we were made to feel that peace with Israel would bring only shame to our Arab pride.

Because of this, the word "Jew" instilled terror and dread into the core of my very being, even though I had never seen a Jew. Even our nursery rhymes and games were something about Jews being dogs. I sang these little songs all the time when I played with my girlfriends. In school, Jews were portrayed as devils, pigs, and an evil, occupying foreign force. We were never told of the Jewish roots in the region. With tears running down their cheeks, older girls whom I admired would stand in front of the class and recite stirring poems pledging jihad, declaring their willingness to give up their lives for the land, and promising to kill the Jewish enemies of God. The sight of these girls in tears had a very powerful effect on the rest of us children.

In fact, we were all required to recite anti-Jewish poetry daily. After reciting the poetry, some said, "May God bless us with *shahada*." The word *shahid* means "martyr." It is the highest honor bestowed on a Muslim and absolutely guarantees entrance to heaven. Shahaida can be achieved by being killed during jihad against the perceived enemies of Islam. Jews, we were told, killed Arab children and pregnant Arab women, and always broke treaties with Arabs. They were hated by God and should be exterminated.

We were taught that nothing was more sacred than the land, not even our own lives or our parents. The words "death" and "kill" were in many poems. We were expected to memorize such poetry without missing a word. Once, when I could not remember one such poem, the principal took me to her office and tried to make me memorize it by force, and when I could not, she hit my hand with a ruler. I went home crying that day.

Our education in Gaza was no different than anywhere else in the Arab world, though perhaps it was more intense, because just over the cease-fire line north of Gaza were the dreaded enemies of God. Our education bred fear, anger, jihad, and extreme criticism and rivalry of other religions. We accepted it and thought it was normal since it came from adults we trusted, from our educators, and was heard on the radio, and in the mosques. It was our whole culture. Even the games I played with the neighborhood children involved danger and violence in general. In one game, children brought knives from their kitchens and flipped them in the air. The one whose knife landed straight down in the sand was the winner. A knife once landed too close to me and I ran home.

I had an independent streak in me. Perhaps it was because I spent time with my maternal grandparents, who were modern, urban Egyptians. Others say I was born with an irrepressible curiosity. I once naively asked the question: "Why do we hate Jews?" The response: "Aren't you a Muslim?" My teacher's answer, delivered in the harshest of tones, was that "people who doubt are traitors and will go to hell." I didn't like the harsh criticism if I did not agree with the conventional wisdom. But I realized that in the Arab world you are either the oppressed or the oppressor. I did not want to be with the oppressed, and I didn't want to oppress, so I ended up pretending. I learned to be more circumspect, justifiably fearing that the same anger and hatred directed against Jews could also be turned on me.

When, on January 16, 1956, Nasser vowed a renewed offensive to destroy Israel, the pressure on my father to step up operations increased. More fedayeen groups were organized, and their training expanded to other areas of the Gaza Strip. Often my father was gone for days at a time. In an attempt to end the terror, Israel sent its commandos one night to our heavily guarded home. My father was not at home that night, and the Israelis found only women and children—my mother, two maids, and five small children. The commandos left us unharmed. I personally did not even wake up or know of the incident until later in life, when I read a book written about my father. After I read it, I called my mother immediately, and she confirmed the story. The Israelis chose not kill us even though the Egyptian-organized fedayeen *did* kill Israeli civilians, women, and children.

As a result of this incident, Abdel Halim, the young Egyptian soldier assigned to our home—the one who fell off the truck on the way to the beach, the one we children loved because he played with us—suddenly disappeared. No one would tell me why he didn't come back. I later learned that he was accused of treason and killed in jail. To this day, I don't know if the accusation against Halim was true.

My father must have understood the personal dangers he faced. (It was said there was a large sum of money offered to anyone who would kill him.) Perhaps that is why he always slept with a pistol under his pillow.

After serving Nasser for several years on the front line of Gaza, my father, weary of his job and increasingly worried about our family's safety, requested a transfer to Cairo. Nasser approved his request but asked my father to stay in his old post for just a few more weeks until a suitable replacement could be found.

During the spring of 1956, the situation in Gaza grew ever more precarious. We often heard the loud explosions of shelling in the night. I would crawl under the bed, thinking it would protect me, my whole body shaking with fear. I prayed to Allah to save us from this horrible place. I longed for the safety of Cairo and my grandmother's home. One morning after a particularly frightening night, my mother comforted us by explaining that soon my father would be transferred to Cairo.

But for our sake, most of the time our parents tried to foster a sense of normalcy. There were pleasant distractions—trips to the beach and frequent outings to the neighborhood movie theater. What a magical place it was. I loved the movies—the handsome Egyptian movie stars, the glamorous screen actresses, the music. During a particularly exhilarating scene featuring belly dancers, I got up from my seat, imitating the dancers' movements, and was pulled down quickly by my horribly embarrassed father. "Only bad, bad women become belly dancers," he whispered harshly. But we loved to watch anyway.

We were two weeks away from leaving Gaza. Nasser had finally agreed on a date for my father's reassignment. It was rumored that my father would be elevated to Chief of Intelligence for all of Egypt. Soon we would be able to move into the villa my father was building in the Heliopolis section of Cairo. On our last trip, we had visited the house. It was nearing completion.

On July 11, 1956, my father dropped off my sisters and me at the movie theater, leaving us with members of his security detail, and then drove on to his office, taking my four-year-old brother with him. Shortly thereafter, we heard an explosion. Engrossed in our movie, we thought little of it. Such noises were common in Gaza. But a few minutes later, security personnel came running into the theater and pulled us out, rushing us home. Everyone was very nervous. But no one explained anything. When we got home, I saw my mother crying uncontrollably, surrounded by other officers' wives. When I asked where my father was, at first no one would give me an answer. Finally someone explained to me that he had been hurt in an explosion and was in the hospital. My little brother had also been injured, but not seriously. The next morning we were rushed to the military airport to be flown to Cairo. "Where is my father? Is he not coming with us?"

My mother said he would come later.

My last trip from Gaza to Cairo was on a military airplane instead of a train. I had never been on a plane before. But the event was surrounded by so much trauma that I remember little of it. Everything was in confusion. The next day at my grandmother's house I noticed everyone was dressed in black, and women were crying and wailing. That is when I began to understand that something very bad had happened to my father. Still no one would tell me. I insisted on an answer. Finally my mother blurted out, "Your father is dead."

My father had been killed by a parcel containing a bomb specifically targeted for him. It was brought into his office by a Palestinian courier, who was also injured in the blast. My four-year-old brother witnessed the whole event but was only slightly wounded. My father had been taken to the hospital after the blast but died of his injuries hours later. He was only thirty-five years old.

My father was hailed a shahid.

My mother, a young and strikingly beautiful Egyptian woman with her whole life in front of her—a woman with five children, the youngest only six months old—was suddenly widowed. We children were disoriented and confused. Even though I was the second oldest of the children, at eight years old I did not really comprehend the finality of death.

The funeral for an Arab military hero—a shahid—is an elaborate and long-drawn-out event with an intense mourning period lasting forty days. We children were taken to a neighbor's house during the Cairo funeral, which was held at my grandparents' home in a large tent decorated with Koranic inscriptions. The grown-ups did not want us children to hear the wailing or see the intense mourning common for funerals in Egypt. Being the kind of child I was, I resolutely refused to go to the neighbor's house. I wanted to stay with my mother; clearly she needed me. Furthermore, I wanted to be part of what was going on, even if I couldn't understand it. This was, after all, my father. But in a culture where children are to be seen and not heard, the family insisted that I be sent off, so I was practically dragged kicking and screaming to the neighbor's house.

In the days following, a steady stream of people, many of them military officers who had worked with my father, flowed in and out of my grandparents' house, as they came to pay their respects to our family. Repeatedly they would tell us children how proud we should be for being the family of a shahid. How lucky we were that my father was now guaranteed a place in heaven forever, they would say. It all washed over me for it made no sense. I didn't want to be the daughter of a shahid. I just wanted my father back.

In the midst of this mourning period, we moved into an apartment in Heliopolis while we waited for the family villa to be completed. One day a representative of the presidency came to us to announce that President Nasser was coming to visit us. That day, the excitement in our neighborhood was palpable. Word had circulated that he was coming, and the street was full of security personnel. Then President Gamal Abdel Nasser arrived at our home to extend his condolences to my mother. I remember sitting on his lap as he praised my father as a hero and promised that Egypt would retaliate. Then he, or perhaps it was one of his officers, turned to us children—we ranged in age from nine years to six months—and asked which one of us would avenge our father's death by killing Jews.

For an instant, the room fell silent.

Nasser was a very popular leader. People adored and worshiped him. I remember everyone cheering for the Egyptian leader as he ceremoniously walked down the street after leaving our home. Nasser's visit was considered a great honor by my mother and the whole family, one we would cherish for a long time. He handed my mother a medal, the Star of Honor, the highest military award, in recognition of my father's services. To this day, it remains in my mother's closet.

The Egyptian president then traveled to Gaza to attend an elaborate military funeral ceremony held there for my father. We did not go but were told that large crowds of the Palestinian people were weeping, wailing, and chanting my father's name. He was much loved and adored by the Palestinians of Gaza, and to this day there is a high school there named Mustafa Hafez, as well as a street that bears his name. The death of a martyr always has the same effect. The anger in Gaza and Egypt seethed, and the culture of retaliation was intensified by his death.

On July 26, 1956, Nasser addressed the Egyptian nation and spoke about my father's death, passionately elocuting his plans for retaliation against Israel. In that same speech, a very famous speech, he nationalized the Suez Canal, an act that led to the major war in 1956 of Egypt against France, Great Britain, and Israel.

But I didn't comprehend or care about the ramifications of my father's death. All I knew was that my father was taken from me. I resented the "honor" of martyrdom, I resented the heaven he had gone to. We needed him more than heaven did. It wasn't fair. At the same time, I felt intensely guilty about these feelings, since God expected us to embrace jihad. So I kept those feelings buried deep inside myself.

The fortieth day after death is marked by another gathering and round of mourning. Once again, family, friends, neighbors, military comrades of my father, and all manner of other well-wishers paraded through the house. On that day, my grandmother, who had functioned as the pillar of strength through the last forty days, began to quietly cry while talking to me about my father's death. And since I still could not comprehend the meaning of death, I asked her, "But when will he be back?"

And then my grandmother wept even harder.

A Koranic verse describing how Allah gives life and sustenance to martyrs was repeatedly recited during my father's funeral, at his burial site, and again at this forty-day commemoration. It would also be repeated on each anniversary of his death. Translated, it is as follows:

But do not think of those who have been slain in God's cause as dead. Nay, they are alive! With their Sustainer have they their sustenance. (3:169)

Recited in Arabic, this verse is very powerful and poetic, and reassured us that my father was in good hands in heaven as a martyr. I always cried hearing it, especially when recited by Muslim sheikhs in their beautiful, hypnotic, classical Arabic. It gave me a feeling that heaven is a beautiful place and better than life.

I am eight years old. We do not talk about my father—the tragedy is still too painful. It is as if he never existed. I try to hold on to his memory. But I remember less and less about him. Many nights in our new home I cannot sleep. I awaken in the middle of the night and steal out of my bed and slip into the living room. Alone in the living room while everyone else is sleeping, I look at a picture of my father on the wall. It is a very official-looking military portrait of him in his uniform. He is looking straight at me. I move to the right. His eyes follow me. I move to the left. His eyes follow me. I run back to my room, and I am crying quietly, trying not to awaken anyone. When I finally fall asleep, I slip into a dream—a recurring dream in which my father is on a train pulling out of some unknown station. Does he see me? I don't know. As the train gains speed, I am chasing after it, calling for my father. But no matter how fast I run, I cannot catch up with the train. It disappears with my father into the landscape.

TWO

Growing Up in Cairo

L ife was suddenly very different without my father. We now lived in a temporary apartment in the crowded city of Cairo while we waited for our villa to be finished. The villa, a project that my father had been so excited about, was being built in an exclusive new neighborhood in Heliopolis reserved for military officers.

A few months after my father's death, the people who had crowded our home congratulating us for our father's heroic sacrifice and fawning over our exalted shahid status disappeared. They were nowhere to be found. We felt so alone. No father, no security guards, no drivers, no army-provided cooks or servants, none of the military pampering we had grown accustomed to. All we had of my father was the Star of Honor, tucked away in a closet, given to my mother by President Nasser when he visited us, and a large photograph of my father on the wall in the great room. My mother gathered us around and explained to the five of us—all girls with the exception of my four-year-old brother—that because we were living in a home without a man we could no longer do many of the activities that we used to do when my father was alive. I did not really understand what that meant.

As my mother became withdrawn and severely depressed after my father's death, we children were cared for by two live-in maids. One of them, by the name of Awatef, had come with us from Gaza. My mother would sometimes disappear into her room for days without coming out. It was a depression that would consume her for much of the rest of her life. Nasser's—and indeed my whole culture's—obsession with destroying Israel had deprived me not only of my father but also of my mother.

In the beginning, as the family of a shahid, we received a generous pension from the government that enabled my mother to send us to the best private schools. She enrolled my sisters and me in St. Clare's College, a British Catholic school in the heart of Cairo run by English nuns. There was no stigma attached to going to a Christian school; in fact, it was quite the opposite. St. Clare's was an exclusive school favored by Cairo's upper classes. Half the students were Muslim. The nuns provided the usual British education— literature, science, math—and in the afternoons, while the Catholic students received their religious instruction, an Islamic teacher came in to teach us the Koran. The Islamic teacher made us memorize and recite verses from the Koran and told stories of how Allah brought victory to Muhammad in his battles against the infidels. And then we returned to our regular classes, where the kind, sweet, "infidel" nuns resumed their instruction.

Before Nasser's revolution, Egypt had many first-class private schools run by English, French, and German educators. However, within a few years, Nasser would nationalize these schools, give them Arabic names, and send the nuns packing. I was privileged to catch the last years of this great British education.

I remember that first day at St. Clare's. My mother was very touched, and, in fact, broke into tears when the nuns, aware of our family's great loss, told her they were praying for her. From the first day, I felt very comfortable and surrounded by love there among people who spoke a different language, with a different religion, and who came from a foreign land. They showed us a peaceful kind of love that wants nothing in return. It was a great comfort.

St. Clare's was very different from Egyptian public schools and the Gaza school I had attended. Unlike at Gaza schools, at my private British school we were never taught hatred. A bad word was never uttered about any group or any religion. Instead, we were taught subjects such as Shakespeare and English poetry.

St. Clare's uniform was similar to the attire of the French children's book character Madeline. We wore blue skirts, white blouses, straw hats in summer and wool hats in the winter. Our day was very structured. When we arrived in the morning, we lined up, and with a polite curtsy began the day by saying "Good morning, Sister." Then we deposited our hats on our designated shelf and filed quietly to our desks. We were always very polite and proper. I loved the structure. In retrospect, it probably helped me get some control over my shattered life and chaotic feelings of loss.

One of the great shocks to my system was the terrible poverty I saw around me in crowded Cairo. Egyptian society has a small, powerful, privileged class and a middle class that is poor by Western standards. But the vast majority of the population is poor, and many are *extremely* poor—the kind of poverty that breaks one's heart. Beggars are very common on Cairo streets. Many of them are children; others are old, handicapped, blind, or missing limbs. None had a wheelchair. The handicapped beggars would lie helpless on the sidewalk with hands outstretched.

Poverty in some parts of Egypt was worse than what I'd seen in the refugee camps of Gaza. We were told that the Jews caused the poverty in Gaza. But what about the poverty in Egypt, I once asked my mother, was that also caused by the Jews? I don't remember what she answered. It did not matter how rich or privileged one was, if you lived in Egypt you could not avoid seeing and dealing with extreme poverty daily. As a child, I used to cry to my mother and grandmother when I saw children begging, without shoes or adequate clothing and malnourished. I remember a school function when I entered the kitchen and saw the waiters eating the leftovers on our plates. It suddenly struck me that the people serving us were hungry.

Living in a society that had this degree of poverty has an impact on everyone, rich and poor. The rich had to go through elaborate behaviors to protect their wealth from petty theft, burglary, and, even more important, from the evil eye. When out in public, at restaurants, hotels, shopping areas, or even simply out on the street, one would often be approached by people who wanted to help for *bakshish*, meaning "tips." Beggars surrounded mosques especially, because they knew people were more likely to give to the poor near a mosque.

My mother was always very touched by the poverty she saw around her. She frequently gave food and clothing to the poor. When my mother gave old clothes to poor women, they wanted to kiss her hands. One time my mother made a large batch of sandwiches for the poor and sent us with a driver to the famous Sayyedna El-Hussein Mosque. As the driver handed out sandwiches, people on all sides suddenly surrounded our car. Some were knocking at the window for food. After the driver finished distributing the sandwiches, he started slowly driving out of the crowd. I was afraid we might hit someone, since people were still circling the car. I remember looking out the back window behind me at the crowd of hungry people as we drove away and saw an old woman in black running behind our car with her hand extended in a desperate gesture. A small child behind her was calling out that she did not get any food. This scene of human suffering made an indelible impression on me. I cried uncontrollably all the way home. Even today I vividly remember the old woman running after us.

Our family buried our pain in those first few months after my father's death by not talking about him. However, we visited my father's grave site in the national military cemetery regularly, especially on Muslim feast days. My mother would prepare a large basket with baked goods, and we would head to the cemetery to spend a half day there. My father's family would sometimes meet us there and give each one of us money, a custom during Muslim feasts. While we were at the grave site poor children would come to beg or sell us something—always very politely, respectful of our mourning—and temporarily I would forget my loss, and my heart would ache for them. My mother always gave them money and baked sweets.

This fenced-in military cemetery is surrounded by a larger cemetery, now known as the City of the Dead, because today it is filled with squatters, destitute people who have moved into the mausoleums, creating a dense district of poverty and crime.

There were some moments of respite from our loneliness and feelings of isolation in that first year. One day a man from Gaza came to visit us with gifts. We were very excited to see him. I saw a tear in his eye when he greeted us. Our old faithful Egyptian driver and cook from Gaza also visited my mother and offered their services. And they began to come by occasionally. Their presence was a great comfort to my mother and was greeted with great excitement by us children. Our old cook, Mahmoud, was promoted to head cook at the home of the head of the Egyptian military, Mushier Abdel Hakim Amer, who was a friend of my father. Mahmoud often told us stories of how Nasser and Amer were like brothers and gathered on holidays with their children, and he cooked for them all. But despite his important new position, Mahmoud managed to come and cook for my mother for special events. On those occasions, I was overjoyed to see him and spent hours in the kitchen helping—mostly for the purpose of talking to him. For me, it was somehow a way to be a part of my father. Mahmoud was a part of our family all his life until he died a decade ago. I was especially happy when our old driver would also visit and take us in a van to one of the small branches of the Nile River and let us run loose. It reminded me of the good old days when they took us to the beautiful beaches of Gaza to play. Their visits were bittersweet.

Not everyone had forgotten about us.

We had been in Cairo only a couple of months when the 1956 war broke out. Nasser nationalized the Suez Canal—in that same speech in which he had praised my father's sacrifice. The move shocked and angered the British and French, who were part owners of the canal. Nasser's bold move held the potential to throw the whole world into crisis. If Nasser began denying access to the canal, international commerce was in jeopardy. Much of the oil the West depended on traveled down the Suez Canal. France and Great Britain attacked. Furthermore, Israel joined the war against Egypt in an attempt to end the Egyptian-led fedayeen raids into its territory.

Our apartment was very close to a military airport, and the shelling and bombing began. It was Gaza all over again, but without the protection of a father and his ever-present military security detail. My sense of safety was shattered. No place on earth felt safe to me anymore. I remember my mother gathered us five children on a prayer rug in the middle of the living room and started praying. We could hear the shells hitting our building as her desperate pleas to Allah resonated in the room. The next morning we saw several holes in our building. An air force plane, shot down during the battle, lay in pieces in the middle of the street only a block from our apartment.

In the weeks to follow, due to pressure from both the United States and the Soviet Union, the British and the French withdrew, their demands unanswered by Nasser. Israel did achieve its goal of ending the fedayeen attacks on its border, and in return, the Israelis withdrew from the Sinai desert. As part of the settlement, United Nations troops were placed on the borders between Gaza and Israel to prevent further fedayeen attacks from Gaza.

President Nasser then declared the negotiated end to hostilities a glorious "victory" over the three evil imperialist nations. No mention was made on the Arab street that the United States and the Soviet Union had actually orchestrated the withdrawal. Nor were we told that Egypt's casualties had numbered in the thousands. Nasser's hero status increased among all Arab nations. His lack of compromise was regarded as a symbol of Arab power against the West.

After the war ended, the bunkers near our apartment were left open for months. With few safe places to play except for some small grassy areas in the center of the street, we neighborhood children commonly played next to the bunkers. While playing hide-and-seek one day, I fell into one of the bunkers and hit my forehead on a rock. I apparently was unconscious for a few minutes. I had to endure several stitches to my bleeding forehead, without anesthesia, and to this day bear the scars to remind me of it.

Eleven months after arriving in Cairo, our lovely new villa was finished, and we finally moved in. To live in a villa—the Middle East's term for a detached, freestanding family dwelling—was very unusual in Egypt, something only the upper classes could afford. Our neighborhood was filled with important people. The head of Egyptian intelligence, Salah Nasr, was our next-door neighbor. He held the post my father had been promised before his assassination. The neighborhood was mostly made up of army officers, who in Nasser's Egypt had become the most privileged class in Egyptian society. They were given their own neighborhoods, country clubs, and many other economic perks.

Our street was named after a martyr who had fallen in the 1956 war. One day, shortly after moving in, as I was walking in the neighborhood, I noticed that all the streets had been renamed after martyrs. I was by then aware of and had visited a major commercial street in Alexandria named after my father. And suddenly it hit me. I recognized that behind each street name was a grieving family such as ours. I was filled with horror as I ran through the neighborhood. Burning in me, something I usually kept hidden, was a deep resentment against the very idea of jihad, for it had taken my father from me. Jihad also took the life of all these men and orphaned and widowed their families. I wondered if any of them felt as I did.

My mother had always been dependent on my father and military drivers for transportation. At some point, fed up with our isolation, she did something very brave and gutsy. In the 1950s very few Egyptian women drove cars, but my mother was no ordinary woman. She started taking driving lessons. Then she bought a small German-made car. She would load us—four young children plus an infant—into the car and take us places. Unfortunately, Egyptian society at that time was critical of a young widow of a shahid driving. Even some family members disapproved. My mother was hurt by the criticism and the gossip that ensued, but that did not deter her. And we children did not care, since we loved the freedom the car gave us. We immediately went on vacation to Alexandria and even took our cat with us. The cat was terrified under the seat of the car.

The car was too small for all of us, and my mother had to stop to stretch many times along the desert road to Alexandria. But we kids did not mind being jammed into the car. We were so excited to be on our way to Alexandria, a great vacation spot. On that trip, as well as many other outings to follow, male drivers would honk at my mother, and some would even shout out compliments. My mother would pay no attention. She quickly learned to hold her own in the crazy streets of Cairo, where no one follows traffic rules. That was the first and last car my mother owned for a long time.

That summer of 1957, when my mother packed us into the little car and headed to Alexandria, she rented—and would later buy—an apartment by a beach called Miami. We spent the whole summer vacation there and returned almost every following summer. My mother still owns this apartment. Our yearly trip to the beach was an act of defiance and bravery. My mother was determined that she would give her girls and young son a semblance of normalcy.

But she did not claim any of that for herself. After my father's death, she was expected to sacrifice her life as well. Society expected the widows of martyrs to live to please society and their children but never to pursue personal happiness. There was no actual prohibition against a widow of a shahid remarrying. It was just that society looked upon it as somehow inappropriate, as if it would dishonor the memory of the martyr. She was to have no life of her own other than that of being a mother and a keeper of the home. Unmarried women are not to mix with men, date, or engage in any fun activities. Single women, widows, and divorcées are looked upon with a critical eye by neighbors and acquaintances. Their honor is everybody else's honor, especially their male relatives'. Martyrdom was not just on the battlefield or against an enemy, but became a Muslim lifestyle for many women who struggled to refrain from doing anything to bring shame to the memory of their martyred husband or his children. An aunt once mentioned an Arab saying, "The back of a man is stronger support than the back of concrete." She complained to us of how her status in society was diminished after her husband died. My mother struggled very hard in a difficult period of Egyptian society in the 1950s and '60s, trying to please society. This took a toll on her happiness. I remember my mother remarking to other women while they watched their children swimming on Alexandria's Miami beach, "Don't you wish we could be a kid again so we could put on our bathing suits and swim all day?"

One woman replied, "We wish, but if we did, we'd all be divorced tomorrow and even strangers would look down upon us as loose women." All they could do was walk along the shoreline fully clothed, wetting their feet in the waves and wishing for what they could not do. None of these women were able to swim with their children.

Despite her occasional sparks of independence and defiance, my mother remained alone and emotionally vulnerable much of the time. In a clanlike, family-oriented society, practically no social structure of support exists for widows outside their families. One's strength and social life comes only from family and especially from male relatives whose role it is to serve as protector. My mother had only one brother, and he worked far away in Kuwait, and her father was too old to help much. And for reasons I cannot even today comprehend, my mother kept her distance from my father's family.

Despite the crowded cities of the Middle East and the closeness of living conditions, people—especially women—are isolated from one another by strict codes and rituals of behavior. There is no genuine social cohesion. People were more concerned with appearances and impressing one another than with genuine interaction. For one thing, the culture is dominated by the idea that "I will be cursed by people who will envy me" to the point of paranoia. People have to keep their distance, sometimes even from their own family members, in defense from the evil eye. We often heard the saying, *"Dari ala shametik te kid,"* meaning, "Hiding your candle will keep it bright." Because of the fear of the evil eye, we rarely heard people expressing happiness over an event. The lyrics to the most famous wedding song in Egypt are, *"Ein el hasoud fiha oud ya halawa; Aris amar we arousto nakawa; We ehna elleladi kidna el aadi,"* meaning, "May the eye of the envious be poked, hallelujah. The groom is beautiful and bride well chosen; Tonight we have teased the enemy and the envious."

While one is continually reminded that envy is mentioned in the Koran, it is never discussed as a sin that hurts the person who is envious, but as a curse that one has to be on guard against. Some even went as far as keeping good news secret and wearing blue beads as protection from the evil eye. My mother, despite her Westernized attitudes, often burned incense called bukhour in our house to ward off the evil eye.

A second factor preventing social cohesion arose directly from Muslim marriage laws. Relationships among Muslim women outside the family are superficial and extremely competitive, because according to Islamic law, sharia, husbands can have up to four wives. Befriending a woman outside of your family—especially a young, beautiful widow—could bring temptation to one's husband. So the wives of other army officers who were once my mother's friends disappeared. Just when she needed it the most, all the emotional support was jerked out from under her. She was now a threat to other women.

Polygamy is accepted practice in Islamic society. However, unlike in Saudi Arabia, where taking multiple wives is common and open, in Egypt second marriages are usually in secret. And they tend to be more common among affluent men. This religiously sanctioned polygamy utterly destroys women's trust in one another, depriving them of a mutual support system vital to women generally, and to a new widow in particular.

It worked both ways—women fearing other women might become rivals for their husbands' attention, and for those women who did not mind marrying married men, it justified their going after another woman's husband. Such women would defend it by saying, "It is a man's right in the eyes of Allah." Therefore, trust between women was utterly destroyed, as husbands are available and fair game for seduction by other women.

In the Middle East a woman's reputation is everything. Neighbors will watch her every step—where she's going, what time she comes home, who visits her. My mother's every move became the subject of scrutiny and gossip. That's why the independence she derived from driving a car fueled speculation and suspicion. My mother endured this her whole life. And as we daughters grew into young women, we were increasingly placed under the same cultural microscope, even by our own family.

One day when my uncle's wife learned that I was taking ballet lessons, she was shocked and asked in front of the whole family, "How can you dance ballet when I see boys carrying the girls and touching them?" Taken aback, I tried to explain that boys did not touch the girls in my ballet class. But I was hurt and feared that I might not be able to continue ballet lessons, an activity I loved. In addition to dancing, I excelled in making clay figures, drawing, and geometry. My grandparents, uncle, and his wife always praised my artistic talent as unique. I don't know if that was just to be nice to me, but it did bolster my self-confidence. I often helped my cousins in their drawing and art projects.

Another time, when I was perhaps eleven or twelve years old, my aunt saw me trying on a new bathing suit and commented that it was not proper for girls to run around wearing bathing suits. She was not trying to be hurtful, but simply repeating what she herself had been told. Nevertheless, I felt hurt. When she saw my reaction, she softened her criticism by joking, "You look like British women—no breasts and no butt." Neither the impropriety of "running around in bathing suits" nor my lack of curves stopped me—or my sisters—from wearing bathing suits all day during our vacations in Alexandria or Suez.

My aunt—my mother's only sister—and her husband lived in Suez, near the Red Sea, and some summers we would vacation there. Her nickname was Zouzou. She herself often joked that she was going to wear shorts and walk on the beach like Western women. But she never did it. Like my mother's, hers was only wishful thinking. Her husband was a businessman who owned a trucking company and bakery, and he was always generous with us. My aunt's family loved the oysters that were sold on carts on the beach. As a child, I could never understand how anyone could eat this disgusting food. Zouzou would rent a cabin on the Red Sea's Sokhna beach for the whole summer. Our visits there are one of my best memories of Egypt. We would stay on the beach all day until midnight, acting as if we owned the place.

Another relative, my mother's aunt, was especially dear to me. We called her "Batta," meaning "ducky." She was a lot of fun and always called us children by funny names, some even nasty, but we loved it. She lived in a huge beautiful villa in the Cairo neighborhood of Hadaek Al Kubba with a maid's quarter and a mango tree. We managed to climb the tree and pick mangoes. In addition to visiting her home, Batta would visit us frequently, often spending the night at our home. Since she had no children of her own, she treated my mother as her daughter. Batta once talked about the strange subject of *tahara*, circumcision of girls. The word *tahara* literally means "cleanliness." In Aunt Batta's generation, and my mother's as well, all girls at around age seven had to go through *tahara*. Batta was laughing while describing how for days young girls could not walk because of the pain between their legs. It did not seem to me like something to laugh about. I noticed that my mother was uncomfortable with the subject and tried to steer the conversation away from it. Fortunately, my mother and much of her generation and class stopped doing this to their daughters. I was relieved that *tahara* was not something that would be forced on me. However, a large number of the uneducated lower classes still practiced this genital mutilation on their young girls in my generation, and tragically, it is still practiced to this day in many Muslim and African countries.

Growing up female in an Arab culture was fraught with complications and contradictions. The whole society imposed very strict standards—no dating, no partying, no mixing with boys, and, above all, no sex outside of marriage. Dating or any kind of relationship—casual or otherwise—between men and women who are not related was simply forbidden. Like most Egyptian girls, I was very conscious of the strict codes of behavior and made every effort to follow them. It wasn't hard or heroic to stay out of trouble. I never smoked, never drank, and had never even seen drugs. And as for sex before marriage, that was out of the question. It never even crossed our minds. Sex was something mysterious that happened in the bedrooms of married couples. Most Egyptian girls I knew were like me. Boys never pushed us to do what an Egyptian good girl should not do. The boys I knew were probably as naive as we were. They knew girls were off-limits.

I remember I could not dare to even smile back at boys when they smiled at me in public places. Yet, despite these taboos, it was common to hear Egyptian men whistle and shout praise and words of admiration (some humorous, some embarrassing) to women in Cairo streets. Women walking on a street without men were considered by some men as easy and fair targets. In fact, some Egyptian men would go as far as pinching and rubbing against women in crowded public buses and on downtown Cairo streets. Their behavior was expected and almost condoned. For us to respond—in any way—was not acceptable and could result in further humiliation. A woman my mother's age told us of an incident that happened to her in downtown Cairo. When she felt a pinch on her behind, she turned around and slapped the man on the face. He slapped her back. She said she was totally humiliated and walked away speechless. A woman without a man in her presence is vulnerable in the Muslim world.

Perhaps the incident that most exemplified these conditions occurred one day when I was fourteen. While waiting on the street after school for my mother to pick me up, a boy attempted to talk to me. He stood some ten feet away. I did not look at him or respond to his questions, even though he was merely being friendly and in no way trying to bother me. As I stood there embarrassed, not knowing how to respond, my mother drove up, sized up the situation, and ordered me into the car. Then she yelled at me, saying, "Don't you care about your reputation, having no father and a boy talking to you on the sidewalk?!"

My mother continued her tirade all the way home. "Isn't it enough, what they say when they see me driving a car?" she screamed. "And then you have to go and shame me by allowing a boy to talk to you on the street?" Her biggest concern was "what would people say," a common refrain in the Egyptian language and psyche—that ever-present notion that appearance is more important than reality.

I was hurt and very angry with her then, not understanding that for her the incident was symbolic of something more. Her anger, while directed at me in that moment, was not really because of me at all. Her outbreak was the culmination of the tragedy of her life as a single, widowed young woman in the Muslim world.

Nevertheless, it was *me*, not the culture, who was grounded.

Despite of all the challenges and contradictions in Muslim society, there is one aspect in the upbringing of girls within the upper and middle classes that I personally remember with a warm feeling—the sense of being sheltered and protected from the harsh realities of life. Parents and educators did not rush to burden children with complex adult realities, forcing them to grow up too fast. As a matter of fact, within our social class, the innocence of children was protected, sometimes perhaps too zealously. However, on the upside, when adults value the preservation of their children's innocence, they end up setting a better example, and that produces a stronger child.

During my childhood, my best times were those I spent with my maternal grandparents, who were themselves first cousins originally. It was the tradition in Egypt at that time for cousins to marry. They actually called each other "cousin" at home. My grandmother was a strong woman, and my grandfather, a gentle, quiet man. He wore a British-style hat, carried a cane, and often spent hours at a nearby coffee shop. I loved spending the Ramadan month with them as they faithfully celebrated the long-held traditions of Ramadan, complete with all the wonderful foods associated with the feast. I recall baking cookies in my grandmother's kitchen. At night, along with all the other neighborhood children, we would parade in the street, carrying the traditional Ramadan colored lanterns while singing *"Wahawy Ya Wahawy."*

Islam has two important feasts. Byram is the feast that marks the end of Ramadan. The second, and the larger feast of the two, is Daheyah, which involves the killing of a lamb to commemorate Abraham's willingness to sacrifice his son Isaac. In this story, at the last minute God allows Abraham to sacrifice an animal instead.

Two weeks before the Daheyah feast, my mother and grandparents bought a live lamb, and we played with it until the first day of the feast when it was time to slaughter it. Some people slaughtered the lambs in their homes themselves. It was regarded as a blessing to the home, but our family left the act to a butcher. On that day, the butcher would come to our house early in the morning, take the lamb, and begin reciting "In the name of Allah, the merciful, *Allahu Akbar.*"

While older children might stick around to witness the ritual slaughter, I could not, despite my curiosity. I would scream and run hysterically into the house, venturing out only when the butcher had finished. We followed tradition strictly: half the lamb went to the poor, and the other half was used to make our family feast.

During the various years of my childhood, we celebrated the Da-heyah feast, sometimes in my mother's home, other times in my grandmother's home. Both my mother and grandmother had a backyard where the lamb could be kept in the days before the feast. But when my grandparents moved to an apartment, they kept the lamb for a week on the balcony, as did other apartment-dwelling neighbors of theirs. The butcher would come to the apartment and slaughter the lamb in the bathroom while everyone watched. Even when I got older, I could never bring myself to witness the slaughter. I do remember on one occasion returning to the bathroom to see what had happened to the lamb. It was already beheaded but the body was still moving in spasms. I started screaming in horror, but the butcher and my grandparents insisted this was a blessing to the home.

Almost from the beginning of Nasser's presidency, life began changing drastically in Egypt. The war of 1956 had cost the nation dearly, in lives and in economic stability. President Nasser had promised my mother that as the widow of a shahid, the government would pay for our education. But when the school informed her in December 1956 that they had not received any payments, my mother called Nasser's office. She was told that the number of martyrs was now very large, and the government could no longer pay for all their children's education. That was a sad day for my mother, who could not afford to keep five children in private schools. However, she did not pull us out of school but decided to dip into her savings to keep us enrolled as long as possible.

Cairo had very little greenery and few parks for children, but there was one very special park that I loved, Anater El Khayreya, near the Nile River. It was a great outlet for children and families, a welcome break from the brutal, noisy, and cramped city of Cairo. I loved the park's huge eucalyptus trees, ancient plants nourished by the rich Nile soil. There was something solid, stable, and sym-bolic about these massive, gnarled trees. We held picnics under their shade and swung like Tarzan from their limbs. However, because of the war, the park was neglected and converted into a military zone with barbed wires, bunkers, and dry grass. The trees suffered and some died as yet another casualty of war. Soon one of the nicest areas of that park became off-limits to the public. It was turned into an exclusive vacation resort for the president of Egypt. Little by little, the militarism of Nasser's Egypt was sapping the goodness out of our life.

My grandmother's radio was always blasting with the stirring songs of Um Kulthum, the famous Egyptian singer who was adored by the whole Arab world. Throughout my childhood, we were bombarded with calls to war and songs praising President Nasser. Arab leaders were treated as gods and they acted as gods. Fear of Allah was transferred to fear of the dictator. My grandfather once dryly remarked that the radio had more praise for the president than for Allah. Singers competed in pleasing Nasser with their songs of adoration for him. War songs glorifying martyrdom and jihad echoed above all other music over the airwaves of Egyptian radio. The song *"Ya Mujahid Fe Sabil Allah,"* meaning "Holy Warrior for the Sake of Allah" was a particularly fiery song that inspired war and violence with the following lyrics:

> *War is the day we all wish for,*
> *Stand up Hero with our swords and join the thousands.*
> *The whole world will witness tomorrow that we are Arabs,*
> *Known for our war heritage that we perfected to an art form.*
> *Hay mujahid for the sake of Allah!*
> *Mujahid, martyrs for Allah.*

Such songs glorifying jihad, Arab land, martyrdom, war, and revenge played all day on the radio, and even when the radio was off, they continued playing in our heads. No Arab could avoid the culture of jihad. Jihad is not some esoteric concept. In the Arab world, the meaning of jihad is clear: It is a religious holy war against infidels, an armed struggle against anyone who is not a Muslim. It is a fight for Allah's cause to promote Islamic dominion in the world.

To ensure this dominion, it was necessary to be in control of the minds, hearts, and souls of all citizens. And nothing was more effective than for Allah's command for jihad to be presented in the musical rhythm of songs, as well as the moving and hypnotic Koranic recitations, which confirmed the call for jihad in Allah's own words.

I liked to listen to the call to worship that rang from the mosques five times each day. These calls, which echoed from loudspeakers on the mosque's minaret, were very beautiful and awe inspiring. But that call was often followed by fiery sermons that exhorted Muslims to destroy the Jews and infidels, the enemies of God. The sheikhs preached that the highest rewards and honor will be bestowed upon those who die in the cause of jihad. The call to war and the pride of giving up one's life for the sake of Allah was everywhere in the popular culture.

Sometimes I was ashamed by my own anger over my father's death in jihad, since that could be interpreted that I was not a good Muslim. I had to hide my feelings and pretend that I was a good Muslim. My mother never forced us to become devout Muslims, since, at that time, Egypt was more secular than other Muslim countries. As did many others in my generation, I rebelled against praying five times a day and fasting during Ramadan. My grandparents and their generation seemed to be the only ones who prayed and fasted regularly. But devout or not, no one could escape the impact of the culture that ruled every aspect of our lives. And while my mother did not require that we be devout in day-to-day practice, she did want us to learn to be good Muslims generally. In fact, my mother sometimes brought in a sheikh to recite the Koran in our home. Even though I did not understand much of the meaning of what he was reciting, I enjoyed the way it sounded and felt good about the blessings the sheikh was giving our house. It helped answer my needs for a connection to something holy. While he was reciting, my mother would burn incense and walk with him all around the house. It made us feel that our home was blessed.

I once asked the sheikh why there were so many poor people, saying that it didn't seem fair to me. He answered that I was not to feel too bad because it is Allah's will and that they deserve the poverty they are in since Allah gives everyone what they deserve. I did not like his answer but did not dare tell him that. As I was leaving the room, he reminded me to always say *"in Shaallah,"* which means "if Allah is willing." I said, "Of course," and then dutifully repeated *"In Shaallah."* But I did so with a sigh of slight revolt. I always hated to be reminded to say it. Everyone around me was so fatalistic. Even as a child, I sensed something wrong with that fatalism. We were expected to say this phrase in almost every conversation, but especially whenever we spoke about a plan or a decision. If I did not say it, I was stopped right in the middle of my conversation and ordered—or "reminded"—that it was not good to speak about plans or decisions without saying *in Shaallah.* Unless you said the magic words, your plans would be cursed and without Allah's blessings.

While the sheikh who visited our home taught that the poor people's condition was Allah's will, I received a very different view of the poor from the nuns at school. That same year, when I was twelve, the nuns took us to an Egyptian village on the outskirts of Cairo, where we visited a mud house. The nuns were very respectful and told us to greet the lady in the house properly. They gave the woman a bag as we left, probably food. I was surprised that the nuns cared about people who most Cairo dwellers, especially the wealthy, looked down upon. These people were a part of Egypt we didn't know.

Social classes in Egypt were very stratified. We never mingled as equals. Furthermore, it was very hard, if not impossible, to move upward from the class you were born into. That was how Egyptian society had functioned for generations. The upper classes treated the lower classes with arrogance and resentment—and sometimes worse. The way a higher class treated the one below it could be very cruel and unjust. I have seen men slap poorer men on the face for the slightest mistake or error. Even women abused poorer women, especially maids. The law did not protect the poor and the weak in society. When we drove by poorer neighborhoods, especially delta villages on the way to Alexandria, it was almost like being in a foreign country. These delta peasants spoke with a different accent than city people, dressed differently, and behaved differently. They lived in mud homes covered by branches and hay. Their children were barefoot, malnourished, and filthy. Women could be seen carrying large, heavy clay containers as they walked to a Nile branch to get water. Some of the women had ankle bracelets called *kholkhal* and tattoos on their foreheads or arms. They washed their clothes as well as drank from these same Nile River branches, even though the water was known to be contaminated with a multitude of germs and diseases. Intestinal *bilharzias* is a widespread disease afflicting many Egyptians, especially peasants who have direct contract with water from the Nile. Despite their harsh life, these peasants seemed content with the life Allah had given them and did not stand up for their rights. The notion of *in Shaallah* seemed to govern at all levels of Egyptian society. Dictators neglected the peasants, called *fellaheen* in Egypt, since their condition was God's will. Ironically, Egyptian fellaheen were actually among the few hard-working segments of the population. Many Cairo people had government desk jobs and avoided hard work, especially when the boss was not around. Despite their extreme poverty and hard life, the fellaheen demanded little from the government and were happy to be left alone outside the sphere of harsh government bureaucracy and mismanagement. The Egyptian word *fellaheen* also had another derogative meaning in Cairo slang; it meant "ignorant," "low class," and "lacking good taste." The fellaheen who fed Egypt were the least respected by Egyptians. And the government neglected these rural areas—at that time most villages did not have electricity, proper schools, or hospitals. By now, Egypt has improved many of the conditions in these villages, but improvements never seem to keep pace in a country whose population multiplies very rapidly.

———

My best friend at St. Clare's was an Armenian girl named Alice. She was gentle and sweet, and her family was more Westernized than many of my Egyptian friends. I enjoyed being with Alice and her family. I felt I could let my guard down around them. When we were sixteen, much to my disappointment, Alice's family left to emigrate to Canada.

While the majority of Egypt was Muslim, there had once been thriving populations of Jews, Armenians, Coptic Christians, Greek Orthodox, and other groups. For centuries, both Cairo and Alexandria were bustling cosmopolitan centers with diverse cultural influences, serving as home to many artists and intellectuals.

Many Jews were forced out of Egypt in the 1950s. Some were accused of espionage after the 1956 war. I was very young, but I seem to recall seeing pictures in the newspaper of two Jews who were hung as traitors. During the 1956 war, some Egyptians called on everyone to turn off their lights, and if anyone did not, it meant that they were traitors who wanted to draw attention so Israeli planes could hit Cairo. The two Jews who were tried as traitors and executed came from prominent, wealthy Jewish-Egyptian families. After the war, most Jews left Egypt penniless, having been forced to leave behind their businesses and homes. When their possessions were auctioned off, the military had first crack at them—one of the many military officers' perks. I remember my mother going off to these auctions where precious furnishings could be had for a fraction of their worth.

With tears in her eyes, my grandmother once told me how her Jewish best friend was evicted from Egypt and how the woman did not want to leave the only country she had ever known. My grandmother described how her friend—one of the kindest and best human beings she had ever known—had to be literally pulled out of her apartment by her family. Other minorities who felt unwelcome after the revolution also left Egypt, many of them by choice when Nasser nationalized all businesses and began pursuing a socialist agenda. The country lurched into a rapid decline—economically, culturally, and politically.

Egyptian Christians (called Copts) with nearly two thousand years of historical ties to Egypt now began suffering the impact of radical Islam as well as Nasser's socialism. They also reluctantly chose to emigrate to the West in large numbers. Historically speaking, Copts could be considered more authentically Egyptian than Muslims, because they were the ones who resisted forced conversion to Islam when the Arabs invaded Egypt in the seventh century. Nevertheless, Copts endured a second-class citizenship and derogative names, such as "blue bone," which harkened to the day when they were forced into hard labor, resulting in blue marks on their bone-thin bodies. Copts comprised about 15 percent of Egypt's population when I was a child. By now, due to emigration, they have shrunk to less than 10 percent.

The once diverse culture of Egypt started shrinking to mostly Egyptian Muslims. Anyone who did not appear 100 percent Egyptian was called *khawaga*, meaning foreigner. Egyptians of Greek and Armenian origin whose families had always lived in Egypt were considered *khawaga* even though they were Egyptians by birth. An Armenian friend once confided in me how unwelcome and insulted her father felt when people called him Khawaga instead of his real name. The few minorities who remained in Egypt into the late 1950s—mostly Armenians and Greeks—eventually began emigrating to the West as well.

By the 1960s, after Nasser's rigid socialist rules began taking effect, even ordinary Egyptians Muslims began looking toward the West. Nasser tried to stem the tide by clamping down on exit visas. It became harder and harder to leave. Until then, emigration was unthinkable among most Egyptians, who valued their strong ties to their land and history. But by the mid-1960s, extreme poverty and the heavy-handed, despotic rule of Nasser forced many Egyptians to seek work in any country that would take them.

The Egyptian film industry in the 1940s and 1950s was thriving, and all Arab countries regarded Egypt as the cultural center of the Arab world. But as talented people—many of them Egyptian

Jews—left the country, the once world-class movie industry deteriorated, ending an important part of the Egyptian cultural scene. The quality of Egyptian movies is now so poor that most Egyptians don't bother to watch them.

I fondly remember the great Egyptian films and movie stars of the 1950s, especially Faten Hamama, the most popular actress in Egypt and indeed the whole Arab world. Faten Hamama was the former wife of Omar Sharif. At the time of their marriage, Sharif was the lesser well known of the two. Born in Egypt to a prominent Lebanese/Syrian family, Omar Sharif was Roman Catholic and converted to Islam in order to marry Faten Hamama. Sharif starred in great classic Egyptian movies, such as *Fi Baitina Rajul.* But he later skyrocketed to international fame when he won roles in *Lawrence of Arabia* and then *Doctor Zhivago.* However, when he played opposite Barbra Streisand in *Funny Girl*, he was branded a "Jew-lover," and his films were banned in Egypt. Another bit of movie trivia: when Elizabeth Taylor converted from Christianity to Judaism, her films were prohibited in the Arab world. So Egyptians never saw the movie *Cleopatra*. Few Westerners can comprehend the degree to which hatred of Jews permeates every aspect of Arab culture.

Long before anyone had heard of Omar Sharif, Faten Hamama was the great movie diva of the Arab world. I adored her. Women and girls throughout the Arab world identified with Faten Hamama's portrayals of Arab women. She played her characters with sincerity, elegance, and class, creating a role model for us all. Her best-known film, *Doa al Karawan* (*Prayers of the Nightingale*) was adapted from a novel by Taha Hussein, a giant of modern Arabic literature. It is both a love story and a tale of revenge. When a girl who worked as a maid is raped by her boss, her uncle cleanses the family honor by killing her. The film resonated with Arab women, not because it was some far-fetched melodrama, but because it described an all-too-familiar tragedy in Islamic culture.

When I was sixteen years old, a new maid who was about my age came to work in our household. I believe her name was Hosneya.

When my mother suspected Hosneya was pregnant, she took her into a room and closed the door and talked to her for a long time. After they came out, my mother looked frightened and distraught. She would not tell us girls what it was about at the time. But later she explained it to us. Hosneya's previous boss had raped her, and when his wife caught him, she kicked the girl out, blaming it all on her. Shortly thereafter, Hosneya came to work at our home.

Our new maid's condition placed my mother in a terrible dilemma. So she sat down with my grandparents to seek their advice. She had to make a difficult decision. If my mother sent Hosneya back to her family, they might kill her. But if we kept her in our home, perhaps one of our male relatives or friends would be accused of causing the pregnancy. My mother came to what she believed was the best decision. She sent Hosneya to a government facility that took in pregnant girls.

Several months later, the domestic employment agent who had originally placed the girl in our home visited us. We asked him how Hosneya was doing. His answer to my mother was "May Allah prolong your life, Madam," which is the polite Egyptian way of saying someone has died. Stunned, we asked him what happened. He simply said, "Her family took care of her disgrace."

To this day I cannot forget Hosneya's face.

Egyptian history textbooks written prior to the 1952 revolution were trashed and rewritten. The new books—and the media— ignored the fact that the same corruption during King Farouk's time was doubled and tripled by the idealistic, inexperienced revolutionary officers who took over the government in 1952. We learned only the negatives of Egyptian history prior to 1952. While the rest of the world's students studied about the glories of ancient Egypt, the pyramids, and the lush agriculture of the Nile Valley, we knew little beyond the vitriolic rhetoric against Zionists and Western imperialists. My contemporaries and I graduated from high school knowing very little about ancient Egyptian pre-Islamic history. Textbooks and Egyptian media glorified defiant and revolutionary figures such as Fidel Castro and Che Guevara. That was especially true after the United States refused to go along with Nasser's plans for increased armaments and the building of the Aswan Dam. Countries that defied the United States, such as Cuba, and later on Vietnam, were seen as heroic states by the Arab media. Any defiance of the United States as a superpower was envied and romanticized by the culture of jihad.

Nasser gradually moved Egypt into the sphere of the Soviet bloc, which was only too happy to cooperate in Egypt's preparation for its next war with Israel. In exchange for arms, the Soviets were often paid with agricultural products badly needed at home by hungry Egyptians. Very little attention was given to building the infrastructure of our country to meet its rapid population growth. The inevitable happened when the economy of Egypt finally hit bottom. Yet despite the extreme hardships and poverty our society was suffering, the Egyptian media had only one agenda, and that was jihad—to destroy Israel. Rather than take responsibility for their mistakes and ineptitude, Nasser and his circle blamed the Zionists and Western imperialists for all our society's ills. I remember cartoons depicting the blood-thirsty Jews who wanted to kill Arabs for fun. Under Nasser's thumb, the Arab news and media outlets turned into propaganda machines of anti-Semitism that worked the citizenry into a frenzy of anger, envy, and paranoia against the West and Israel.

Even as a child I could not buy into this mentality. I don't know why. I grew up with anger and struggled for a long time to keep my sanity. My trust of people and sense of security had been shattered as a young child, and it did not heal. Somewhere deep down, I could not accept a culture that was willing to orphan its own children in its obsessive hatred of Jews, that was ready to sacrifice lives and the health of its family structure over a few miles of land. Egyptians acted as though the West Bank and Gaza were taken from them, even though they were never Egyptian land. However, even if I could, I dared not give words to my feelings. But in my mind, as I grew into my teenage years, I continued to question the culture of hatred that snatched away my father for nothing.

I felt Egypt was just looking for trouble with Israel. It needed an enemy to blame. It treated Israel as it treated its minorities, as it treated its fellaheen, as it treated its orphans and even its own history. On some primal level, I related to Israel. Israel was the object of hatred, fueled by the arrogance of power and petrol dollars of the Arabs. It could do nothing to please this culture, other than cease to exist. Similarly, I felt I could do nothing to be accepted in my own culture if I didn't hide my feelings and live to please those around me. The only other thing I could do, would be to cease to exist.

The Soviets were only too happy to stoke the fires of Arab anger at the West. They helped Egypt build the Aswan Dam and behind it Nasser's new lake. Construction began in 1960 when I was twelve and would not be completed for a decade. All Egyptians were spoon-fed the notion through the media and schools that the dam was Nasser's greatest achievement. All of Egypt was expected to be very grateful to Nasser for this ambitious project that would supposedly provide all the electricity that Egypt needed to become a top industrial power. This, we were told, would solve most, if not all, of Egypt's economic and agricultural problems. However, the hoped-for prosperity from building the dam never materialized. Egyptians even today reject the assessments of experts—predicted before the dam was built and sadly borne out by later reality—that the negative ecological results would outweigh the positive. The dam submerged most of southern Egypt's archeological treasures, except for the collosal and magnificent temple at Abu Simbel, which was saved by the United Nations, not Nasser's government. The huge surface of the lake allowed a significant part of the Nile's precious water to evaporate uselessly, while the dam prevented the rich mud, called *tamii*, from enriching the delta soil. According to some scientists, the Nile Valley's agricultural productivity subsequently dropped below its previous levels.

We even began to notice the changes when we vacationed at the Miami beach in Alexandria. The beach was being eroded. The water began reaching the cabins, and the sand area was nearly gone. I was told that was because the Aswan Dam did not allow enough of the *tamii* into the Mediterranean, thus the sea water had nothing to stop it from expanding onto the beach.

As Nasser moved closer to the Soviet bloc, he instituted many Soviet-style socialist "reforms." For one thing, he nationalized all big business, and people became totally dependent on the government for employment, which led to all manner of corruption. Jobs became dependent on who you knew, not what you did. In this climate, productivity in all sectors of industry and business took a nosedive.

Compounding the economic problems, most of Egypt's resources were directed to the military and Nasser's preparation for the next war with Israel. Egyptians started suffering from shortages of food, medications, and many vital goods and services. The government began rationing food products, such as cooking oil, rice, tea, and sugar. I remember craving a cup of tea one day in the winter, and there simply wasn't any left. I took a taxi to my grandmother's house, and she brewed me a cup of precious tea. Even wealthy families started feeling the pinch. I remember seeing food lines in front of government-run cooperative markets even though they had very little on their shelves. Egyptians were beginning to spend a great deal of time waiting in line for food.

Nasser also enforced a harsh new rent control law in 1960. The end result was that people stopped investing in apartment buildings, and a huge shortage in rentals and housing forced many Egyptians to live in horrible conditions with several families sharing one small apartment. The effects of the harsh rent control is still felt today in Egypt. Mistakes like that can last for generations.

My mother became a victim of that rent control. After my father's death, she used money from a life insurance policy to build a three-unit apartment building so the rent she collected could subsidize her income and help keep us in private schools. It was the way we survived since the government shahid pension was not enough to send five children to private schools. Each apartment rented for forty Egyptian pounds per month. Nasser's new rent control law ordered the reduction of rents to a quarter of their previous amount. Furthermore, the rent was not allowed to increase as long as the tenants remained. The law also forbade evictions. Overnight, my mother's income was reduced from 120 to 30 Egyptian pounds a month, a devastating blow to our family's finances. I often wondered how my mother could withstand my father's death and all this injustice—and somehow raise five children. Despite the dark days of her reoccurring depression and the obstacles she had to overcome in a society that does not look kindly on a woman alone, she made it. She kept us in private schools. She kept us fed and clothed. She made sure we had vacations and most of the normal activities and joys of childhood. She would make sure we had access to a college education. She coped heroically amid a society and economy that was falling apart around us.

She even sent my older sister Soheir to America as an exchange student in 1963, a gutsy thing for any Egyptian mother to do at the time. Soheir was gone for nine long months, and I missed her terribly. But when she came back she had so much to tell us, so much to share. She loved her American family and told how parents leave candy under their children's pillows when they lose a baby tooth. Soheir came back with Bermuda shorts, T-shirts with writing on them—we'd never seen such a thing before—and records of the Beatles, Louis Armstrong, Eartha Kitt, and Johnny Mathis. We loved wearing the shorts and T-shirts, and we played the music all day long. My grandfather—like grandfathers everywhere—didn't like the Beatles. He frowned, stroked his big, meticulously trimmed mustache, and wondered whatever happened to our generation.

As I was approaching my last year in high school, St. Clare's was nationalized, and the government was about to begin enforcing the Egyptian government curriculum. I wanted to quickly get a British high school diploma, called a GCE, so I began attending an English school that offered classes at night. While at that school, we took a field trip to Gaza, one that I will never forget.

At the time, Gaza was still under Egyptian rule, and many Egyptians poured into the city for shopping because Gaza had more freedom to trade with the outside world than Egypt. Egyptians who could not find necessary goods to buy in Egypt went to Gaza for a shopping spree.

As we traveled by bus through the desert of the Sinai, I stared out the window at the landscape I had not seen since my last train trip eight years earlier. When we approached Gaza, the bus was required to stop at a couple of checkpoints. At the first one, soldiers came on the bus asking to see "the daughter of Mustafa Hafez." One of the teachers proudly introduced me to them. At the second checkpoint, the same thing happened. When we reached Gaza, I asked the teacher if I could see our old home. The bus drove by slowly but did not stop. The house looked so different and so strange. There were no soldiers around it, guarding it like there used to be.

In the hotel in the center of the city where we stayed, I was surprised when several visitors came by asking to see me. Somewhat perplexed at the attention, I received them graciously. Many people of Gaza told me that they had my father's picture proudly displayed in their homes. I discovered there was a city square, a street, and a school named after my father.

The next day we toured the Mustafa Hafez High School, which still exists today. At an assembly, there was a speech about my father. I wasn't expecting it. During the speech, as I heard my father's name spoken, I began to shake uncontrollably and struggled to hold back my tears. They went on and on about their love for him. I was filled with emotions I could barely contain. I had no idea that the people of Gaza still remembered my father, much less loved and appreciated him so much.

They were talking about a military hero. Someone whose portrait hung in their living rooms. A larger-than-life man. A father— *my father*—whose memory had begun to fade into the background of my life. Until I was jolted into remembering.

On the way out of the school, students followed me to ask:

"Are you really the daughter of Mustafa Hafez?" One boy asked, "Why are you coming back to this hellhole? Living in Cairo must be much better."

I did not answer him. I did not explain to him that living in Cairo was not such a wonderful thing either.

I left Gaza and never set foot in it again.

Three | Living in Two Worlds

I started college in 1964, at age sixteen, when I became a student at the American University in Cairo (AUC), a small island of American education in the heart of the Egyptian capital. Most of the students were Egyptian, but a considerable number of foreign students—Americans, Europeans, Jordanians, Kuwaitis, and Palestinians—also attended AUC.

This was yet another phase in my Western education after St. Clare's. It presented me with a great opportunity to meet students from other countries at a time when many minorities had left Egypt and it was rare to meet non-Egyptians or non-Muslims. I am very grateful to my mother who sacrificed so much to send my siblings and me to such a distinguished university.

I was very young when I entered the university because I had rushed to get my high school degree in order to avoid the state schools after Nasser nationalized education. I was perhaps a little too young at the time to fully appreciate all that was offered to me as an AUC student. Nevertheless, I saw a window of opportunity to look at things from a new perspective, a Western openness that did not exist in Arab culture. At the American University of Cairo, I found a respect for knowledge and a level of honesty, simplicity, and appreciation of the truth that I found lacking in my society.

I majored in sociology and anthropology because my anthropology professor, Dr. Cynthia Nelson, was the most interesting of all my teachers. Her classes opened my mind to viewing different cultures and societies in a new light. I observed my teacher's sensitivity and eagerness to learn about other societies that were less advanced or different from her own. Professor Nelson was equally enthusiastic about her studies of Egyptian society. When a Virgin Mary sighting in a Coptic church in Zeitun, a suburb of Cairo, attracted crowds of people nightly, both Muslim and Coptic, Dr. Nelson visited the church several times to document this phenomenon. I also visited one evening, as the Coptic church was across the street from my grandparents' house.

My sociology and anthropology studies at the American University were in sharp contrast to my own culture, which was judgmental and intolerant of non-Muslim countries. I began living in two worlds: the world of American education advocating tolerance, respect, and understanding; and the opposite world outside the campus, a world that blamed all its misfortune and shortcomings on *Istemaar*, meaning imperialism, and especially our arch-enemy, Israel. All of the Western world—essentially all non-Muslims— were viewed as people interested only in occupation and tricking Arabs. Even buying products from the West was a sign of weakness and shame. Outside the university walls, I lived in Nasser's Egypt, an Egypt that was saturated with propaganda, misinformation, and hate mongering. The bulk of that hate was focused on one small country—Israel. Hatred of Israel and the Jews has become part of the identity of being an Arab. This hatred was just a reflex, something that no one thought of questioning. We knew nothing about Israel, its society, or the Israeli point of view. Even at the American University, Israel was a taboo topic never to be discussed, probably so as not to upset the Egyptian government. But even though Israel was never discussed in my classes, in my mind I was curious about this country that my culture demonized and blamed for all the world's problems. I started looking at this hatred of Israel more objectively and from a new paradigm. I looked back at my family tragedy, my father's assassination because of the jihad against Israel, my mother's unhappy life, and my brother, who was having to grow up without a father. I loved my younger brother dearly, and I often felt deep sadness for him as I watched him enter his teen years. It is especially hard for a boy to be without his father's guidance at this time in his life. I too missed my father, his guidance, and his mere existence in our home. What did he die for? Arab hatred of Israel and Jews was destroying so many lives. Why? I started questioning anything and everything said about Israel, with the benefit of my university education, analyzing the hate speech, the racism, and the anti-Semitism. What was wrong in allowing a few million Jews to live among us in peace? Arab land was plenty. They had only a small sliver of land, in some places only thirty kilometers wide. But the hatred and anti-Semitism was frighteningly prevalent in our society.

At the time I did not know—no one in the Arab world did—that Israel had a history on that small strip of land going back thousands of years. Nor did we comprehend that Jerusalem was the point of origin for two great religions, Judaism and Christianity, religions that had existed long before Islam even began. This was not taught. We were taught that Muhammad was the final prophet and that Islam was the true uncorrupted religion, unlike Judaism and Christianity. We were taught that "Zionists" were foreign infidel invaders bent on taking Muslim land and our destruction, and that they must be destroyed.

It's strange, actually, for Egyptians in general did not trust their government or believe their media. Yet, paradoxically, they kept repeating the government and media lies they were fed since they had no other sources of information. It was all they had learned, even though it often made no sense.

Even misunderstandings and disputes between Arab nations were blamed on a Zionist conspiracy. In his speeches broadcast on the radio, Nasser inflamed the public with his defiance and ridicule of the West. Egypt's problems were regarded as a result of the evil of the outside world. Egyptians were never told it was their responsibly to solve their own problems. The villain was always an outside force. This scapegoating was true on the national front and it was true on the personal level as well. The concept of taking responsibility for oneself was completely foreign. To admit one's flaws and errors and to correct and repent challenges a person of any nationality. In Muslim culture, however, it is inconceivable. To acknowledge one's shortcomings or errors was a sure way to invite severe punishment, shame, and dishonor. In our culture, those who admit fault, even unintentional guilt, are regarded as naive or foolish. Avoiding taking any responsibility has thus become part of the national character. The phrase *malish dawaa* or *wana mali*, which means "none of my business," has become the all-purpose excuse, the ready explanation for not involving oneself in solving problems that might get a person in trouble.

Nasser's vision for Egypt and his obsession with the elimination of Israel was initially very popular among the rest of the Arab world as well. He worked to bring everyone on board in his plans to eliminate Israel. He railed against the *Istimaar*, the colonialists and their agents, the Jews represented by Israel. He saw Jews as the only barrier to the dream of a United Arab Republic that would include all Arabic-speaking countries, and that was why they had to be eliminated. Nasser in fact relentlessly attacked Arab leaders who did not follow his political line. King Hussein of Jordan, who maintained ties to the West, as well as the Saudi kings, were among those Nasser criticized and ridiculed in his speeches. I remember listening to one of his speeches in which he was chanting "*taale lommo,*" meaning King Hussein was "his mother's boy" or "like his mother." In the Arab world, it is a big insult for a man to be like his mother and not like his father.

In this climate, war to eliminate Israel was the highest priority and became the national goal in and of itself. No other topic was

allowed to even get close as a priority—not the economy, education, or political system. Everything was on hold until Israel could
be eliminated.

And so, as I attended classes at the American University, im-
mersing myself in the pursuit of knowledge and understanding of
other cultures, on the outside where I actually lived the war drums
were beating with euphoria. Everything was leading up to war.

I remember a discussion I had with a young navy officer who
was the son of a family friend. He was very excited and happy about
the impending war to get rid of Israel. I told him that I did not
feel good about this war and that I thought Egypt and the other
Arab countries would lose. He laughed at me and assured me that
I was wrong.

Although I admired him, his typical Egyptian bravado and cer-
tainty did not assuage my fears. I had a very bad feeling about yet
another war and viewed it as another potential round of death and
destruction. As the drumbeat for war grew louder, foreigners began leaving Egypt. But most Egyptians believed in Nasser's power,
and their expectations for victory were very high.

Ever since the 1956 war with Israel, Nasser had been attempting to unite the whole Arab world into a military alliance to attack
Israel. He made no secret of it. In 1966 Egypt convinced Syria to
sign a military pact that basically promised that one would join in
if the other went to war. Nasser attempted to get the same agreement with Jordan. In the spring of 1967, Nasser publicly announced
his plans to remilitarize the Sinai. One problem: the United Nations was stationed there as part of the cease-fire arrangement after
the war of 1956 to prevent such a thing. On May 17, 1967, Nasser
demanded that the UN forces be pulled out of their position between Egypt and Israel. Amazingly, UN Secretary-General U Thant
complied, and Nasser, with the whole world watching, immediately began amassing tanks and troops on the border with Israel.
About that time, border skirmishes began breaking out on the
Syrian-Israeli border. Then on May 23, Nasser closed the Straits

of Tiran in the Red Sea, Israel's major shipping lane for oil, and blockaded the Israeli port of Eilat. Now it was more than beating drums, rhetoric, and posturing. War was imminent.

Historians say that this was the first time a U.S. president actually picked up the famous red phone to talk to Moscow. The United States pleaded with the Russians to use their influence with Nasser to avert war. The Soviets, despite their decades-long military support of Egypt, attempted to convince the Egyptians to at least not be the first to strike.

Jordan's King Hussein, who feared that Nasser's plans would bring instability to the region, knew that most of his country supported Nasser's vision, and he caved in rather than face an insurrection on his own streets. On May 30, Jordan signed a mutual defense treaty, joining the alliance with Egypt and Syria. Only days earlier, President Nasser had called King Hussein an "imperialist lackey," among other insults. But now Hussein was on board. King Hussein even "allowed" an Egyptian general to come in and take command of his armed forces. This was an important part of Nasser's plan. From a strategic place on the Jordanian border, it was only seventeen kilometers to Israel's coastline. In only a matter of minutes or hours Israel could be cut in half as a first step to finally casting the Jewish state into the sea. Nasser declared for the whole world to hear: "Our basic objective will be the destruction of Israel." The Egyptian public was elated. Adrenaline flowed.

On the morning of June 5, 1967, the Six Day War began.

Some 400,000 Egyptian soldiers were sent into battle, among them my military officer friend. Once again a major war with Israel was on, and once again my family and I had to live through alarming sirens warning us of possible air raids on Cairo. Once again we were sitting in total darkness at night listening to faraway bombings. I was frightened.

In Cairo we stayed tuned to our radios night and day to hear news of the war. The Egyptian media fed us lies. Songs of triumph on the radio proclaimed that we were winning the war against the

Jews and the Zionist enemy. "Very soon Egypt will occupy Tel Aviv," was the heady prediction heard on the streets.

As Egyptians scanned the radio dial to hear the news of the war, many of us knew that we were probably hearing lies, and we began searching for foreign radio stations, such as the Voice of America, to learn the truth. The reception for the BBC and Voice of America was very weak and often jammed. But this did not stop us from listening eagerly.

And we began hearing a different story. We heard of a devastating defeat and the loss of the Sinai. Even though I had predicted this result, I still could not believe it could happen that fast and that easily. The loss was a blow to Egyptians as they learned what had really happened the morning of June 5. The Egyptian Air Force, the largest, most modern of all the Arab forces, with more than 300 Soviet-built aircraft, had been destroyed on the ground by a pre-emptive Israeli attack. About 300 aircraft were demolished, 350 combat pilots were dead, and the runways shredded so the few remaining planes could not take off. Ironically, the Israelis had struck at a time when the Egyptians had turned off their air defense radar to perform an inspection.

Egypt did not fare much better on the ground in the Sinai despite 100,000 troops, more than 1,000 tanks, and all kinds of state-of-the-art, Soviet-built artillery. Israeli paratroopers landed in the heavily fortified area of Abu-Ageila and destroyed much of the artillery, and combined Israeli forces attacked the Egyptians from the front and the rear. The battles were fierce and continued for three and a half days before Abu-Ageila fell. When Egyptian field marshal and war minister Abdel Hakim Amer heard about the fall of Abu-Ageila, he panicked and ordered all Egyptian units in the Sinai to retreat.

Israeli forces attempted to block their retreat in the mountain passes but were only partially successful. Some Egyptian units made their escape across the Suez into safety. But fighting all along the escape route was heavy. It had taken the Israelis only three days to capture the entire Sinai.

Besides the truth leaking out to us across foreign radio waves, there was the personal knowledge Egyptians were hearing from family members. In our case, my aunt's whole family as well as her in-laws had to flee from the city of Suez as fighting reached there. The city of Suez was on the southern end of the Suez Canal where it joins the Red Sea. About twenty adults and children took refuge as guests at my grandmother's house. They were sleeping everywhere.

For many years before the 1967 war, my siblings and I had enjoyed carefree summers in my aunt's cabin on the Red Sea resort of 'Ein el Sokhna. My aunt and her family never returned to Suez after the 1967 war, since the apartment building she owned, with its breathtaking view of the Red Sea, was totally destroyed along with most of the city. Suez and most of the other canal cities were ruined and became ghost towns. Most of the population of these cities moved permanently to Cairo or Alexandria, placing further stress on these two crowded cities. It was especially hard on my aunt's husband, who lost his business and source of livelihood in Suez. He died of a heart attack before the year was out.

After the war, the once blue beautiful beach was contaminated by several oil spills, its once clean water covered with black crude. The Suez Canal itself was closed to navigation for many years, littered with broken ships hastily docked and left there. The good days at the Red Sea beach that we had looked forward to every summer ended because of the war. Only memories remained.

It was no better for other Arab countries. In the first few hours of the war, when Nasser convinced King Hussein that Egypt was winning the air war, Jordan agreed to attack, moving against West Jerusalem, even temporarily occupying the UN Government House and shelling the city. They also fired in the direction of Tel Aviv. But their early successful attempts were cut short. Israel soon destroyed the entire Royal Jordanian Air Force and beat back the ground forces, capturing East Jerusalem, the Western Wall, and the Temple Mount. Within two days, Israel had pushed Jordanian forces back and captured the West Bank. The Syrian front fared no better as Israel took the Golan Heights, even though other Arab nations such as Iraq had joined the fray.

In a mere six days, the Arab nations were handed a humiliating defeat. While such numbers were never admitted to, around 10,000 Egyptian lives were lost (some estimates placed it as high as 15,000), not to mention thousands more wounded or maimed. Those 10,000 families knew their young men did not return. If every dead soldier had 100 extended family members plus close friends, there were at least a million Egyptians who knew the truth firsthand. It was impossible to hide that many deaths, let alone the fact that Egypt had lost the entire Sinai.

The truth about the Arab's devastating defeat came out after the war but was twisted and repackaged with many lies by the government and a corrupt media. Yet there was no public outcry over those media lies. Only through Arab media outlets can a military defeat be rewritten as a military conquest.

After Arabs convinced themselves that their defeat was not really a defeat, they started making demands of an enemy who just resoundingly won the war. They truly expected Israel to immediately and unconditionally turn back all the lands conquered in the 1967 war. In this delusionary environment, Arabs actually believed that after each war Israel should hand them back their marbles in order to allow Arabs to get ready to start the next round of wars against the Jewish state. The thinking went that perhaps next time, if Israel does not "cheat" by defending itself, the Arabs would succeed and win.

Even the educated Egyptians, myself included, did not comprehend why Israel was not immediately withdrawing from the occupied territories. They had done so after the 1956 war (at the insistence of other world powers unbeknownst to us), and we expected them to do it again. It was only "fair," or so we thought.

United Nations Resolution 242, which grew out of the war of 1967, was portrayed in Arab media as an order from the UN for Israel to give back occupied territories. Arab media never told the public that the resolution also required peaceful negotiations that would provide Israel with security guarantees. To this day, Arabs ignore that half of the resolution and only discuss "the occupation," refusing to hold up their end of the bargain to achieve their goals. The only true and consistent goal in the Arab mind was to get rid of Israel.

But even more bewildering, despite the devastating defeat, there was no public demand for an investigation of what really happened. People only whispered about Nasser's bad choice of the military leadership of Amer but never dared to blame Nasser for it. Arab media managed to portray Nasser and Egypt as the victims of Israeli aggression rather than the perpetrators of the war. The bigger the lie, the more believable it becomes to the average Arab citizen. Thus, Arab media never fail to be less than outrageous. They blamed the defeat on none other than Israel, as though self-defense and self-preservation was not a right to be exercised by the Jewish enemy. They simply accused Israel of wanting to conquer the Arab world and that would become the excuse for conducting one unsuccessful war after the other. They also claimed that American and British warplanes had actually attacked Egypt from aircraft carriers and bases in Libya, and that American and British troops also ran support on the ground. The claim was patently false, yet to this day, many Arabs believe it to be true. It came to be referred to in the West as the "Big Lie."

It was not the first time Nasser had successfully manipulated his population by using the technique of the Big Lie. Nasser's revolution had explained away the 1948 defeat in their war against Israel by claiming that King Farouk and the British were traitors who conspired to cause the Arab defeat by giving Egyptian soldiers defective weapons that fired back at them instead of at the enemy. That's what we were told in school, the media, and movies. It was particularly touching when we saw a movie about how the poor Egyptian soldiers were getting killed by their own weapons. I truly believed the story as a child—after all, it was in our school textbooks. But I was later amazed that what we had seen in the movies was not confirmed by any army officers who participated in that war.

Nasser used this propaganda to make Egyptians feel victimized in a war that he claimed would have otherwise been winnable. That kept an opening and a yearning in the minds of people to correct the results of that war by getting into another one, but next time with the best possible armaments from the Soviet Union.

The Big Lie to explain away the defeat in 1967 was that the Egyptian Air Force was actually destroyed by American and British warplanes, not the Israelis. Based on this lie, which was accepted without question in every Arab capital in the Middle East, oil-producing states announced an embargo on the United States and Great Britain and in some cases stopped all shipments of oil to the West.

It's true that in the postwar rumblings, Nasser attempted to symbolically resign from his position, but the Egyptian people poured into the streets asking him to remain in power. To many he was the Great Daddy who needed to comfort his children after the defeat—a defeat that they still continued to deny happened.

Despite his "symbolic" gesture, Nasser failed to take responsibility for the national disaster of that war or the strategic blunders of his administration. Instead he blamed others, placing several top government officials under house arrest. Given the up-to-date weaponry supplied by the Soviets, this time Nasser could not place the blame on "defective weapons," as his revolution had done in the 1948 defeat. However, Nasser never failed to find reasons outside of himself for Egypt's problems, which were piling up on all fronts.

The head of Egyptian intelligence, Salah Nasr, who was our next-door neighbor, was one of those placed under house arrest. Government police replaced his security guards around his house, and some of them were positioned in part of our own side yard. Later Salah Nasr was taken to jail, where he remained for many years. My mother, who comforted his wife, reminded us that my father was supposed to have held Salah Nasr's position had he lived. My family could not help but wonder: Had our father not been killed in Gaza, might he have ended up in jail like Nasr, a scapegoat for Nasser's failures?

Such arrests and political intrigues were not unusual in Egypt, which had become a police state under Nasser.

Another mistake Nasser never admitted to was his poor choice for head of the Egyptian armed forces, Mushier Abdel Hakim Amer, who was such a close friend of Nasser's that they named their children after each other. Our cook from my father's days, Mahmoud, who had become Amer's cook, used to tell us how Nasser and Amer were very close family friends. Amer was a known womanizer who indulged in many pleasures, including regular use of hashish. He had at least one famous movie actress as a second wife and with whom he had a son. But despite their supposed "close friendship," Amer was blamed by Nasser for losing the war and was placed under house arrest. Amer was later found dead from a gunshot wound. Despite the claim by the government that Amer committed suicide, many Egyptians believe that he was murdered by Nasser.

Nasser believed his own propaganda. Blinded by his obsessions, he overestimated his own power and his military's readiness, competence, and commitment to the goal of destroying Israel. But, according to military analysts, he also failed to pick the right person to head the Egyptian military in order to achieve these goals. Amer was a popular figure in the military and known for keeping the officers happy. Nasser's choice of Amer as the stabilizing factor in the military was more important to Nasser than having a competent man for the job. His choice of Amer kept Nasser safe from a military coup, which is very telling as to where Nasser's priorities lay. But Amer's friendship and loyalty was meaningless in the end. He died a convenient scapegoat.

Another reason why the Arabs lose wars is that they are not fighting for survival. As a result, they lack cohesion and the sense of working as a team. In 1967 Egyptian soldiers were not fighting a war for Egypt's survival. Israel, however, *was* fighting for its survival. The class factor also played a crucial role. The majority of Egyptian lower-rank soldiers were very poor peasants who were underpaid, illiterate, malnourished, and held in low regard by their leadership. I witnessed this dynamic in 1976 at a 3M demonstration to the Egyptian military when I was working as a translator for the 3M Company in Cairo. After the event, there was a banquet given for the top officers, while the lower soldiers were treated as their servants. Egyptian military lower-ranking soldiers are often literally treated as servants. Many end up as household help in officer's homes and are sent on personal errands. That dynamic of relationships in the Egyptian military does not produce the cohesion and unity necessary for armies to win wars. Rank-and-file Egyptian soldiers had little motivation to fight Israel since their true oppressors were, in fact, their superiors within the army. In this aspect, the Egyptian military suffered from the same social and political problems of the larger society.

My navy officer friend later admitted to me that I was the only one he knew who had rightly predicted the outcome of the 1967 war. Nevertheless, my officer friend remained a loyal military man, totally committed to the Egyptian obsession to annihilate Israel. He would later participate in the War of Attrition between 1969 and 1970, as Nasser maintained a constant state of military activity against Israel along the Suez Canal. My friend was involved in many covert operations against the Israeli soldiers who were stationed on the eastern side of the Suez Canal. He once showed me a very fancy pair of boots he was wearing and proudly stated that they were made in America. He had taken them off the feet of an Israeli soldier after killing him. My friend then nonchalantly added that the Israeli boot was of a much better quality and far more comfortable than the boots provided by the Egyptian military.

My friend also participated in a relatively unknown war started by Nasser, the Egyptian war on Yemen. That was a war against a brother Arab Muslim nation. Many atrocities were committed in that "little" war that the world didn't notice, and many were killed on both sides. Egyptian military officers, such as my friend, were happy to participate in the war against Yemen because it brought them additional and desperately needed income. Profiting financially from the war against Yemen was the only motivation for many Egyptians to go to war. My friend told me he was able to save a lot of money from the Yemen war.

People in Egypt never asked "why" about any war, even if it was against another Arab Muslim country. When a dictator decides he has an enemy and takes the country to war, the people go blindfolded. To this day, it is not clear to most Egyptians why they went to war against Yemen.

My military officer friend might have become a romantic interest in my life—there was no such thing as dating in our culture—we were friends and able to talk only because our families were friends. But, even as I confided in and enjoyed his confidences, it was clear to me that I was not really part of the culture that he wholeheartedly accepted, a culture that glorified war and wished to eliminate Israel. Furthermore, I had no desire to follow in my mother's footsteps and become an unhappy, sacrificial widow to our wars against Israel. I was already the unwilling and resentful daughter of a shahid.

Four | Marriage and Family Dynamics

My mother had four daughters to marry off.

I was just a teenager when they started coming: nervous fathers and mothers with an embarrassed son in tow, sitting on our salon couch making polite conversation with my mother, looking for a suitable wife and daughter-in-law.

We girls would look on through a crack in the door, trying to suppress our giggles as we surveyed and made fun of the young men who were our marriage "prospects." There would be sneers of "eeuw," nearly all of these boys were distasteful to us. We had dreams of romance and true love dancing in our heads, not financial negotiations and practical considerations.

Fortunately, my mother always came up with polite excuses. Her girls were too young. They were in school. They needed to finish college. I would console myself that I was safe from the fate of an arranged marriage at least until I graduated from the American University in Cairo.

Before these visits, the older women in the family would give us advice on how to present ourselves in front of the potential groom's family. Stay quiet, we were told. My grandmother always empha-sized that young ladies should never give opinions or talk back. Just offer coffee or tea, sit up straight, don't cross your legs, and smile. She always said, "The best one is the quiet one, the one that is hardly seen or heard, the one that does not argue or rock the boat, the one that wants to please." I was often admonished, "Look at your cousin [or this or that girl]. She sits quietly like a lady when there is company in the salon [our name for the guest living room]." We were told those who are quiet and obedient get the good hus-bands, and those who are not, get what they deserve! I often did not meet these criteria. I asked too many questions and had a big mouth compared to some of the "good" girls I was constantly be-ing compared to. Even though I knew that my mother and grand-mother loved me and thought I was very talented, their advice often hurt and confused me. Our upbringing did not allow us to convey dissatisfaction or learn how to say no or express hurt feel-ings. All of that was taboo for a nice young Muslim girl.

In the Muslim world, most marriages are arrangements be-tween families. This is simply how you get married. Muslim women have very few choices when it comes to marriage as compared to Western women. We are deprived of dating, falling in love, and even innocent communication with boys. Furthermore, Muslim women often face an array of family tragedies that result from Is-lamic marriage and divorce laws. These laws are simply stacked against women while giving total freedom and power to men. It is a tragedy that begins with oppression of women but ends up in a complex family dynamic that negatively impacts the whole family—men included—and indeed Muslim society as a whole.

After graduating from college, I began wondering about how and when I would get married. I did want to someday marry and have children. But I hated the idea of marrying someone I didn't know, arranged through the family, no matter how well meaning the effort. I looked around me. I didn't want to be condemned to the same destiny as the many unhappy married Egyptian women I knew. However, I understood the reality of the Middle East and that I was probably going to get married the old-fashioned way, through the family.

After college, at age twenty-one, I finally yielded to the idea of marriage and accepted an engagement with a perfect stranger who was recommended by my aunt as a great catch from a wealthy family. After the engagement party, his parents invited me to their home and we were supposed to go out to a restaurant for dinner. His mother handed her son and me a shirt to iron for him before leaving. First of all, growing up with maids to perform most of the household duties, I didn't really know how to iron. But I gave it a try. How hard could it be? Nervous and excited, and busy talking with my new fiancé, I burned the shirt. His mother came in and had a fit, sarcastically saying that obviously neither one of us could take care of ourselves, let alone be responsible for a home.

To make a long story short, the next day I handed back the ring. It was one of the shortest engagements in the Middle East.

Egyptian girls are no different than girls all over the world. They long for love and romance. One could always hope and dream, for there were some exceptions in which marriage took place after a secret love relationship. Sometimes girls and boys fell in love and would meet behind their parents' backs, in dark movie theaters or street corners where they hoped they would not be seen by relatives or family friends.

However, carrying on such a relationship involved serious risks. If they were seen by a friend, neighbor, or relative, the girl's reputation could be damaged for life and impact her whole family, especially the males in the family, whose honor depends on the chastity of the women in the family. And in Arab cultures, a young woman's chastity can be called into question for nothing more than being seen with a man.

If a couple who is in love survives the risks of such a relationship and decides to get married, the formal proposal has to come from the man and his family to the family of the bride. The final say and approval is in the hand of the parents, since marriage is not a personal matter, but a family affair. After acceptance, the next step is making the financial arrangements, a major part of marriage in Egypt. There are many factors to consider in a country with housing shortages, unemployment, and poverty. The parents immediately start discussing the dowry—which the groom pays the bride's family, the financial responsibilities of the bride and the groom, and the hardest of all, the apartment. In my generation, many young men and women could not get married because of lack of finances and the shortage of apartments. As a result, I saw many engagements broken, and the marriage age began to rise. In the sixties and seventies, because of all our wars with Israel, there was compulsory military service for all young men. They had to serve for up to seven or eight years with very little salary. Many marriages had to be postponed while men were in the military service. Even when discharged from the army, if they survived the war, these men often had little income with which to begin married life. Only the very wealthy were able to get married and afford apartments. The majority had to wait, and many who did marry were forced to live in small crowded apartments with their parents and other siblings.

For many girls and young women in Arab societies, an attempt to follow their hearts has dire consequences and does not usually lead to marriage. The young man with whom she is infatuated could very well end up being the first one to expose her and ruin her reputation. That is why girls have to think twice before entrusting a boy with as innocent a thing as a smile. It is very common for Middle Eastern men to gossip about girls whom they accuse of being "loose" or "easy" for the slightest flirtatious glance. Boys often ruin a girl's reputation after an innocent date by telling friends and even perfect strangers that the girl seduced him. How does a Muslim young woman know whom to trust? The answer is often no one when it comes to her good name. That's why dating—or any contact with boys—is such a risky act. Many girls fell in that trap and found themselves in terrible conflicts with their families and male relatives as a result of vicious accusations and lies.

A friend once told me that a certain young man that I hardly knew was claiming I was his girlfriend and that I had initiated a sexual encounter with him. I was shocked by the news. He was someone I had merely seen once at work. I had never dated him. He had never even asked me out. It was a sobering lesson for me to not trust young men.

Boys have an advantage that girls don't have in such social situations; their reputation is intact or even enhanced if they have relationships. That gives boys and young men a lot of power over girls in a boyfriend-girlfriend relationship. The girl is always the one to blame when things go wrong. The young men can and often do say, "She's a loose woman; she has no shame."

But even a careful woman, who shuns relationships, can find herself ruined, particularly if she is poor, with no family, especially no male family to provide protection. An Egyptian young man I knew bragged to me about an incident with a woman he called a "known prostitute." He said that when he was about twenty-two years old, he and a friend saw this "prostitute" on the street at night and wanted her to go with them to an apartment. When she refused and fled, they chased her down a street. She ran into a police station. They followed her into the police station and somehow convinced the officers to hand her over to them. They were able to take her out of the police station, into their car, and to an apartment where they both raped her. That woman was simply poor and had no male relatives, therefore no protection, and no respect. Worst of all, the male policemen to whom she went for protection saw nothing wrong with handing her over to her pursuers. Furthermore, the man recounting this story saw nothing wrong with his actions. When I asked him how could he do something like that, he said, "She asked for it."

That means if you are a poor Egyptian girl, without a father or brother, and decide to wear Western clothing or not cover your head, you are "asking for it." For this reason, many young women, even though they are secular, chose to cover their heads simply to avoid being looked upon as whores or be subject to rape.

That is the Egypt I did not experience personally since I came from an upper-middle-class family with power and influence. However, women of all classes in Arab society carry a terrible burden: their bodies, their "chastity."

Ironically, at the heart of Islamic fundamentalism lies the most precious and important object, the woman. She is the source of pride or shame to the Muslim man who rules and is ruled by the most despotic, tyrannical, and humiliating forms of governments on earth. It is a supreme irony that in the world of the Muslim man, the female in his family is the one object over which he may have power.

The Arabic word *harim* describes women and *hormah* is singular for a woman; the word's literal meaning is quite telling—it means "prohibited," "forbidden," or "untouchable." A woman's physical appearance is a public statement. She is covered and concealed, her virginity is subject to public verification, she suffers ritual female genital mutilation (female circumcision), she is prohibited from exercising most rights enjoyed by Muslim men, and is shackled by sharia (Islamic civil law). Adding insult to injury, she suffers the humiliation of polygamy, a privilege reserved for men.

Honor and sex are very closely tied in Arab culture. Men's honor is totally dependent on their female blood relatives. Honor is not perceived as being primarily based on personal character, honesty, integrity, and hard work, as it is in many other cultures. It is not even totally dependent on wealth and power. It's true, that with good character—as Arabs interpret it—a man can enjoy great respect and honor. And wealth and power also command respect. Yet all respect, honor, and good standing in society can disappear in a heartbeat if a man's female blood relatives do not conform to the strict sexual mores of Muslim society. And the *appearance* of improper behavior, and not just actual sexual acts, can be just as damaging. When a father marries off his daughter, a virginity check is the traditional requirement in Muslim weddings in order for the father and brothers to declare they have handed the daughter to the groom with honor. But the notion of a man's honor does not stop with his daughter. Even cousins and other far-off female blood relatives can bring shame and dishonor to a man. This creates incredible paranoia in a culture obsessed with sex and controlling it. No man can command absolute control of all the womenfolk in his extended family twenty-four hours a day.

It's in fact quite unfair when you think about it; that men's respect in society could be more dependent on the sexual behavior of their sisters, mothers, wives, or daughters than on their own personal behavior. Thus men feel compelled to monitor the way their women dress, whom they communicate with, who visits their home, and all their comings and goings. It also sets up another case of Muslim culture allowing men to avoid personal responsibility by blaming others.

The Middle East is a place of many contradictions, most of which spring from the extreme compartmentalization of the different roles people play within Arab culture. For instance, despite the extremely prudish moral code on one hand, the overt sexuality of belly dancing is accepted and appreciated by both men and women. This sensual dance is performed at weddings and in all Arab nightclubs, often in the presence of all family members, including children, who sometimes get up and mimic the dancing, as I once did at a Gaza movie theater. However, women who belly dance are looked upon by society as prostitutes. Belly dancers belong to a different and separate class that has very different values and behavior. Arab society sees nothing wrong with such compartmentalization, splitting the good and the bad and seeing each as fulfilling a legitimate role. Only recently have Muslim extremists, who are now very powerful in Egypt, moved to prohibit the centuries-old tradition of belly dancing.

Many of the Arab/Muslim social problems stem directly from the institution of polygamy. The pre-Islamic tribal desert culture in the Arabian Peninsula practiced polygamy for centuries. When Islam came upon the scene in the seventh century, instead of abolishing the practice, it codified polygamy into Islamic law, limiting men to four wives plus any number of slave women. And so this ancient Arabian form of marriage, practiced long before Muhammad arrived, ended up becoming the law for Muslims around the world and in all cultures to this day. A complex of Islamic marriage and divorce laws, designed to protect men's "honor" and maintain their total control over women, compounds the devastating consequences of this practice.

In addition to the actual laws, a whole array of taboos and social restrictions on women were created to help men control their female flock and thus their honor. These taboos and laws undermine women's sense of security and respect as partners in marriage, and their relationships to their children, in-laws, and other women, as well as increase women's dependence on their original family when things go wrong.

In more moderate Muslim countries like Egypt, second marriages are not encouraged but tolerated. And they are usually shrouded in secrecy among the more educated classes. In Egypt, Sunni Muslims practice three forms of marriage. The first is the typical public, official first marriage duly recorded in the courts. A second type is called an *urfi* marriage, usually done in secret with witnesses but unrecorded with civil courts. Many men who have second marriages prefer urfi marriage because it's harder for first wives to discover it. A third form is a temporary marriage contract called *mutaa* marriage, literally meaning "pleasure marriage." Technically, it is available to both married men and single women, but in practice it is an action initiated by men. This form of marriage, also usually done in secrecy, is for the express purpose of having sex, often for a one-night stand. Under this form of marriage, men can satisfy their lust over any woman for one night, usually in exchange for money (calling it a dowry), and still feel that it is acceptable in the eyes of God. This practice usually boils down to little more than legalized prostitution. Under Islamic law, men have the freedom and many choices to actually legally cheat on their wives, while wives are unable to get a divorce or have a relationship, even when their husband has left them.

How does this affect the dynamics between a husband and wife? Men do not even have to exercise their right to additional wives for the damage to be done. By allowing men to be "loyal" to up to four wives, the stage is set for women always to distrust their husbands. Nor can they trust women friends. Any other woman could shamelessly become an eligible "bachelorette" for one's husband. Instances of women marrying the husbands of their best friends and having his children behind the first wife's back do happen.

A single Muslim woman with an eye on a married man can say: "He is a man with a free will to exercise his religious rights to marry another woman. Our marriage will still be blessed by God, just as that of the first wife. He is within his rights to have both of us." I have actually heard some Muslim women say that. Any man, married or not, can be regarded by a single women as available. Men whose wives are unable to have a baby right after marriage, regardless of who is responsible, are especially likely to seek second marriages. Egyptian movies often reflect such real-life dramas. Situation comedies are filled with women who seek the help of fortune-tellers or give potions to a husband without his knowledge in an effort to retain his love and keep him from seeking a second wife who can give him the prize of a son. Such comedies reflect the fear of a second wife by desperate first wives.

Many famous movie stars, politicians, doctors, and other wealthy Muslims have more than one wife and many are kept secret. Most presidents, dictators, and men of power in the Arab world have second wives and some even more. Famous examples are the men of the Saudi royal family, Osama bin Laden, and Saddam Hussein.

The end result is an environment that sets women up as adversaries against one another, causing much unnecessary distrust and caution. Competitive relationships among women also deprive them of forming support groups to stand up to the many injustices they are all suffering under. Thus relationships among women in Muslim countries become haphazard, strained, and even hostile. Few Muslim women venture to form relationships outside the family or clan, and very often husbands discourage it. Western-style women's groups and organizations working for a common cause and to influence change are almost nonexistent in the clanlike Muslim culture. The problem is compounded by fear of envy and the evil eye in Arab society, which is a major Muslim cultural phenomenon. Muslim women, as a result of all these roadblocks, end up having no moral pressure or political muscle to work together to make polygamy unacceptable. Expressing disagreement or any attempts at change are viewed as subversive behavior and outright attacks on Islam.

And, of course, fear of polygamy makes it impossible for a wife to form a bond of trust with her husband. When a husband starts earning more money, a warning bell starts ringing in a woman's head, since he can now afford the second wife. I remember hearing conversations among Arab wives advising one another to "pluck up his feathers," meaning spend his money as fast as possible before there is extra for another wife. Women relatives sometimes advise a woman to hide some money behind his back with her family, as a form of security in case of a second marriage. "Hiding money for a bad day" does not sound like a bad plan in such an insecure situation.

Women's financial insecurity can affect many areas of family life, such as the raising of children, since child support can be very difficult to collect when there are other wives and their children involved. That is why the first wife is often left in the dark about the second wife. However, usually the man's own family and some of his close friends know of a second marriage and willingly cover up for him. I have heard numerous horror stories of women discovering the existence of a second wife and other children after the death of their husbands, with whom they now have to share the inheritance as equals. Some end up holding separate funeral services for the same man.

A Muslim wife is threatened by single women in a way that no Christian wife can imagine. It is true that Christian husbands can and do cheat on their wives, but the threat of a mistress and the threat of a legal wife in the eyes of society and God are two very different things. Under Islamic law, a second wife—and third and fourth—are legally equal to the first in every way, including inheritance. This is very different from an affair in the West where a mistress has no rights and is discouraged by religion and society from making or accepting advances from a married man. If a Western man chooses to marry his mistress, he must first obtain a legal divorce from his first wife and settle any financial issues with her before he can marry a second time. That makes all the difference.

I will always remember hearing the wife of a family member crying to her husband after an argument, "Go ahead and have affairs, but please, for the sake of the children, don't take a second wife." Her voice still rings in my ears after the passage of decades as a sad lesson on what was to come when it would be my turn to get married. She feared the existence of another wife and children would not only end her role as the sole wife, but also be an unfathomable blow to her stature and pride. The second wife would be regarded as equal by law and society.

In order for Arab women to live and function around the social injustice and oppressive marriage laws, they had to develop elaborate manipulative behavior to get a modicum of respect and power. Arab fairy tales, such as those in the famous *Tales from the Thousand and One Nights*, reflect the impossible life of the main character, Shahrazad, a woman struggling to survive by telling tales to please the king. Every year, during the holy month of Ramadan, we listened on the radio to thirty shows featuring the tales of Shahrazad. Every evening, at the end of each story, my cousins, sisters, and I would be on the edge of our seats, worried and anxious about Shahrazad. Will the king like tonight's story and spare her life? Or will she be killed like the rest of his harem? Shahrazad's struggle was to keep the king amused and never fully satisfied; she always had to end on a note that kept him—and the listeners—eager to hear more. If she failed to amuse him or he became bored, then she would be killed. So we all hoped and prayed for an even better story the next day so her life would be saved. We heard Shahrazad nightly pour her talent, charm, deceit, distrust, fear, and female sexual manipulation into the effort to save her life. We girls were learning the lessons of manipulative survival from these stories, getting ready to shoulder the burden of Muslim women on how to survive in a cruel culture with few options and no loyalty expected from our life partner.

Even as children we were aware that Shahrazad was not a wife but one of the king's harem forced into sexual slavery. Even today, Islamic law allows men many choices to have sex. Beside the three types of marriage and the technical allowance of up to four wives, the Muslim concept of *ma malakat aymanahum* permits men to have sex outside of marriage with women he "owns," such as slaves. In that case a woman has to tolerate sex against her will by a man who considers her his property. Of course many Muslims will say this concept is irrelevant because slavery is no longer practiced in the Muslim world. Yet its legacy lives on. For example, household help may be considered in the eyes of some men as "owned" and thus the concept of *ma malakat aymanahum* can apply. That is why we see an epidemic in rapes of maids in Muslim homes, a fate many Filipino maids in Saudi Arabia have endured. The Muslim north in Sudan does enslave the Christian south and thus Sudanese Christian women are frequently forced by Muslim men into having sex. Non-Muslim women living in majority-Muslim countries have very few laws to protect them.

The same culture that allows Muslim men many outlets for sex—even forced sex—tacitly permits honor killing of women and, in some countries, death by stoning for women who have sex outside of marriage. Compare two cases: a man who forces sex on his maid and an unmarried woman caught sleeping with her lover. In both cases, sex outside of marriage has occurred, but one is not punished under Islamic law and the other is very severely punished. A review of the stoning cases in hard-line Muslim states will show that it is *choice*, not the sex act itself, that brings a death penalty. Choice is solely a man's prerogative. A woman can be forced into a slave-master sexual relationship—that is not considered against the law. But should a woman exercise control over her body, should she choose to have sex, and, even worse, choose her partner, she has committed a sin punishable by death. Islamic laws by design give women very little control over their bodies and their sexual and marital relationships, perpetuating the epidemic of humiliation and degradation of Muslim women.

The sense of powerlessness women feel can manifest in bizarre ways. Since blaming their men for misbehavior will get women nowhere, it is easier to blame it on the evil eye or the female victim of a man rather than the true male perpetrator. This is also often done to save face in front of friends and neighbors. For example, my sister's neighbor caught her husband, a hajj who had just returned from the pilgrimage in Mecca, raping the young maid. After the scandal became known to the whole building, the wife denied the rape, blamed the maid, and kicked her out on the street. She later said that all of this was the result of the evil eye from neighbors who envied her husband's successful business.

At all levels of Islamic society, the sharia laws turn the relationship between husband and wife from that of partners to one of slave and master. Women of the lower, uneducated classes are especially vulnerable to polygamy's effects. I heard many horror stories from our maids, sitting in our kitchen, listening to their stories and trying to comfort them after their husbands had abandoned them for a second wife. They would complain that their husband's income now could not take care of two wives and two sets of children. And they now had to work very hard to provide for their own children. They had in essence become "single mothers." The strength and resilience of some of these women amaze me to this today. The story of Om Ali was especially sad since she had breast cancer and needed extraordinary help and medical care. She would talk to me about her pride in her son Ali, who was now the man of the house and did not talk to his father anymore.

Very often these maids would show me their bruises from beatings they were subjected to. A notorious verse in the Koran, Surah 4:34, advises Muslim husbands with regard to wives from whom they fear "rebellion," to admonish them, abstain from laying with them, and beat them—*wa-dribuwhunnu*. Because of that verse in the Koran, many Muslim men feel that it is within their legal and religious right to beat their wives.

Physical abuse of women in Muslim culture is very common and occurs at all levels of the social ladder. Slapping women on the face and pushing them to the ground are common scenes in many Arabic TV shows and movies. Even educated Arab producers include wife beating as a normal part of arguments between husband and wife. I once heard an educated Egyptian man proudly say that when his wife asked him for a divorce after an argument in their first year of marriage, he slapped her on the face. He then added that she never asked him for a divorce again. He spoke about the incident with pride, as having fulfilled his obligation as a man in control of his woman. This same man was later discovered to have a second wife in secret. Wife beating, which is justified in Islam under certain conditions, can end up being used by Muslim men as a tool to silence the first wife into tolerating polygamy. Wife beating thus adds yet another layer and dimension to the built-in anger within the Muslim family.

Even in the United States, I hear many complaints from Arab girls who are physically beaten by their brothers and fathers. A twenty-four-year-old Jordanian coworker, a U.S citizen who lived at home, once confided in me that she was beaten by her father and brother and showed me the scars on her body. My daughter had a Jordanian high school friend who was known by her close friends to be physically abused and not allowed to leave the house or invite girls from school to her home. Physical abuse in the Arab Muslim community in the West often goes unreported to the authorities.

Polygamy wreaks havoc on the whole family and touches all classes. As a teenager in Egypt, I remember our neighbor came to us one day crying because she had discovered that her physician husband had been married for years to one of his attractive young patients and already had a little girl with her. The couple, both of them very distinguished physicians, had been married for twenty years and had two teenage sons. The husband, whom I called Uncle

Maged, was very charming and an overall nice man whom I greatly respected. He was well traveled and liked by everybody. When our neighbor woman confronted Uncle Maged with her discovery, his response was "What do you want? I am within my rights." She asked him to divorce the other woman. He refused. She told him, "Then you have to divorce me," thinking he would back down. Maged called her bluff; the next day he divorced his wife of twenty years.

Even a nice man like Uncle Maged was corrupted by his right to polygamy. The distinguished woman physician was reduced to a helpless woman because of a law that destroyed her beautiful family. Her marriage ended up not much different from the poor, uneducated maids I used to comfort in our kitchen.

Divorce under Islamic law is very easy for a man and is accomplished by the husband repeating the phrase "I divorce you" three times. That's it! A woman on the other hand may ask (or beg) the man to divorce her but cannot do it herself. Unless the husband grants the divorce, it simply cannot happen. While it was little consolation for our physician friend, she at least was granted a divorce. That, ironically, is more than many abandoned wives get.

This area of sharia law does not differentiate between the most educated or sophisticated Arab women and their illiterate village sisters. Any Muslim woman can end up being one of two, three, or four women all married to one man with or without the knowledge of the first wife. And if the first wife objects to her husband marrying, she has no recourse in the legal system. Even though she has essentially been abandoned, she has no right to divorce him and still needs her husband's permission for many activities, such as travel. While he has remarried and is having a normal married life and children with the new wife, she is forbidden from doing the same thing and cannot remarry until four months after he divorces her, if he ever does.

One day a young woman friend and coworker in Egypt confided to me the details of her divorce horror story. She, like me and all other Egyptian young women, lived with her parents. Five years earlier, she had been married, but it was a very unhappy situation. When she asked her husband for a divorce, he refused. He sent her back to her family but kept her legally married to him in retaliation for his wounded pride. At the same time, he married another woman with whom he had a couple of children. He could have divorced my friend in a minute if he had wished, allowing her to resume her normal life and perhaps remarry. But he refused to give her a divorce even when her parents begged him for it. Here she was, an attractive young woman in her twenties, unable to have relationships with other men because that would be *zina*, meaning "having sex outside of marriage," which is punishable by law. In Arab countries, the zina laws are usually used against women since men's sexual freedom is regarded as part of their manhood and easily facilitated by their legal rights to have extramarital sex through urfi and mutaa marriages. You can't take him to jail for that, but you can certainly take a Muslim woman to jail if she has premarital or outside-of-marriage sex. My friend ended up unable to remarry, become engaged, or have any kind of male relationship from age eighteen to twenty-four. She had to go through years of unsuccessful court procedures until finally her family convinced him to divorce her by bribing him with a hefty sum of money.

But even beyond the divorce issue, sharia closes all doors for women who seek to live an independent lifestyle. *Beit el taa*, meaning "house of obedience," is a law in Egypt that causes much fear in women. Under that law, a man can be given permission by the court to sequester his wife at home as punishment for disobedience. This controversial law has been the subject of many jokes and is poked fun at in many Arab comedy movies. But to the women who have suffered from it, there is nothing humorous about beit el taa.

Another block on women's freedom is their limited choice in marriage. Muslim men have the right to marry non-Muslim and foreign women. Muslim women have no such right and can marry only Muslim men. (When Egyptian men marry foreigners, their wives are automatically granted Egyptian citizenship. However, if Egyptian women marry foreigners, even if they convert to Islam, these husbands do not get citizenship.) This inequity gives men a larger range of women to choose from and causes a gap of availability of men to Muslim women. The end result is a large number of unmarried women who have a limited and much smaller population of Muslim men to choose from. In fact, Egypt has a large female population who have remained unmarried into their forties and fifties, usually living with elderly parents or other family. This is due in part to the losses in the wars with Israel in the 1960s and '70s, creating more Muslim women in this age group than men, plus, the fact that Muslim men have the right under Islamic law to marry non-Muslim women, which also contributed to the shortage of available men.

Foreign non-Muslim men find it hard to get to know, let alone marry, Muslim women because dating is prohibited in Muslim countries. Furthermore, a non-Muslim man who wants to marry a Muslim woman has to convert to Islam before the marriage can take place. On the other hand, there is a new trend of Muslim men marrying non-Muslim women for the purpose of spreading Islam. Many men also find it easier to marry a non-Muslim foreigner: he does not have to pay a dowry or follow strict family courtship rules, and the wife's family isn't likely to bother him by looking after her interests.

Muslim women living in the West who marry a Western Christian man must hide that fact from the Muslim community, especially when they visit the old country. According to Islam, these women are no longer Muslims and could be punished harshly. Without the protection of Western society, these women could even be killed in their own countries for marrying non-Muslims. While Muslim men are rewarded for marrying Christian and foreign women for doing a good deed by spreading Islam, Muslim women are denied the same right. Muslim women must remain loyal to Muslim men and society even if at the expense of never finding a husband.

Practicing Muslim women who live in Judeo-Christian societies are certainly happier living under Judeo-Christian laws that
prohibit polygamy and wife beating and give them equal rights
with their husbands. That is why we see many attempts by radical
Muslims to bring their sharia civil law in marriage and family
matters into the West. Canada has recently refused to enforce
sharia family laws and in the process had to adjust many of its own
laws pertaining to other groups and religions so as not to appear
discriminatory.

On the other hand, Western women who marry Muslim men
and choose to live in the Muslim world are no longer protected by
the Western legal system. They discover, when the marriage ends,
after it is too late, the desperate situation in which they have become entrapped. They cannot bring their children back home to
the West and are often prevented from seeing them at all. In Islam,
the father has the right to keep the children after a certain age.
Very often Muslim men residing in the United States will leave
their American wives, take their children, and go back to their
home country to be wed to a new wife without even having given
their Western wife a divorce. We have all heard the horror stories
of American women falling victims to sharia laws and never seeing
their children again. These children, who end up living in Saudi
Arabia or Iran, are taught that their mother is an American infidel
and a loose woman because she does not cover her head.

There may be unpleasant surprises ahead even for those American women who marry Muslims and stay in the West. They are
often not prepared for the way in which their husbands might exercise control over every aspect of their lives. I once received an
e-mail from an American woman who was married to a Muslim
man in Texas. She told me how wrong I was in my views, that she
is now a covered-up Muslim, happy to please her husband, and
that Islam is the best thing that has happened to her. I congratulated her and wished her good luck. A few months later, the same
woman wrote me another e-mail complaining about her husband
and his family and desperately asking for advice. I reminded her of

the e-mail she had written to me a few months earlier, in which she told a completely different story. She insisted she had had never before sent me an e-mail, but she remembered that after reading one of my articles a few months earlier her husband had reprimanded her for doing so. He angrily took the article away from her. The article had my e-mail address on it, and she realized he must have used her e-mail account to send me that e-mail himself. We developed a short Internet friendship, and she wrote to me a year later saying she had obtained a divorce and was back with her family and her church in Texas.

Every Western woman needs to understand both the negatives and positives of marrying into the Middle Eastern Muslim culture before taking a step that might change her life forever. She has to fully understand sharia law before stepping into Saudi Arabia or other Muslim countries. Unfortunately many vulnerable American women are still lured by love, money, and promises. A good book on Arab culture and law might save them a lot of heartbreak later on in their marriages.

I realized at a young age that there were very few happy marriages around me. With few exceptions, it was a miracle of extraordinary good luck for a woman to find happiness and security in a Muslim marriage. If a husband stays married and faithful to his first wife, then it is a sign of his generosity and good graces. That wife should then thank her lucky stars and be eternally grateful to him and his whole family. For her good fortune, she becomes the envy of other women. However, in the back of her mind she is always in fear. Security for Muslim women in marriage may come later in life when a man gets older and more dependent on his wife. A Muslim wife can try to demand her husband's exclusive loyalty and faithfulness, but their marriage contract does not require it, and there are no guarantees that his loyalty will hold in the face of the inevitable challenges to any relationship.

In modern Muslim societies, objections to this inequity are frequently dismissed with comments like "So what? Most Muslim men have only one wife anyway." Some Muslim men jokingly say, "We can hardly even take care of one wife, let alone four, so why should we reform these laws?" However, these comments are insincere and do not address the terrible consequences of polygamy. They miss the point, which is the effect sharia laws have on all of society by virtue of their existence, even upon monogamous families.

As a teenager, I vividly recall watching the scene of a church wedding in an old Hollywood movie. I was very touched by the holiness of the marriage vows, especially when the husband promised to love, honor, and cherish his one and only wife "till death do us part." And they said their vows to each other as two equals before God. That scene struck me so deeply that I wept over the beauty of those words. After the movie, I asked my aunt, "How come we don't have weddings like that?" Her answer missed the point. "We do have very glamorous weddings too," she said defensively, as if the issue was glamour or romance. I nagged her, without comprehending why. "No! We don't have weddings like that!"

I now realize that my innocent mind was touched not only by the romance of the marriage vows but also by the way a Christian woman was honored and elevated by her husband and society, and by the stability and comfort that a monogamous union promised to offer a man and a woman—and their family.

In sharp contrast, Muslim weddings are more about sex and money. They do not convey the holy covenant of marriage. The traditional virginity check of the bride is no longer practiced among the upper classes but is still common among the less educated classes. In these more traditional weddings, there is an exchange of the dowry between the groom and father of the bride, and then the belly dancers lead the bride and groom to the bedroom for the virginity test. (Hymen rebuilding operations are sometimes done in the Muslim world to prevent a scandal or a tragedy on the wedding day.)

The Judeo-Christian culture has greatly contributed to humanity and the order of things in Western civilization by its insistence on the value of one man, one woman, joined in holy matrimony. It has resulted in a far more stable social order. Even though Islam is supposedly rooted in the Judeo-Christian tradition, the commandments and exhortations for monogamy seem to have been completely lost to the desert culture of Mecca. In matters of marriage and family, one society protects its citizen's human rights and dignity and the other does not. The Western man lives as an equal partner with his one and only free wife. The Muslim man lives with up to four wives as a dictator.

For all the ills suffered by women because of polygamy, men are negatively impacted as well. Polygamy deprives men of the intimacy and security that belonging to one woman offers. A man knows deep down in his psyche that his loyalty to his wife "in sickness or in health, in wealth or poverty, till death do us part" is secondary. But deep down, he also knows that he cannot count on her emotional loyalty to him "in sickness or in health, in wealth or poverty, till death do us part." If she cannot feel secure in their relationship, neither can he.

A man may decide to be faithful to one woman and never marry another, but in the back of his mind he always knows that his faithfulness is not required by God. While men may like fantasizing about having more than one wife, I believe that the majority of men do need the stability and intimacy of a relationship limited to only one woman. In the end, having many wives can have the same effect on a man as having none at all.

Polygamy made legal has a corrupting effect on men and becomes a burden and a temptation they cannot avoid in times of trouble. In practice, when the inevitable conflicts of marriage occur, many Muslim men resort to a second wife, or threat thereof, as their "solution" instead of working out the problem. Polygamy offers them an easy escape from their marriage when times get tough. Not only does it set up a disincentive to solve the inevitable crises of marriage, but it also robs marriage of the healthy give-and-take between partners, which adds to the stability of a marriage and teaches children about relationships and conflict resolution.

There is yet another negative effect of polygamy and Islamic marriage laws for men. Poor Muslim men have to compete with older, wealthier married men for single women. You see them, the throngs of angry, restless, young men who make up the seething Arab street. First, these young men are sexually repressed by the extreme Islamic sexual morality codes. And second, economic realities make it difficult for them to get married. In order to marry they must pay a dowry and provide an apartment in an economy where only the children of the rich can afford such things. After marriage they need to support their wives and the many children their society encourages them to have. Polygamy is unfavorable to poorer lower-class Muslim men and contributes to this imbalance, because many young women would rather become the second wife to an older, richer man than take a chance with a young, poor, possibly volatile man who is likely to become abusive, or at a minimum behave like a spoiled brat.

In the current climate, these young unmarried Islamic men are ripe for fundamentalism and jihad. Repressed, disaffected, unable to marry or afford an apartment, unable to get a job or unhappy in an abusive job, these young Muslim men see heaven with seventy-two virgins to service their every sexual fantasy as a tempting lure. After all, that is what they hear from their religious leaders day in and day out in their neighborhood mosques.

Married or unmarried, many Muslim men become pawns in a dysfunctional society. They are asked to give up their lives and become a shahid for the sake of jihad. Even their mothers and wives who love them are encouraged to show pride when they die in war or sacrifice themselves in acts of terrorism. The political and religious leaders who encourage them to do so have no intentions of dying as a shahid themselves.

One cannot help but ask: Why are there so many Muslim men ready to give up their life for shahada? Why would they choose to abandon their dominant role inside their home and the freedoms

Islamic marriage law grants them? Could it be that they too are unhappy under the Muslim marriage contract? Is heaven with its promise of unlimited sexual pleasure their rescue from life's disappointments and unhappy family life on earth?

It's true that Muslim women have to juggle a complicated web of injustice, limitations, harm, and deceit. The Muslim marriage laws skewed in favor of men leave women in a very weak position, but that injustice obviously does not come free of cost to men and has a devastating impact on every aspect of Muslim society.

Marriage and divorce laws have numerous and profound effects not just on women and men, but the family unit, children, secondary relationships, and ultimately Muslim society as a whole. One of the basic roles of religion is to regulate the codes of behavior that will stabilize this sacred marriage union for the benefit and good of children and of the greater society. For many centuries, polygamy has delivered a devastating impact on the healthy function and the structure of loyalties of the Muslim family. The source of all loyalty in the family is the one between husband and wife. Relationships extending out beyond the marriage depend on the stability provided by that man-woman unit.

Islam asks men to be fair and just among the wives and to treat them all equally. Perhaps the nomadic tribes in the desert found a way to achieve a just balance a thousand years ago. Perhaps it is an ideal that has never happened. In reality, a man's loyalty thus divided between multiple wives can never bring peace, stability, and trust to any of the parties involved, including the children.

Beyond being unfair to women, polygamy has much deeper, unintended, damaging consequences to the healthy upbringing of children, including male children. As infants and children, Muslim men are raised by their oppressed mothers until an older age when the father takes over. A first wife's loyalty to her husband is completely undermined if he takes a second wife or if she fears he will, and the woman ends up shifting her loyalty to her firstborn son and her own blood relatives. The son becomes her man and her defender, very often against his own father, whom he blames for marrying a second wife. At the same time, he has learned from his father and male relatives a sense of entitlement. These sons on one hand may be mama's boys, and on the other hand, arrogant "spoiled brats."

In addition to needing the protection and support of her eldest son against unjust treatment from her husband, frequently a woman's father or brother will step in to settle disputes with her husband, even after many years of marriage. The unit of loyalty in the Muslim family is then transferred from husband-and-wife to mother-and-son or to mother-and-her-family versus husband-and-other-wives and husband-and-his-own-family, who very often cover up for his second marriage. The end result is that family cohesion and structure is fragmented, and loyalties become tangled in endless complications. Distrust and anger prevail, and elaborate behavior on every side takes place to protect everyone's rights. None of this would be necessary if marriage was considered a holy covenant between one man and one woman, which would transfer the loyalty and trust to the basic nucleus of the family from where all trust comes: the husband and wife.

Even a woman's name reflects the confusion in the family structure. Women in the Middle East do not change their last names to that of their husbands after they get married, as is common in the West. That is not because they are "liberated," but because they live and die with their honor and loyalty belonging to their blood male relatives—their fathers and brothers. Unofficially, Muslim women become known by their son's name such as *Om Muhammad*, meaning "Mother of Muhammad" or *Om Ali*, "Mother of Ali." Their first son becomes their new identity, their true man and defender.

This mother-son bond leads to especially strained and bizarre relationships between mothers and daughters-in-law. When a son marries, a mother who had transferred her loyalty to her son suddenly may feel her position with her son is threatened. In some instances, she chooses the son's wife, which helps place her in a powerful position in relationship to her daughter-in-law, especially in the first years of the marriage. The new wife must please her mother-in-law—as much as she must please her husband. Often the couple lives in the house of the mother, and the daughter-in-law ends up having to "serve her" more so than the mother-in-law's own daughters. There are even cases among the poorer classes where the new wife is abused, both verbally and physically, by her mother-in-law—particularly in Islamic Pakistan.

In this messy sea of interlocking loyalties, the new wife is faced with a dilemma: by pleasing her mother-in-law, the wife might guarantee her in-law's approval and consequently secure her support to convince the son not to marry another woman. On the other hand, the mother-in-law might encourage her son to get a second wife if she feels her daughter-in-law is not obedient enough. I have seen many such examples in Egypt even among educated and middle-class families. If this all seems confusing, that's the whole point. It's a disaster!

When Westerners criticize Muslim society's discrimination against women, many Muslims proudly claim that women in Islam have more property rights than Western women. They say, "With all the oppressive laws to control women, how is it that their property is protected? After marriage a Muslim woman's property is still hers." That claim is misleading and taken out of context. Yes, women keep the property they inherit from their family—the concept of community (marital) property does not exist in Muslim culture, which I believe is due to polygamy. The personal property of a woman after marriage remains hers simply because her husband has the right to marry up to three other wives, and therefore her family has to protect their family property from going to additional wives and their children. These property laws, in fact, prove the point that a Muslim married woman is never secure as a result of polygamy laws. The woman and the man are two legally separate entities, and the finances of the two have to be separated. That's because a wife must protect herself and her family's assets from becoming the property of three other wives and their children.

Her male relatives (brother and father) are still her protectors after marriage, and because of polygamy, she must entrust only them with her wealth. So the claims of Muslim scholars that Muslim women have more rights in regards to their property than Western women is only a partial truth. Furthermore, just as in court her statement counts as half the value of a male, a woman is also half the worth of a man when it comes to inheritance. Yes, under law, she receives half the amount of inheritance of a male relative.

In addition to other wives, a man's father, mother, and siblings also share his inheritance with his wife and children. I remember my aunt asking her husband, a wealthy businessman, who had parents and many brothers and sisters, to give her a will to transfer all his wealth to her and her five children at his death. He refused, saying that he wanted God's sharia inheritance laws to stay in place. Then he jokingly asked, "Why? Do you want to be a rich widow and remarry?" When my aunt's husband eventually died, his mother, father, and siblings shared his inheritance with her and her children. My aunt ended up with only about 20 percent of the inheritance.

There are, of course, many exceptions to the marriage and family tragedies in the Muslim world. I am sure there are Muslim women who are happily married. There are also many good Muslim men who are faithful to their wives and treat them as equals. You will also find rich Muslim widows whose luck changed later in life, even though they started their lives as typical oppressed Muslim women. Their lives usually changed over the years after a large inheritance, which allowed them to achieve independence.

But for the vast majority, the changes needed at a grassroots level have not yet happened in the Muslim world. In order for Arab feminists to succeed in their attempts to achieve reforms for women, they have to take their cause not just to the courts, but also work within the larger context of political and social reform to achieve democracy. Many think that time will cure fundamentalism and radicalism in Islam. However, we have seen just the opposite to be true. In recent decades, the clock has turned backward, and reform has become more difficult.

Tightly controlled through various religious laws and taboos, Muslim women are left blind to their natural human rights. Under the thumb of an authoritarian society, they live and die never knowing of any other options, totally ignorant of the rights that many women in other societies enjoy and even take for granted.

The majority of Muslim women see no escape route from their plight. Even after death, in the paradise of Islam, women are given the short end of the stick. The idea of heaven is a lustful man's dream and a woman's nightmare. Since men who die as shahid are promised seventy-two virgins, a woman in Islam's heaven is supposed to be servicing men's sensual desires together with about seventy-one other women. Islam has once again been extra-generous to men at the expense of women. Polygamy follows them in heaven.

The natural reaction for women to resolve this repression could be either to revolt or to end up becoming *even more* radical and religious than her male counterpart. Revolting is regarded as anti-Muslim and against Allah's commands, and that makes it out of the question for many Muslim women. For some, the solution ends up being, "If you can't beat them, join them." The only door left open for them to achieve power and respect is through compliance and becoming a part of the larger system that oppresses other women. To many the veil then becomes a woman's symbol of honor, power, and respect; her female form of jihad.

Ironically, compliance thus becomes a technique for escaping discrimination and a way out of oppression. Many Muslim women themselves have no tolerance for Muslim "feminists" who want to change the system. Some even go as far as exposing "the bad Muslim women" who do not adhere to the rules of proper behavior. Hence, most attempts for change by Muslim feminists end up rejected, ridiculed, or diluted. They are accused of apostasy and obscenity.

Attempts to reform sharia marriage laws are quickly silenced by today's Islamic religious tyrants. A secular couple in Muslim society is viewed as a great threat, thus Muslim law can divorce them! This has even gone as far as attempting to impose a divorce brought to the court by a third party upon an unwilling couple as punishment for their holding secular views. A scholar by the name of Nasr Abu Zayd faced such an attack in court and had to flee Egypt with his wife.

Several brave, moderate Muslim women's groups have risen and fallen, and few remain standing to fight for reform and change. Most often they are blocked by dead-end courts and *fatwas* (death warrants) issued against outspoken Arab women. Farag Foda, a human rights activist and an advocate of women's rights in Egypt, was accused of apostasy and gunned down in front of his Cairo office in 1992 by Islamists even though he had never criticized Islam. His killers defended the murder by calling it a "righteous act."

Arab feminists are not succeeding because the majority of Muslim women are silent and afraid of change. Furthermore, often they have to fight not just the law, but those Muslim women who feel their only way to gain respect in society is to become radical and cover up from head to toe. When attempts are made for some equality and justice in the lives of women, we often hear the "good" conformist Arab Muslim women say, "No, we are happy this way." Some who say that are sincere. Those who are truly content are the few who have professional or oil-rich husbands who have the power to keep them well protected and treat them well at home. But that is certainly not the condition of the larger majority of the population, especially the poorer masses.

Feminism also fails in Egypt and other Arab countries because it is regarded as a creation of the West, but Muslim women can and should forge their own brand of feminism. Too often Arab women equate female independence with a narrow and negative perception of the West. They judge Western values from the Hollywood movies that portray an insane, violent American society rife with sexual excesses, drugs, and crime. That is their only window onto

American life. They do not understand the justice, integrity, equality, and honesty of Western culture. They do not see the virtues in everyday American families, the hard-working, law-abiding, decent American communities living largely peacefully in diverse religious and racial harmony.

Change is resisted because it is feared that it would come at the expense of men's honor or women's chastity. Resistance to progress then results in stagnation, and an entire Muslim region becomes largely dysfunctional—politically, economically, socially, and culturally.

To complete the picture of the dynamics of the Muslim family, we have to address the negatives of being a Muslim man who holds all this power over his female relatives but has to endure the injustice, humiliation, and insecurity of living under the brutal totalitarian regimes of the Middle East. This political reality also has an effect on family life and the treatment of women. This chain of oppression and brutality operates between all levels of social classes, from top to bottom. Muslim men create and also live under dictatorships such as that of Saddam Hussein, Hafez al-Assad, the Taliban, and Muammar Gaddafi. That is very different from Western men who create their own destiny within a system of democracy that allows them to benefit both financially and socially from hard work, dedication, and loyalty to family.

In the minds of many Muslim men in the much-feared Arab street, their rights on earth do not come from their creator, Allah, but from the dictator whom they have learned to appease for survival. It is amazing how the most radical religion on earth has a population that seems to fear their leaders more than Allah. We have all seen the pictures of torture of men by Saddam Hussein. Tragically, there is much more that goes unreported in many other Muslim countries. The supposedly educated men and women who control the Arab media are participating in suppressing such stories. Sadly, perhaps women symbolize a man's only chance for honor. For Arab men's personal honor is daily snatched from them by the brutality of the outside world, where they have to deal with abusive bosses, police who demand bribes under threat of jail, and all manner of other extortionist government bureaucrats. Dictators like Saddam understood this dynamic and acted upon it to get men's confessions by having their wives and daughters raped during the interrogation process. That is the worst punishment you can give an Arab man. Saddam took away these men's only connection to some honor and self-respect embodied in their wives and female family members.

Is it any wonder that Muslim men desperately cling to their women's honor, submission, and obedience? Taking away sharia marriage and divorce laws from men without reforming the oppressive dictatorial system under which they must live would bring down upon them an unbearable sense of failure.

Muslim men of power and wealth carry their authoritarian control at home into the workplace. Arab bosses are commonly rude and even brutal to subordinate workers, to a degree that goes far beyond typical Western workplace complaints. During a construction project in my home in Egypt, I once saw the contractor slap one of the workers on the face. Others workers surrounding urged him to control himself and not return the slap. The worker did not strike back; his livelihood was in the hands of his boss. The end result is that workers have to compete to please the boss and even step on one another's rights to curry favor. I often saw in the streets of Cairo young teenage boys or children in menial jobs being beaten by their bosses. They take it because their families need the job for survival. Abused at their jobs, such men have only one consolation; when they get home, they are the bosses.

The chain of oppression then trickles down to the home, with women and children at the bottom of the food chain in a giant machine of oppression from one level of the social structure to the next. Even children cannot escape this cruel system, which perpetuates much anger inside Muslim families. Child abuse occurring within the home is hardly discussed, and when it happens, it's regarded as "good upbringing." In Arab society, child abuse is neither recognized nor understood and is never reported simply because there is no interest, even by the police or legal system.

Some of the anger within the family is, in fact, rooted in cultural child-rearing attitudes and practices that on the surface seem acceptable and normal. My grandmother, like all Arab mothers, based her upbringing philosophy on shaming and criticizing children by using the word *eabe*, which means improper or disgraceful behavior, or the expression *ellet adab*, meaning lack of proper behavior. We heard these two words all the time from our elders. Many normal childhood behaviors—even laughing out loud—was considered improper. If we giggled, we were told *"El dihk men kheir sabab ellet adab,"* meaning "laughing for no reason is lack of proper behavior." This code of proper behavior is enforced by everyone. No one is spared the disapproving microscopic examination by the eyes of Arab society. In Arab society, it is the duty of all adults to shout *eabe* and *ellet adab* to the children. The word *haram*, meaning "forbidden by God," brought another dimension to shaming. With this word added, it became "God will curse you" if you misbehave. I believe this attitude toward child rearing is one of the underlying reasons why Arabs are so sensitive to criticism and tend to blame others rather than accept responsibility for their actions. As children, those who admitted fault were severely punished. Doing so opened a whole can of worms. Telling the truth and taking responsibility was simply unacceptable. That cultural stricture can have the effect of paralyzing progress. Unique and spontaneous behavior is the basis of innovation and progress, but anyone who did anything out of the ordinary or in any way promoted change or deviation from the norm was called shameful names and ousted from respectful society.

I truly believe that the anger that is pushing the wheels of Islamic terrorism can be traced back to pent-up anger within the Muslim family. For any reform to be achieved, a good starting point would be the family unit and reforming the Muslim marriage contract giving both men and women equal rights to marriage and divorce as well as instituting monogamy. However, these reforms can be sustained only within a democracy that will end the instability, paranoia, and inequity in Muslim society. A Muslim man's loyalty to one wife and a true, nurturing family unit to live for will be a stabilizing factor and motivation for loving life and not escaping from it.

Five

The Invisible Wall

In 1970 I was now a young woman, and like most Egyptian single young women, I was still living in my mother's home. By then we had moved from Heliopolis to Maadi, a nice suburb of Cairo close to the Nile River, a neighborhood with more greenery than the rest of Cairo. Cairo at that time was a dusty city with very few trees. The city was overpopulated and traveling from one area to another was brutal.

My first job out of university was working at the English desk of the Middle East News Agency, a government agency that, among other things, served the foreign press in Egypt. I served as an editor, translator, and censor. Part of my job was to translate government press releases from Arabic to English to give to English-language correspondents. In my censorship duties, I was somehow supposed to decide what an English-language foreign journalist was or was not allowed to report. Being naive and inexperienced, I followed a simple rule: If the sentence mentioned anything about the military, I took my pencil and crossed it out. We were all overly cautious about our censorship duties for fear of getting in personal trouble for not catching something. The foreign correspondents were able to work around it by dictating their stories over the phone. At that time there were no fax machines or computers in the Egyptian media.

There were ten of us working at the English desk doing what was essentially the job of one person. This was typical of Egypt at the time. The government tried to mask unemployment by massive overhiring to fill government jobs. This led to boredom, and in most cases gross inefficiency. With many people charged with doing the same work, the work often didn't get done at all. This is why productivity in Egypt was at such an all-time low. However, at the English desk at Middle East News, we were falling over one another trying to get the censorship work, especially from the most enterprising foreign journalists, because these foreign correspondents were our sources of knowledge, our only window onto the world, even for what was happening in our own country.

The Egyptian minister of information in the 1970s was Youssef el-Sebaee, an old friend of my father's. When I met him at his office he spoke very highly of my father. He asked me if I would like to travel. Of course I said yes. So he helped further my career by sending me to several international conferences. El-Sebaee was not just a senior government official, he was also a famous novelist. He wrote many romantic novels that later became memorable movies. I remember eagerly reading most of his romantic novels; many made me cry. He wrote with such passion and sensitivity. Due to el-Sebaee's help, I was able to travel as an interpreter to countries such as the Philippines and Iraq. On my own, I also traveled to London and France, where my older sister then lived. These trips opened my eyes even more to the outside world and other cultures.

All journalists in Egypt were government employees. Being one of them, I learned firsthand about the sad state of Arab media. The Arab media does not inform its citizenry of anything other than what the government allows. I once asked why Egyptian newspapers at the time did not inform the public about the dangers of smoking. The answer from a reputable journalist was that the Egyptian government does not want the public to panic, since smoking was very widespread in Egypt, even among physicians.

On the other hand, Egyptian and Arab media as a whole did all it could to encourage another kind of panic: fear of certain outside forces, namely Israel and Western countries. An outside enemy was necessary to foster Arab cohesion and keep the Arab public preoccupied with news of dangers and threats. Thus, the press kept up a constant bombardment of stories that blamed Israel for all the troubles within the Arab world. The effect was to decrease the pressure and deflect criticism of Arab governments. How can people criticize the government internally when a giant threat is ready to attack our borders?

The public was continually told that the Jews and Israel wanted to conquer the Arab world. Golda Meir was portrayed in Egyptian cartoons as an ugly, blood-sucking woman with dangling breasts, messy hair, and blood dripping from her mouth. All Jews were supposed to look like that—holding bloody daggers after killing little Arab babies.

I once told a fellow journalist that in one of my travels I had met a Jew who "seemed very nice." The answer was, "You know what happens to those who communicate with Jews outside Egypt. They come back to Egypt in a box." That scared the hell out of me, the fact that even saying I met a nice Jew could bring such a horrific threat.

I also learned that Arab unity was just a myth and a facade. Arabs did not really like one another. At the same time that Arab media was trying to portray Arab unity to the rest of the world, endless political crises, mutual antagonisms, and media wars between Arab governments and leaders continually erupted. Arab countries fenced themselves off from one another despite their slogans and songs proclaiming Arab nationalism and unity. Egyptians were not well treated by oil-rich Arab countries such as Saudi Arabia. And when these Arabs visited Egypt, many in our country regarded them as foreigners from backward radical Muslim countries who covered their women from head to toe.

Although Saudi Arabia and most of the oil-rich Gulf nations had the economic strength to absorb large numbers of other Muslim populations, and, in fact, relied on them as workers in their oil industry, there was no inclination to accept them into their society. Herein lies a great hypocrisy that continues to this day. While the religious schools of such countries as Saudi Arabia teach the children from the poor, less-developed Muslim countries that all Muslims are brothers, they are not accepted as such. The oil-rich Arab nations are quite obsessed with maintaining "ethnic purity." Many Egyptians who worked in Saudi Arabia and Gulf states complained that they could live and die in Saudi Arabia and never be given citizenship and always be treated as a foreigner. The Gulf War exposed such undercurrents in Kuwaiti society. Thousands of Palestinians have been living in Kuwait for several generations, providing the necessary hard work in the oil fields, but they have not been granted Kuwaiti citizenship and have no hope of achieving it. The same could be said about the modern-day Yemenis working and living in Saudi Arabia for generations. Interestingly, if those migrants had instead decided to seek work in the United States decades ago, their offspring would have been "full-blooded Americans" already. The Palestinians living within the borders of Syria, Jordan, Egypt, Kuwait, Saudi Arabia, and other Arab countries for generations have been denied citizenship or the rights that would include. This of course has contributed to the conflicts, stalemates, instability, and volatility of Middle East politics that continues to plague the world. That is by design.

In addition to traveling abroad, I learned about other cultures through befriending foreign students and visitors. Many times while at American University, I took American students to see historic neighborhoods and to eat at typical Egyptian restaurants so they could partake of our culture. I suppose I picked up this attitude from my mother. She loved to entertain visitors from other countries and put on elaborate feasts for them. My sister had been a foreign exchange student in America, and when some of her American friends came to visit Egypt, we entertained them in our home and showed them our country.

So, quite naturally, when through my work I met a very kind American man who was interested in Egyptian ancient history, I invited him over to meet Baba Abbas, the family friend who had functioned as a surrogate father for me as I was growing up. Baba Abbas knew a great deal about ancient Egyptian history and had many interesting books, so I wanted my acquaintance to have a chance to talk with him. As soon as the American left, Baba Abbas immediately told me that my friend was definitely a CIA spy. I felt extremely offended because he was in effect telling me that my American friend was in Egypt for evil reasons. I felt that Abbas was attempting to make me doubt my friendship with a person from another country and culture.

Baba Abbas's paranoia over Americans and foreigners in general was not uncommon in Egypt. Young Egyptian men who be-friended a foreign Western woman were warned that she could be an Israeli agent. Every foreign man was "CIA" and every foreign woman was an "Israeli agent." Once, when my American friend and I took a taxi in Cairo, the taxi driver looked us with an accusatory expression. His eyes were saying, *How dare you go out with an American infidel man?* I have heard stories of taxi drivers asking Egyptian women customers who got into the cab together with a man actually asking such questions: "Who is this man? Is he your husband?" In the Muslim world your business is everyone else's business. Even a taxi cab driver who is a total stranger feels justified at being concerned about the relationships between his female and male customers.

A friend at work had a Coptic boyfriend. Both were around twenty-six years of age. She told me of a very bad experience they'd had in a hotel in Port Said. They had taken separate rooms in a hotel while visiting the city. But when she visited his room once, the police knocked at the door and arrested both of them. The scandal almost ruined her reputation.

That story hit home with me because I too had a Coptic boyfriend and could not imagine the horror of something like that happening to me. I knew we had to be very careful. We were planning on getting married as soon as he was finished with his military service. He was planning on converting to Islam so we could be married, and we would move to America to join his family, many of whom were already in California. But we had to put our plans on hold until he finished his military service.

My friendships, any friendships—with men or women—were suspect. Throughout my travels I noticed that in foreign countries women gathered and formed groups and organizations to work on a shared goal. Those goals could be political, recreational, or social. That did not exist in Egypt or the Arab world. Some men made decisions for their wives on whom and whom not to befriend. I often heard stories of husbands prohibiting their wives from associating with this or that woman because she looks this or that way, or did not wear proper clothes.

As a young woman, I felt that I was locked in a box, living to satisfy someone else's criteria of morality and social behavior. I was only to befriend Egyptians, preferably Muslims and women like me, and even those friendships presented problems. For instance, we were not to mix socially with people in lower and poorer classes. That kept my choices of friendships very limited. Any relationships outside the family were supposed to be superficial and more formal.

There is an old Arab saying: "My brother and I against our cousin, but my cousin and I against a stranger." I was constantly reminded of this Arab proverb not just verbally, but also through people's attitudes and behavior. The message was always to stay "in the tribe" and never trust strangers. And, of course, I should not befriend—let alone marry—infidels who supposedly are only befriending me for evil reasons.

Although the Arab world did not have a Berlin Wall, we were

enclosed by a rigid psychological wall. The religious and political leadership wanted nothing less than total control over their citizen's thoughts, behavior, and, indeed, all their choices in life. That is worse than a physical wall. A wall made of bricks can be brought down for people to cross over. But in the Arab world, terrible consequences awaited anyone who tried to breach the invisible wall of social, religious, and political constraints. The key to survival was to conform—or at least pretend to, never rock the boat internally, and keep pointing at Israel as the villain.

I once visited a Christian girl friend in a Cairo neighborhood called Hadaek El Kubba. My friend and I both heard the Friday prayer sermon through the loudspeakers of a nearby radical mosque. We heard the preacher, Sheikh Kishk, say: "May God destroy the infidels the enemies of God. We are not to befriend them or make treaties with them." We also heard worshipers responding, "Amen." My Christian friend looked frightened, and I was ashamed. As I tried to put myself in her shoes and think how it made her feel, I realized that something was very wrong in the way my religion was taught and practiced.

Just as my world had expanded by visiting other countries and befriending foreign visitors, my worldview was also opened by visiting another part of my own country. My sister had become a doctor and was practicing in a small village in the delta. When I visited her, as we walked through the narrow village street, the peasants greeted us with respect, and nearly everyone we saw in front of their homes invited us in for tea. It was the kindness and generosity Egypt was famous for. These simple peasants, whom middle- and upper-class Egyptians shunned, were wonderful, warm people. My deep feelings of respect and love for the Egyptian peasants, the people who feed all of Egypt and whose life has changed very little over the centuries, was reinforced by this experience.

Politically, Egypt was in the doldrums. The defeat in the 1967 war with its loss of lives and the loss of the Sinai had left the country demoralized. Israel became more and more the scapegoat for

Egypt's problems. Add to that the deteriorating economic conditions, and the nation was on the verge of bankruptcy. Nasser was under a great deal of pressure, not only within Egypt but also among other Arab nations, the Soviets, and the Palestinian movement, a movement which was largely created by Egypt and other Arab neighbors.

In 1970 Nasser suddenly collapsed and died of a heart attack. The country was stunned. The grief of the Egyptian people was overwhelming. His failures and shortcomings were their failures and shortcomings. The emotional grief over Nasser's death certainly also applied to me; Nasser was the only president I had ever known even though I never really liked him. Even today, many Egyptians look back at the Nasser period as the "good old days" of reform and reestablishment of Arab pride, both inside and outside of Egypt. It was a time in our nation's history when colonialism was overthrown and Egypt became independent. As the nation grieved, many forgave Nasser's many military blunders and disastrous economic policies that had turned Egypt into one of the most economically depressed countries in the region. But there were also others who perceived Nasser's policies as that of a careless militarism that led Egypt from one defeat to another rather than to peace and economic prosperity. Once he was dead, some people finally felt free to express their disappointment in him and their doubts about the direction he had taken our country. After Nasser's funeral, I remember somone mentioning that "we get the leaders we deserve," and "absolute power corrupts." I certainly agreed with that last assessment.

Nasser's death gave Egypt a new presidency with Anwar Sadat, who brought a new perspective and new solutions to a country that desperately needed change. At first, Sadat was underestimated by Egyptian citizens, who perceived him to be weak. The country actually knew very little about Anwar Sadat. Born in the delta village of Mit Abul Kom, he came from peasant roots, and his mother was originally Sudanese. He had been one of the first students to attend a military school established by the British. When young Sadat graduated from the military academy, he was sent to an obscure military post, where he was to meet Gamal Abdel Nasser. Sadat became one of the young officers to form the fledgling revolutionary group that would overthrow British rule. For these activities, Sadat was twice sent to prison. The second time, he took the opportunity to teach himself French and English. After being released from his second imprisonment, Sadat turned his back on military life, trying out an acting career and then various business ventures. But eventually he reestablished contact with Nasser and the strengthening revolutionary movement, and became a member of the Free Officers Organization, which staged the coup that overthrew King Farouk.

Anwar Sadat's style on the international scene was very different from Nasser's. Shortly after he took over as president, he pressed the Soviets for additional military aid to replace the losses from the 1967 war. When they ignored his requests, Sadat expelled the Soviets, a bold move that surprised the whole world and won Sadat respect and praise from the Egyptian people. There was another reason Sadat expelled 20,000 Soviet military advisers. The Egyptian government was afraid that the Soviets might leak secret Egyptian plans to cross the Suez, which was in the early planning stage.

This was at the height of the Cold War era, when most nations were aligned either with the United States or the Soviet Union. While careful to officially keep Egypt "nonaligned," Sadat opened the door to American interests, playing one side off the other. Many Egyptians were happy that under President Sadat's regime Egypt's ties with the Soviet Union were weakening and its relationship with the United States was improving.

Sadat allowed American companies to begin doing business in Egypt, and American tourists also began flocking to Egypt. Shopkeepers in Cairo's bazaars who did not like the poor Russian tourists were now ecstatic about the friendly and generous American tourists.

Despite the anti-American rhetoric we'd been fed for many years, most Egyptians were very happy to receive President Nixon on his visit to Egypt in 1972. They spilled out voluntarily into the streets with American flags to enthusiastically greet Nixon, who at that time was in the midst of the Watergate scandal. We felt sorry for him and could not comprehend how the power of the presidency in such a world superpower could not stop his attackers. After all, it would have been very easy for Arab dictators to crush such opposition. Furthermore, from what we knew of the so-called Watergate scandal, Nixon's actions were not only ordinary in Middle East politics, but also very mild compared to what our leaders did.

Egyptians who suffered for decades from a closed economy and denials of exit visas to leave the country looked to Nixon as a symbol of hope and of an open economy. I was happy to see Nixon and felt the same way as the rest of Egypt.

After the demoralizing Arab defeat in the 1967 war, Egyptians were dealing with the occupation of the Sinai. They knew that getting back the Sinai this time would not be as easy as in 1956. Regaining the Sinai was at the top of President Sadat's agenda, probably for more than one reason. In order to put in place the reforms necessary to turn around the stagnant economy, he needed to gain the respect of his people. Some Egyptians, in fact, were upset that two years into his presidency, Sadat had not yet gone to war with Israel. Early on, in 1971, Sadat had signaled a willingness to consider entering a peace agreement with Israel if they returned the Sinai and Gaza—which Israel had refused. Now in 1972, Sadat publicly announced that Egypt was committed to going to war with Israel and was prepared to "sacrifice one million Egyptian soldiers." But such posturing and talk of war, often to ply aid from the superpowers, was not surprising in the Arab world and was not taken seriously by Israel. However, both the Soviet Union and the United States were concerned. They had no desire to see the world come to the brink of a world war over conflicts in the Middle East.

Sadat was indeed serious about going to war with Israel to re-cover the Sinai. But he went about it differently than Nasser had. This time the preparation for the war was quiet, and we did not hear the war drums of euphoria we Egyptians were used to.

The War of Attrition had never really stopped since the end of the 1967 war. There were always border clashes and military pos-turing at the Suez. On October 6, Yom Kippur, the holiest day of the Jewish year, while Israelis were fasting and attending syna-gogue, Egypt and Syria launched a surprise attack. The Egyptian army breached Israel's first defenses and quickly crossed the Suez Canal, in what Egyptians would come to proudly call "The Cross-ing," and advanced fifteen kilometers into the Sinai.

The Egyptian public was skeptical about the early reports of our gains. From past experiences Egyptians did not trust what was being said by the Egyptian media, and many wanted to know the truth from international sources, which was hard to get.

Bloody battles ensued in the Sinai with heavy losses for both the Israelis and the Egyptians. Other Arab nations were part of the effort. Iraq lent a squadron of fighter jets to Egypt and sent 18,000 troops to the Golan Heights. Libya, which had already given Cairo more than $1 billion in aid to help Egypt rearm, also sent Mirage fighters to reinforce our air force. Algeria, Tunisia, Morocco, Ku-wait, and Saudi Arabia also helped. Palestinians shelled northern Israel from Lebanon. Even Jordan's King Hussein, who had been kept uninformed of the early plans, sent two armored units to help Syria. It was all-out war once again: all the Arab nations against Israel.

The October 6 War, as we called it in Egypt, did not bring the Sinai back, and the two armies ended up entangled, but it was still called a victory by Egypt. We were told that Israel crossed the ca-nal and was a few miles from Cairo, and at the same time the Egyp-tian army took back parts of the Sinai.

An organized cease-fire, brokered once again by outside pow-ers, went into effect October 26, but military tensions remained high, with sporadic clashes breaking out now and then. Our third army remained surrounded by the Israelis in the Sinai desert. Henry Kissinger, who was handling negotiations for the Americans, was surprised to receive a message from Egyptian national security adviser Hafez Ismail. Egypt would be willing to enter into direct face-to-face talks with the Israelis if they agreed to allow nonmilitary supplies such as food and water to reach their army and agreed to a complete cease-fire.

An American journalist I met years later told how she had been taken to the front shortly after the cessation of the fighting. Her Israeli military escort had allowed her to wander for some minutes on the battlefield where the highest casualties of the war had occurred.

As far as the eye could see, the Sinai sand was littered with helmets, bits of clothing, and shoes. She told me she was struck by the fact that every helmet, every shoe, had once been on a soldier, either an Israeli or an Egyptian who was now dead. She realized that for each pair of shoes strewn across this battlefield there was a mother, perhaps a wife or sweetheart, grieving for the young man she had lost.

She described it as one of the most sobering moments of her life. "I was not a journalist right then," she told me. "I was a woman thinking of other women. There was no politics, no territory, no point. Just a lot of dead men."

Later she was allowed to view from afar the large white tent where Egyptian and Israeli generals were meeting at that very moment. She remembers thinking: Do these men realize what they must do? Do they realize what they owe the grieving families in their countries? My friend reminded me that the grief was the same on both sides, the Israeli and Arab side.

After I moved to America I would later learn many more details about this war and all the other wars with Israel. But what we knew then was that Anwar Sadat was heralded as the "Hero of the Crossing." But the problem of the Sinai remained unsolved. Sadat would eventually make an extraordinary move to get it back. The lesson the war taught this seasoned military man was that war was not worth its high cost to his country in economic or human terms. There had to be another way.

The Egyptian public might have been distracted temporarily by the war, but its internal economic problems soon boiled over. A huge, violent, anti-government food riot erupted in Cairo. I was standing on a friend's balcony on Ramsis Street, near downtown Cairo, and saw poor Egyptian young men rioting and running in the streets out of despair. They were demanding an end to the increases in the price of an Egyptian loaf of bread. Bread prices were decided by the government. I heard the slogan: *"Ya batl al-abur, fen al-futur?"* which translated was "Hero of the Crossing, where is our breakfast?" Bread was the last thing they could afford to buy to eat, and even that was going up. Even the famous Egyptian "focul," which is beans, was getting too expensive for some to buy. From that balcony I saw hungry young Egyptian men whom the upper classes mistreated and used as fodder for jihad yet gave them no respect. Now they were starving them, depriving them of the very basics of life. I felt very sorry for them.

It was also very sad to see the end result of socialism, rent control, nationalization of industry, and war—the failures of a regime that came to power to help the poor and ended up starving them after making them totally dependent on government. The economic, social, and political problems, which had been compounded over the years by the revolutionary military leadership, had prevented our nation from joining the competitive world community.

The Egyptian economy was destroyed long before Sadat took office, but it was a difficult battle to reverse the desperate plight of a society that had been stagnant for so many years.

While I, in my twenties, was personally financially secure, nevertheless, everyone was economically impacted. It was difficult to be young and have any hope for a future in the climate of those times. My government salary at that time paid sixteen Egyptian pounds a month. Almost all Egyptians at that time depended on the government for work. University graduates in 1970—if they were lucky and had lots of connections—could get a job with a starting salary of sixteen Egyptian pounds. My salary covered transportation to work and back and nothing else. It was just enough for me to take a private or a group taxi to work. Taking a bus was out of the question. Riding public buses in Egypt has become a humiliating experience; passengers were crowded like sardines, and no respect was shown for women or the elderly. But I still wanted to work, even though it paid for no more than my transportation to work, since staying home was the last thing I wanted to do in a culture that already denied many activities for women.

The influx of American companies that began in 1972 was a bonanza for someone with my bilingual education. Because of my English-language skills, I was able to get a job as a secretary in a very small office of the 3M Company. Later I took a job with Citicorp. I was paid $75 a month, which was an enormous salary. At the time, $75 was equivalent to 150 Egyptian pounds. By comparison, 60 pounds a month is what a high government official might pull down as a salary. I was making ten times the normal amount for office work, and more than twice the sum of a high government official or business executive.

I am often surprised by the naïveté of people who protest that American companies are paying slave-labor wages to workers in other countries. They do not understand that while the salaries seems small by American standards, they are often huge in comparison to what those workers would normally receive from similar jobs. In fact, American companies can create very unstable and inequitable situations if they pay workers proportionately too much in comparison to the local economy. International economics is far more complicated than many imagine.

My boyfriend's military service was prolonged as a result of the 1973 war. That meant that we had to postpone our marriage. During that time, I would visit his home, where he lived with his mother and brothers. His mother was a very kind and devoted woman. Christian Egyptians knew they were a minority and were very careful not to upset Muslims. My boyfriend's father changed his Christian last name to a more neutral name that could pass. At that time, many Egyptian Coptic Christians were leaving to live in the West—those who hadn't already left under Nasser's rule. The pressure from radical Islam was pushing them to leave. In 1976 my boyfriend was finally released from the army. After that, it took him almost a year to get releases from the government to allow him to leave the country. Our plan was that after he got his immigration papers and left for America, I would follow later on a tourist visa. He would convert to Islam and we would be married.

While we were waiting to realize our "escape" dreams, a great deal was happening in Egypt. In the aftermath of the 1973 war, Sadat became convinced that peace with Israel was the only road to solving Egypt's severe economic and social problems. In an extraordinary speech to the Egyptian parliament in 1977, Sadat stunned the world and his own countrymen by saying he would go anywhere, anytime, to negotiate a peace with the Israelis. The Israelis took him up on his offer, inviting him to Jerusalem to speak to the Israeli Knesset.

In 1977 my heart was pounding with joy as I watched on television and saw President Sadat's plane land in Israel. It felt as if a heavy burden on the shoulders of every Egyptian had been lifted. It was a great day of reconciliation and pride for President Sadat, who did the right thing and who realized that peace with Israel was the only way for prosperity and the improved welfare of Egypt. However, that did not sit well with the enemies of peace in the region, the Muslim extremists, and other Arab countries who viewed Sadat's initiative as treason. In retaliation, the Arab League suspended Egypt's membership and moved its headquarters from Cairo to Tunis.

Sadat's bold move eventually led to the Camp David Accords in 1978, which finalized the peace agreement with Israel. After the peace treaty with Israel was signed, the Sinai was returned to Egypt. This was the second time Israel handed back the Sinai to Egypt after a war. As Egyptians got a glimpse of the returned territory, many were in awe of what Israel had done with the Sinai Peninsula. Previously, Egyptians viewed it only as a buffer and a military zone. During their occupation of the Sinai, Israel had managed to develop an infrastructure, building hotels both on the beautiful Red Sea and the Mediterranean beaches. They even dug oil wells in those few years. In its thousands of years of history on this land, Egypt had never thought to make the Sinai habitable or use its beautiful coastlines for resorts. They thought it only fit for habitation by Bedouins, people whom Egyptians did not really recognize as part of Egyptian society. Israel had managed to change Egypt's perception of the Sinai and set an example of how that large peninsula could be turned around from a desert sandbox for the military into a multipurpose useful space that could help defuse the crowding in cities around the Nile Valley. All of this thanks to the peace treaty with Israel that resulted in the Sinai becoming a demilitarized zone.

However, even though the Sinai was now back in Egyptian hands, the "treasonous" peace plan horrified the extremist Islamic fundamentalists who had been gaining more and more support during the years since the 1973 war. Radical Muslims, who for years were indoctrinated to hate Israel, simply could not switch gears and accept a peaceful existence with Israel. It was unthinkable. They simply did not want peace and regarded Sadat as a traitor to the Arab cause.

My father's friend Youssef el-Sebaee, the famous writer and minister of information, was one of Sadat's companions on his 1977 trip to Israel. A few months after he accompanied Sadat in his famous trip to Israel, he was gunned down by terrorists in front of a hotel in Cyprus. A wonderful, gentle man who wanted nothing but peace was assassinated for daring to support Sadat in reaching out for peace with Israel. I was devastated, again.

The peace-hate machine represented by extremist Islamic groups would eventually succeed in assassinating President Sadat in October of 1981, ironically during a military review celebrating the 1973 Suez crossing. I was already in America then. He was killed by the fanatical Muslim Brotherhood. (Bin Laden's second-in-command, Ayman al-Zawahiri, was a member of that group.) The message that many Egyptians got from such assassinations was loud and clear: *Those who work for peace and recognition of Israel are going to be killed.* The radical Islamist movement then spread very fast all over Egypt.

With Sadat's assassination, I realized that tyranny in the Muslim world does not just come from the leadership but also from the society itself and the radical elements in it. That is why Arab governments are constantly struggling to stay in power and always under the threat of a coup d'etat. If they befriend the United States, they have to do it in secret. Leaders like Sadat who want peace, an open economy, and less government control are killed. The Arab League and Arab media will gang up against such leaders. That's why only tyranical governments can survive in the Arab world.

The billions of dollars in aid the United States sent to Egypt as part of the Camp David Accord did not bring America much appreciation among the Egyptian public. Attitudes toward America began changing. The Egyptian public's perception of the United States as the savior when Nixon was received in the early 1970s changed to one of regarding the United States as the Great Satan due to Islamists and Arab secular leftists in the Arab world media who bombarded the Arab street with misinformation, propaganda, and outright lies. Even foreign media in the Arab world played along, not daring to expose the realities of the Middle East to Arab citizens for fear they would be ousted and their offices closed. The gap between the reality of what was happening in the international arena and what Egyptians knew was very wide and created just the right climate for Islamic fundamentalism and extremism to grow and flourish in Egypt. In addition, the great wealth from oil in Saudi Arabia was being used to spread its Wahabi Islamist agenda in Egypt as well as in other moderate Arab countries. That was not difficult to do in a desperately poor country just emerging from several wars in total defeat. Saudi Arabian Wahabism and the Iranian civil war, another coinciding event, succeeded in changing and radicalizing all moderate countries in the Arab world. On the Arab street, desperate Egyptians chanted, "The answer is Islam."

As the radical Islamist movement gained power, it began affecting the upper classes as well. I began seeing changes in people I knew. Baba Abbas's wife started covering her hair for the first time in her life. Her sister followed. Then I began seeing many other women cover their heads. An older woman I knew criticized me for having long manicured nails. She told me that if you shake the hands of a man you might scratch him and that could be very seductive. I started getting lectured on the virtues of Islamic head covering. Some said, "We have to tell the world we are Muslims and we are proud." That was very unusual in Egypt in the seventies. Only peasants and the uneducated classes covered their heads. Everything was changing.

Despite the gradual improvement in my work situation because of Sadat's more open policy, I still felt I wanted to leave Egypt. I needed to get away from it all, the total control over the minds and behavior of citizens, the culure of jihad and the hatred of Israel and the increasing Islamic fundamentalism. I felt the Middle East was a ticking time bomb that would soon explode. The mid-twentieth century had seen three major events that had contributed to this dangerous level of confrontations in the Middle East. Saudi Arabia has suddenly started enjoying unprecedented wealth from oil, a wealth that came without lifting a finger of hard work or innovation. A poor nomadic tribal state with a mission to conquer the world to Islam suddenly has the money and power to do it. At almost the same time of Saudi Arabia's dream of expanding Islam, Israel became a state. I often wondered if the Arab-Israeli conflict would exist today if Israel had been established as a state a century earlier. At the same time, the British and French were losing their power to keep the peace between all these nations, minorities, and tribes. They lost their large empire and evacuated their presence from the region also by the mid-fifties. Regardless of the negatives or positives of the British and French presence, their departure marked a point in Arab history where no neutral authority was present to keep the peace.

In January of 1978, my boyfriend left for California to join his brother and cousins. He called me several times asking me to come and join him. I began finalizing my plans to leave. My mother and family were very understanding and wished me good luck. My mother planned on coming to America to attend our wedding. Some friends and relatives told me they wished they could do the same.

It took a few visits to the Mugamaa, the Egyptian government office that handles passports, to renew my passport. It was a simple thing, yet it was tied up in endless red tape. Every time I went to the passport office, no one knew where my paperwork was. (Part of it was that Egyptian policy of hiring ten people to do the work of one.) But finally fed up, I went to the office and gave them two or three Egyptian pounds. And somehow my paperwork was then miraculously "found."

In November of 1978 I left for America.

Our old military driver, Hassan, volunteered to drive me to the airport when he heard I was leaving for America. He had retired from the army but still drove my mother and our family for special occasions. The drive to the Cairo International Airport from Maadi was long in the heavy Cairo traffic. I started reflecting over my thirty years of life in Egypt and Gaza. I saw very little change in the lives of people. Most people lived and died in the same apartment, worked the same government jobs, and struggled to feed their children. They rarely complained publicly or blamed their government for starting unnecessary wars or for controlling every aspect of their lives. They treated their rulers as pharaohs for life. They let off steam by using that famous Egyptian sarcasm and self-pity, but did very little to change their conditions. Yet Egyptians, coming from this ancient culture, are probably one of the most content, durable, and adaptable people on earth. Sadly, mistakes from Egypt's five-thousand-year history keep being repeated, and no one seems to learn from history's lessons. But, despite all the misery, wars, and poverty, the Egyptian people, my people, are still predominantly good, decent, and law abiding. Like people everywhere, all they have ever needed was a job and an apartment and the ability to take care of their children. Cairo, in comparison to many cities around the world, was safe to walk the streets in the late hours of the night. Driving to the airport, I wept as I was looking at my fellow Egyptians on the streets of Cairo. I felt deep love and respect for my people and wished them peace and a better future.

But as for me now, I was on my way to a new life in America. I was finally able to jump over of the invisible wall. It wasn't easy, but I did it.

Six

A New Beginning in America

I arrived at Los Angeles International Airport in November of 1978. I loved America even before seeing it. My first experience was with airport workers who graciously helped me as soon as I asked for assistance. When I cleared customs and made my way into the waiting area, my boyfriend's whole family was waiting for me with flowers and big smiles. I could not have asked for a nicer reception. I basked in the kindness and generosity of this wonderful Christian Coptic family who had left Egypt for freedom from oppression and was now welcoming me into their family.

As we drove from the airport, I looked out the window of the car in fascination, marveling at everything I was seeing around me—Los Angeles, its bright lights, its freeways and mountains looming in the distance. Coming from a flat desert country made me truly appreciate the green mountains and hills of Los Angeles. Everything seemed so large—streets, stores, buildings. Traffic seemed to move very smoothly, compared to Egypt or even Europe. I noticed that drivers respected pedestrians and stopped for them—very different from how pedestrians were treated in the Middle East.

Respect for the individual was evident everywhere. I marveled at how spread out the city was, giving people privacy and plenty of room to breath. Californians, and Americans in general, clearly preferred living in single-family homes rather than apartment buildings, which gave Americans a style of life that is different from the rest of the world. Family life included things like outdoor barbecues and entertaining and simply more freedom and privacy. Homes were built with wood frames and slab foundations that made the homes part of the landscape and close to the outdoors.

It was a truly an eye-opening experience to have lived half my life in one country then suddenly move to a totally different culture. Coming to America after living until age thirty in the Middle East was like a *Back to the Future* film experience. I left behind an old society with archaic customs, values, and expectations for a new, more comfortable, and easier life. The discovery process in itself was fascinating and exciting, but what made it special was that this new country was welcoming, accepting, and gracious.

A few days after arriving in America, my fiancé and I then went to a Los Angeles mosque where he converted to Islam. His face was white when he came out. Something about the experience was troubling to him, but he never talked about it. He was doing this for me and my family. It would assure my safety if we returned to Egypt for a visit, as we would later discover. We then were married in a private ceremony in his brother's home, held just for family and close friends. My mother came from Egypt to attend the wedding and gave us her blessing, which meant a great deal to me.

My mother stayed for a few days to sightsee and was fascinated with America. She loved it as much as I did. I don't remember ever seeing her that happy. Before leaving the United States, my mother shopped for the whole family, especially her grandchildren. When she looked at her receipts, she realized that she was being charged tax on her merchandise. I remember her response. She said that in America one is allowed to question the government about where the tax money is going, and she could certainly see that it was going to good use to build this wonderful country. That is something

Americans often forget, the extraordinary infrastructure and services they enjoy in this country—their taxes at work.

At that time, Egypt did not have supermarkets. Most markets in Egypt were very small and specialized in a few things. Many had empty shelves after the wars. My mother loved the large variety the supermarkets offered. She said it was a pleasure to do grocery shopping. Egyptian women we knew rarely went to the market themselves. They usually sent their maids to shop for them. In fact, I never saw my mother go shopping for food in the marketplace in Cairo by herself. I found the price of food in the United States in relationship to income to be very reasonable, even for new immigrants like us. After seeing a special aisle for dog and cat food, my mother remarked, "Even animals have more rights in America," which she followed with a hearty "Long live capitalism."

Before leaving to return to Egypt, my mother handed me my inheritance money to help me buy my first home in America. After it was converted into dollars, the money was just enough for a down payment on a home with a swimming pool.

From the very first, I wanted to learn as much as I could about my new environment. I bought maps of Los Angeles and California and studied them. Los Angeles is a very well planned city with wide streets and divided lanes that made driving a pleasure. I noticed that streets mostly ran north and south or east and west, which made it very easy to find your way around. That was very different from a very old city such as Cairo, where streets are usually narrow and zigzagged with little planning and with no concept of direction. I was quickly able to drive and find my way around. Because I was hesitant to drive on freeways with their entrance and exit ramps, I hired a driving instructor to help me learn how to negotiate the road system. All I needed was some guided practice, and I was soon comfortable with L.A. freeways.

I was also able to quickly find a job—in fact, on my very first interview. I started work as a secretary in a small business. I thanked God for my British education and degree from the American University in Cairo. My mother-in-law was amazed at how quickly I found a job in America, and she jokingly told people, "If you want a job go with Nonie." The owner of the small business I worked for was Jewish. He was a kind man with a great sense of humor. His parents were a lovely couple, and I was impressed by how much they seemed to adore each other, even after so many years of marriage. I heard the husband call his wife "Dolly," "Darling," and "Sweetheart." Western men and women freely expressed affection for one another in public. That was not allowed in Egypt, where even a husband cannot express affection for his wife by a hug or holding hands in public. In the Middle East, men who do that are regarded as wimps. An Egyptian man who is affectionate with his wife in public is often ridiculed, especially by the women in his family, who say that his wife is controlling him. Being controlled by one's wife is a source of shame to an Arab man. As a result, Egyptian men will often be cold or authoritarian with their wives in public, especially in front of their own families.

When my husband and I rented our first apartment, my boss's parents came into the office one day with a big box for me. It was filled with extra dishes and kitchen utensils they wanted to give me. I was very grateful for their kindness and generosity.

America is now the country I choose to call home. I was surprised at how totally I was accepted as part of this great nation and how quickly I began to feel at home. I was like a child discovering everything. I was amazed at how friendly, generous, and decent ordinary Americans are. I want you to look at Americans through the eyes of a newcomer from another culture.

Friendliness and helpfulness: I had never before seen perfect strangers on the street smile at you and say good morning. In the markets and stores people go out of their way to greet you. There is always a "Good morning," a "Hello," or a "Thank you." It is very uplifting and makes you feel good all over. I noticed this on my very first day in America. I stayed at my brother-in-law's home in the San

Fernando Valley and was surprised when neighbors who saw me walking the next morning came over to welcome me. When I went jogging people who passed me said "Good morning" or "Hello." I was totally unaccustomed to such a thing. And appreciating this great tradition, I also began saying hello to strangers with whom I came face-to-face. The customer service in most department stores and supermarkets also amazed me. I loved the "May I help you" and "Thank you." It showed they recognized me as an individual and a customer that counted to the store. I compared that to my poor treatment in the stores I had visited in France.

Courtesy: Common courtesy was another surprise for me. In the United States, if people bump into you they immediately say "Pardon me" or "Sorry," something seldom heard in Cairo, a crowded and densely populated city, where people bump into each other all the time without saying a word.

Diversity and multiculturalism: Americans love to learn about other cultures and express respect for diversity and differences. When Americans met me, they were very interested in Egypt and its history, and they wanted to know all about me and my culture. Universities and workplaces considered diversity of workers and students to be a source of pride. In Egypt and the Arab world it was just the opposite. Anyone different from the majority is shunned as Khawaga. But in America, I soon realized that people of different nationalities, backgrounds, and religions routinely mixed socially. And I was very happy to be part of that. One of the other employees at my workplace was Jewish, and he became my husband's best friend. His name was Larry. I invited Larry, his girlfriend, my boss, and his parents all to my little apartment for an Egyptian dinner of lamb, moussaka, and stuffed grape leaves. As I was cooking and cleaning for the dinner party, I suddenly realized how dependent I had always been on maids. I had to ask for a quick lesson in housekeeping from my sister-in-law. The simplest thing like washing dishes was a mystery to me. But I saw American women routinely cleaning and cooking, easily and quickly. I realized that in America, people take care of themselves and are self-sufficient.

Self-sufficiency, pride in labor: I noticed Americans are not ashamed of physical labor. I saw them sweep and clean in front of their homes and do their own repairs. In fact, they were proud of such abilities—it was a value, not a shame. In Egypt, manual physical labor is looked down upon. My mother once rented our house to a British couple and was surprised to see the woman openly sweeping the floor in front of the house. Physical work to middle and upper classes in Egypt is very demeaning, and it is viewed as a sign that you are poor and uneducated. Even the poor are ashamed of physical labor, and as soon as they become more successful they want to avoid physical labor. Everyone wanted to be an *effendi*, which is a title for a more educated Arab who usually works at a desk, or *bahawat*, "upper class." Even poorer classes try to avoid hard work when no one is looking.

Generous, honest, and open: Americans are generous, ready, and eager to help someone in need, and they are also able to graciously ask for and accept help when they need it. In Arab culture, to be needy causes loss of face, a grave loss of honor. The proper response is denial of need, and if one gets a little help, deny you ever asked for it. My grandmother always said: *"Rabena ma yehwegni lehad,"* which means, "May God bless me with never needing help from another human being." This oft-repeated phrase in Arab culture is one that I particularly dislike. It is a shame to need, to ask for help. Therefore, to ask for a favor one has to go through elaborate behavior to conceal one's need. If someone actually does need a favor from someone else, they must go about it in a dishonest way, which involves later concealing the "shame" by denying they asked for it and insisting and that they accepted the "favor" only to please the person. One has to save face. This creates an awkward situation all around. Egyptians who are on the giving end then often turn around and complain about the ingratitude of people for whom they did a favor.

After this kind of elaborate social posturing, the frankness and openness of Americans was not only refreshing, it was also a great relief to me. I was surprised by the fact that not all Egyptians felt the same way. When other Egyptian immigrants asked me how I was able to make friendships with Americans so quickly, I didn't have an answer. But I soon learned for myself that my personality was more compatible with the American culture than it was with Middle Eastern culture. What was considered a negative in the Middle East was a positive in America. For example, my natural openness and frankness earned me nothing but negative reactions in Egypt, but it was greatly appreciated by my American friends. My wish to learn about and respect other cultures and religions was not appreciated in the Middle East, but in America it was. To many Middle Eastern Muslims, Americans seemed very naive because of their honesty. That label was often applied to me. Now I was finally liberated in America; I no longer had to deny, lie, or hide my feelings.

The whole issue of truthfulness and honesty in Arab culture is a multilayered mystery to most of the Western world and is integral to the misunderstandings between our cultures. For this reason I want to attempt to explain it further. In Arab culture, being truthful is not only considered to be naive, and stupid, but it is also considered—believe it or not—rude. In a culture where one's business is everyone else's, it is often regarded as rude to set limits in one's relationships by saying either yes or no. Thus Western culture's "virtue" of honesty, in the eyes of Arabs, is not a virtue at all but an opportunity to take advantage of the naive Westerners. They are, after all, "opening themselves up" to be taken advantage of. For example, Muslim men look at the honesty and openness of Western women as an invitation—she's being "easy." If she talks openly about her life and preferences and goes to lunch with him, then she must be asking for sex! Then when the man is later rejected sexually, he is deeply insulted and blames American women for being deceptive and acting like sluts.

In the West "yes" is "yes" and "no" is "no." But when Arabs hear
the word "no" from an American they often take it as an insult.
That is because Arabs don't say the word "no" directly. Very often
they say *"in Shaalah"* when they mean "no." In dealing with Westerners, an Arab may say "yes" when they really don't mean it, and
that gets them in a lot of trouble with Westerners. More than one
American president and countless diplomats who tried to negotiate with Arafat were confounded by what they *thought* Arafat had
said. These perception problems are especially difficult in political
relations and peace negotiations between Arabs and the West.
When Arabs are asked if they want peace with Israel they always
say "yes," but the truth is that when the next terror group strikes
another blow against peace, they will defend it and make excuses
for it. This is not understood by the West, but it makes perfect
sense to an Arab. Even in Arab-to-Arab relations, leaders may fall
into this game. President Nasser of Egypt told King Hussein of
Jordan that "yes," we are winning the 1967 war even though the
Egyptian army was almost destroyed. King Hussein accordingly
joined the war and the lie cost him the West Bank.

For the most part, in the Arab community, we *know* not to take
"yes" seriously and use our instincts. However, it takes its toll on
our interpersonal relationships, creating a lot of distrust in Arab
relations at all levels. In Arab culture these language games are
very common. If you have become lost or confused by the above,
that only further illustrates the difficulties in understanding the
Arab mind-set.

Lying to protect family, community, or your culture of origin
from being exposed to outsiders is actually considered a virtue.
Under such circumstances, lying is respected and rewarded. It is a
game that most Arabs develop very early in life and so it comes
very naturally. My mother-in-law proudly tells us that when her
husband made a mistake he would always say he didn't do it. She
viewed this as a virtue. She saw it as a sign that he loved her and she
believed that his denial of wrongdoing was his way of saying "sorry"
to her.

I have seen the signs of avoidance of truth even in myself. As a young woman I found myself defending the Arab-Israeli conflict and Islam, regardless of the truth or of the facts presented to me. Family pride was also an issue worth protecting in Arab culture at the expense of the truth or of one's own happiness. After my father's death, my family situation was very difficult, especially with my mother's severe depression and our inability to talk about our pain. To hide the pain I had to lie. After all, my family pride was on the line. I was in denial to protect my family honor and myself. So I kept my pain to myself and hardly ever talked about it to anyone. I wanted to keep up the facade of the happy family life we used to have when my father was alive. Sensing my pain, a schoolteacher once asked me if everything was okay at home. I responded by saying, "Yes." Perhaps the only person I confided in was my grandmother, and even with her I made sure not to tell everything so as not to upset her.

It was very different from American culture, where people talk freely about their shortcomings and pain without shame. Furthermore, they find satisfaction in helping someone else in a similar situation. Americans join support groups to seek help for all sorts of problems. That is unheard of in the Arab world, where one family member's shame can hurt the whole family, and one member's pride can boost the pride of the whole clan. Individual and family relationships are not a personal matter, and preserving the family honor is more important that happiness and a healthy life.

In Egypt, domestic abuse of women and children is common but never reported. And if it was reported, the victim was often the one to be blamed. Telling anything negative about your family can bring down severe condemnation, both from society and the family. A friend of my sister's who had a lot of family problems was once told to see a counselor. Her response was, "If I talk to a stranger, my family will be disgraced in society and they will never forgive me." It is unthinkable to most Arabs to speak any negativity against their family, even if they are suffering from severe abuse. Thus people have no choice but to lie. They will even lie about having a disease such as cancer. Cancer sufferers in Egypt feel a great deal of shame and will often deny it because people fear the evil eye and may avoid severely ill people out of fear of being envied for their health. Bottom line, being truthful in Arab culture can get someone in great trouble from many sources, so the wisest way to protect oneself is to lie. It was fascinating when I first came to America to see my American friends share their most intimate problems and see their friends respond with great compassion. I saw many seek help and treatment and face their problems with great courage and without lies and shame.

While American-style honest interaction and simplicity was a great relief and was far healthier for me and other Egyptian immigrants as well, we just did not practice it with one another. Many still kept up the facade in their Arab-to-Arab relationships but had more open and honest relationships with Americans.

Western-style soul searching or examination of beliefs is almost unheard of in Arab culture. Such behavior would bring about shame and loss of honor. And no subject is more sacred and protected from analysis or criticism than the Koran or Islam. Muslims can get violently angry if that is done. To a lesser extent, if a family member, tribe, nation, or culture is perceived to be under attack, then excuses, justifications, misrepresentations, and outright lies are the only honorable thing to do. Remember, this is a culture based on pride and shame. This phenomenon can be seen when Muslim women are questioned about their status in Muslim society. Westerners often hear even educated and respectable Muslim women defend and boldly deny verifiable facts and statistics. They will, for instance, deny that women are being stoned in Iran when the whole world has seen the pictures of women buried to their waist in dirt being stoned to death. Saving face is a very strong motivation for Arabs, and lying is a virtue when there is no other choice in order to save face. Westernized Arabs who engage in honest, open discussions admit to shortcomings in their culture, and work toward solutions are rare. Those who do so are ostracized and even called traitors.

Problems arise when Arab immigrants choose to live in the West but never assimilate or make an effort to understand or appreciate the simplicity of American values such as truthfulness. They may be mystified by the openness of Americans and cannot comprehend taking what Americans say at face value. But for me, the openness of Americans was a welcome relief. I loved it.

Informality: Americans easily bypassed the formalities in their friendships that we Egyptians were accustomed to. When I had American guests in my home, I did not need to make the house look perfect, cook a feast, or be extra careful to please. Around Americans, believe it or not, I was more relaxed, since they were less judgmental and more accepting and appreciative.

We did, of course, also move in the circles of other Egyptians who had come to this country. Among many Egyptian immigrants—but of course not all—there was plenty of gossip, envy, suspicion, and watching one's back. I heard many Egyptian Americans, especially Muslims, openly say they did not want to do business with one another. Some even avoided one another in public. I felt so sad for my community that they could not shake this sense of distrust. Even in this new place—especially for those who immigrated together with their large extended family—newcomers found themselves once again stuck mostly with family relationships out of distrust of others. In the early years, I often felt lonely, because in Arab culture, without your family, you are like a fish out of water—and you are made to feel so. I had no family—that is, no *blood relatives*—in America. But, looking back, I think that was a blessing in disguise. Without the constraints of family, I was given more of a chance to explore and immerse myself in the big melting pot of America.

Women's relationships: Perhaps the greatest cultural difference I noticed as a newcomer was the way American women relate to one another. First, I noticed that American women have a no-nonsense attitude about life and men—they certainly don't put up with abuse, most of them, at least. But it was amazing to see how women support other women, as well as work together for the good of their communities. Many of my American coworkers and neighbors belonged to women's groups, which were social, recreational, or political. When things went wrong in their community they got together and took a stand. Retired women and men volunteered their time, effort, and money to many causes—hospitals, churches, schools—wherever they found need. These were not rich people, but people who cared about their community. This might seem ordinary in American society, but to a newcomer from the Middle East, where women restrict their activities to within the family, it is very noticeable and was quite impressive. As for other Egyptian immigrants, I don't think they even noticed.

I do not want to confuse this with saying that Muslims do not help the needy. Yes, Muslims give to the poor, as required by Islam, but it is often done in a condescending manner and sometimes even with disgust, giving only what is left over or no longer useful, rather than what the poor need. The attitude is: Some food during the feasts and that is it. There is a famous Arab saying, *"Ettaki sharra men ahsanta elayh,"* meaning "Beware of evil from those to whom you give charity." This is just another layer of the pervasive distrust that permeates all Arab relationships. It is no wonder that needing help is a shameful thing to express or that elaborate, pretentious behavior becomes necessary to protect one's "pride."

American women also support one another on a personal level. Many of them act gracious toward each other, ask about each other's welfare, compliment one another—at least that is the "acceptable" social behavior. In sharp contrast, among most Egyptian women, being gracious with one another would signal that you are weak or needy. Egyptian women, even those who have immigrated to America, do not hide their feelings of jealousy, envy, and competitiveness. You can walk into a room and another Egyptian woman might say, "What have you done to your hair? It looks awful." And she will mean it. An American woman, if she uttered such words, would be teasing. A full-figure Egyptian friend of mine told me that she hates going to Egypt because every time she visits, she is reminded of her weight problem by other women. They constantly greet her by saying, "What happened to you? You gained so much weight!" She also added that one woman told her, "That is why God wants you to cover up with an Islamic dress—to hide your fat!"

Even though Egyptian women in America no longer have to worry about their husbands legally taking second or third wives, the legacy of competitiveness and distrust plagues their relationships with other women and keeps them from enjoying the support and warmth of female friendships that American women take for granted.

Child rearing: American parents' traditional upbringing standards are also very different. First of all, they instill in their children—boys and girls equally—the American values of respect, thrift, hard work, and honesty. These teachings reinforce the societal values that became the cornerstone of American democracy and society's respect for human rights. I see them teach these values in a very concrete ways. American parents will encourage their children to earn money early in life by washing neighbors' cars, mowing lawns, or babysitting. They know it contributes to the upbringing of independent and responsible children. I heard many Egyptians criticize American parents as being too hard on their children when they expected them to help around the house or get part-time jobs as teenagers. But it is such early lessons that contribute to Americans' being self-sufficient, hardworking, and responsible, both within the family and as citizens.

American parents also encourage their children to follow their best instincts—to give of themselves, volunteer to help others in need. In Egypt, a country in desperate need of many services and volunteer work, people mostly stay at home watching TV, cooking, or doing nothing. Volunteer work is unheard of among the large number of Egyptians living on government pensions while the masses are suffering.

Work ethic: I also realized that in order to succeed in America one has to work hard. I was ready for the hard work and knew that it would pay off in the future. My freedom and new life was well worth the hard work. That was one notion I shared with all the other Egyptian immigrants. Many had come penniless to America, but they found good jobs, started businesses, worked hard, and were able to buy homes. They also encouraged their children to do well in school.

As I looked back on my first year in America, I felt lucky to have made friends so quickly. These new friends included some Jewish Americans—the very people we were taught to hate all of our lives in the Middle East. That was when I realized that the indoctrination into fear and hatred of Jews that we Arabs grew up with was just a big lie. I started questioning my upbringing and the Arab propaganda I'd been fed all my life. I asked myself, Why the hate? What purpose does it serve? What are Arabs afraid of? Why do they want to spread lies and propaganda against them? Why can't they live with Jews and Christians in the Middle East—a land so vast it stretches from Morocco to Iran? I realized that the Arab-Israeli conflict is not a crisis over land, but a crisis of hate, lack of compassion, ingratitude, and insecurity.

I started blocking out my past. Whenever I saw broadcasts of the Middle East that showed violence and terrorism, I turned off the TV. I simply could not bear to see it or live with it anymore. I would tell myself: "I am now safe in America—the land of the free and the home of the brave. I am now free to pursue the American dream." The U.S. Declaration of Independence says: "We hold these Truths to be self-evident, that all Men are created equal, that they are endowed by their Creator with certain unalienable Rights, that among these are Life, Liberty and the Pursuit of Happiness . . ." One of the youngest nations on earth realized "the self-evident truths" about human rights and human nature. In the most powerful nation on earth your human rights are not granted to you by the president or Congress, but by your creator, whomever you may believe that to be. You are respected and have rights simply because you exist as citizens. As I looked around, I saw that respect for the individual permeated the culture of this country, my newly adopted country, in every aspect of life. I read the U.S. Constitution—not only to pass the test to become a citizen but also because I was genuinely curious to see what this nation was built on. I was in awe of what I was reading, because I realized that if a nation respects the rights of its citizens it would also respect the nations outside its border. As I studied this document, I wondered why the whole world wouldn't adopt similar principles. After becoming an American, and looking at it from an American perspective, I was all the more sad to consider how vulnerable minorities such as Christians and Jews are in the Middle East.

In Los Angeles, I met many Coptic Egyptian families who immigrated together—including grandparents, aunts, uncles, and cousins—with almost no one left behind in Egypt. These Coptic Christian families had survived years of discrimination in Egypt, where they were trained to take the abuse, keep their mouths shut, and move on. Here, basking in their new freedom, they could be who they were, and they were happy and fun to be around. I enjoyed being included in that circle. The large Coptic Egyptian families gathered together almost every weekend, either in their backyards or at Southern California beaches or parks for barbecues. These Egyptian families worked hard on weekdays to achieve the American dream, but on the weekends they cooked, joked, laughed—thoroughly enjoying their new freedom. Most of them came to the United States penniless but soon succeeded in finding good jobs and owning their own homes. They encouraged their children to quickly learn to speak English and to be proud Americans. Yet even though they were no longer an oppressed minority, they were still afraid to speak about their oppression as Christians in the Middle East. They wanted to put all of that behind them.

Coptic churches were popping up in many neighborhoods in Southern California. Egyptian Copts do not teach the Old Testament as part of the Bible. I noticed some anti-Semitism among them, which was understandable, since in Egypt they had been bombarded with the indoctrination of hate and fear of Jews. But others among the Copts were aware of how closely their former persecution was related to the experience of Jews in Egypt. Once after hearing news of violence against Christian churches in the Middle East, I heard an Arab Christian say, "First the Jews, second the Christians."

Yet I was amazed at how Egyptian Coptic immigrants would speak in quiet tones when they relayed the news of violence against their own people and their churches in the Middle East. If *my people*—Muslims—suffered violations of rights or injustice in any way, in any place on the globe, our protest was vocal and often violent, accompanied by outrage and calls for apologies. Arab Christians, on the other hand, were so accustomed to suffering quietly, that even here in America, they spoke about the worsening situation for Middle East Christians only in quiet, secretive tones. The reaction was so ingrained that most could not shake the habit of suffering in silence and were consumed by fear of rocking the boat.

I noticed other "ingrained" cultural habits among the immigrant community. Egyptian newcomers often viewed Americans through the prism of their former culture. For instance, the wife of an Egyptian doctor who lived in a wealthy suburb of Los Angles once complained to me about her "envious" American neighbors who objected to her building a Mediterranean-style home with Roman-style statues and fountains in the front yard. She concluded that her neighbors were extremely jealous of her new home. When I went to visit her I immediately realized why her neighbors objected. The home was grandiose and tasteless, totally out of place in a neighborhood with elegant, low-key, Tudor-style homes. It never occurred to her that their objections were not out of jealousy but out of wanting to preserve the look of the neighborhood. When inevitable construction problems occurred during the building of her little mansion, she attributed it to the evil eye of the neighbors.

In November 1980 I had to travel back to Egypt to handle some family matters and also to conclude my immigration papers at the U.S. Embassy in Cairo. An Egyptian Muslim woman, a former coworker of mine, worked at the embassy. We had a lot in common. Like me, she was the daughter of a shahid. Her father also died fighting Israel. She had been brought up by her father's family after her mother abandoned her.

When I gave her my marriage certificate, which was necessary to obtain the visa, she looked at it and said, "I want to talk to you in the reception area." She spoke in a serious tone, and a certain angry look in her eyes worried me. I left the area behind the counter to join her in a corner in the reception area. She was not being courteous or friendly as one might expect from a former coworker who hadn't seen you in a long time. I was puzzled. She sat down next to me and asked me point-blank: "Did your Coptic husband convert to Islam?" My heart sank, and for a moment I felt that my life was in her hands. I told her, "Yes, of course, and I have the conversion certificate to prove it at home." I did not have it with me, but I told her that I could get it for her.

She asked again, firmly, "Are you sure he converted?"

I almost began crying. I insisted, "Yes, he did."

She asked, "Does he *practice* Islam?"

Again, I said yes. Only then did she get me the papers I needed to complete my visa requirements for the green card.

After returning to my mother's house, I realized how unethical this woman had been. As an employee of the U.S. Embassy in Cairo, she worked for the American government, and she had violated a basic American principle. She had no right to ask me those questions, or appear to threaten to withhold my documents over the issue of my husband's religion. However, I did not dare report her or expose her actions since I was not in America. I was still in Egypt. I realized anew how fragile my life and my happiness were in the hands of this culture.

I had planned to stay in Cairo for a few more days to have more time with my family. But after my experience with the woman in the embassy, I wanted to leave immediately. That night I had a dream that I lost my passport and all my papers and could not go back to Los Angeles to join my husband. I woke up and changed my airline ticket reservation, said good-bye to my family, and went one last time to visit my aging grandmother before leaving. She looked frail and a lot older, but she was just as alert and loving as she had always been. We kissed, hugged, and said good-bye. That was the last time I saw my grandmother.

My grandmother's words echoed in my mind as I left Egypt yet another time: *Rabena ma yehwebni lehad*—may God bless me with never needing help from another human being. That expression grew out of a culture that was ruthless against the needy and the powerless. Respect was given only to the powerful and the arrogant. I was eager to get on that plane and once again leave behind this culture of arrogance, pride, and shame. I wanted to be comfortable in being imperfect and be able to express my need for help if I wanted. I was now leaving again, but I knew what I was returning to—a country and culture where I was accepted and where I need never be ashamed to show that I am a human being with weaknesses and needs. I could hardly wait to get back.

During my first two years in America, my sudden exposure to freedom of religion and social and racial equality made me realize to what degree Muslim society oppressed, shamed, and manipulated its citizens. It was crippling to a healthy life. For the first thirty years of my life, I had lived in oppressive dictatorships, among people who were afraid to speak their mind. Any new immigrant to the United States who has come from repressive regimes will certainly understand what I am talking about. Not many Middle Eastern immigrants talk about this gift that America gave us, about their sudden enjoyment of democracy and freedom, free self-expression, simplicity, honesty, and the American way of life. Moving to America was like being catapulted to another time in history. America for me was not just a place for making money, having a job, a house, and car, it was a place for becoming a human being. Other immigrants who feel this way may not talk about it, but because of the way I am, I cannot stop thinking about it and talking about it.

Home now was Los Angeles, California, far away from radical Islam and people like the Egyptian woman at the American Embassy. The 1980s was a time of immersion in both work and family. I gave birth to two beautiful children, a boy in 1981 and a girl in 1983. They were the miracle in my life. I worked all through my pregnancies. My mother came for a year to help me take care of my children while I was working. For the next decade, I was like most American women, juggling work and raising a family, with all the joys and challenges that entails.

My escape from radical Islam to the open arms of America did not last for long. As we moved deeper into the 1980s decade, I began to see gradual change among the Arab Muslims around me. To my surprise, the radical aspects of Islamic culture from which I had escaped were starting to grow in power right here in America.

Seven | The Journey from Hatred to Love

I prospered in America, with my two beautiful children—a boy and a girl—and a lovely home. But something was missing. I lacked a spiritual life. And I felt a deep hunger.

In Egypt religious life and one's relationship with God was not a personal matter. Our religious destiny was assigned to us by birth. Even though I came from a time in Egypt where radical Islam was not yet in control, Islam was our identity. Our knowledge of Islam was based on memorization and compliance, and not on study, debate, or asking questions. We all believed Islam was part of our genes: We were born with it, like our hair or eye color. It was not a matter of choice. You were Muslim, period. Those who did not want to practice—and they were many—simply did not talk about it. Rejecting or changing one's religion was unthinkable. We were led to believe that those who left Islam were killed, and they deserved it. Even knowledge about other religions was forbidden; those who attempted to learn about other religions were accused of apostasy.

Everything around us reminded us we were Muslims—our

identification cards, licenses, passports, and even college IDs. We felt Islam's presence everywhere, and this led to a feeling that there was no need to "practice it." In fact, many Muslims among all classes and educational levels did not practice, but were nevertheless very careful to avoid any behavior that is *eib*, meaning "improper," or *haram*, meaning "sinful," at least in public. In the days before I left Egypt, most of my fellow students and coworkers were nonpracticing Muslims. Yet we were locked in "Islam's closet," following ritualistic behaviors such as saying *in Shaallah* in every conversation.

As Middle Eastern women, we never attended mosques or had any ties to religious institutions. I liked listening to the call for prayers from mosques and hearing certain Koran recitations. But, like all Egyptian girls at that time, I never attended a mosque for the purpose of prayer. The only mosques I ever entered in Egypt were three historical sites in Cairo—Muhammad Ali Citadel Mosque, Sayeda Zeinab Mosque, and Sayyedna El-Hussein Mosque—and these visits were as a tourist or for the purpose of giving to the poor.

Mosques were part of a man's world, one that women simply did not experience. Women were supposed to practice their religion at home, and since no one was looking, many did not pray regularly. A common joke in Egyptian society was: "Women are lacking in brains and religion." Women's knowledge about religion was limited to whatever they could grasp from family and school and was not learned from religious institutions. Islamic society had nothing similar to America's traditional Bible study or prayer groups. I am not sure why women were prevented from receiving institutionalized religious education beyond what was taught in religion class in elementary school. Perhaps the fear was that if women got out of their homes and met in groups and formed alliances, it would encourage questioning and debate, and eventually that might lead to women, as an organized group, making demands to improve their conditions. I cannot help but think that women's religious isolation was by design and not by coincidence.

During my childhood and young adult years in Egypt, middle- and upper-class women did not cover their heads except in rural Egypt and among lower classes with peasant roots. Peasants, both men and women, covered their heads for protection from the blazing Egyptian sun while working in the fields. For them, head covering was a practical matter and was regarded as more traditional than religious.

At the time I left, Egypt had a 70 percent illiteracy rate; thus most Egyptians could not read the Koran, let alone understand it. Among this huge illiterate population, especially women, there was very little knowledge of the Koran, or even of Islam in general.

This must be very hard to understand by Western standards. Outsiders assume the Middle East is very religious. It is, after all, known to be the land where radical Islam rules, but many in the Middle East have never even read the Koran or interpreted it. How can someone live in the heart of the Muslim world, where the famous historical Islamic institution Al-Azhar University is located, and know so little about Islam? But that is precisely the point. Most Muslims have little or no education in Islam. Why? Such education would end Muslim leadership's total control over the minds and behavior of the masses. Their objective is to maintain a Muslim army of followers who fear to ask questions or to engage in debate or dissent. Muslims are safe as long as they are loyal followers and obedient to the national goal of jihad against the non-Muslim infidels, especially the Jews next door.

In the Muslim world there are no real distinctions between moderate or radical Muslims; all are Muslims. Some practice and some don't, and the ones who don't may have views as radical as those who do practice. They also try to do all they can to publicly behave as good Muslims in order to keep the radicals off their backs.

The Muslim masses have been prevented from any exposure to other ideologies or religions. A good Muslim must never look at other religious books such as a Bible. We were told it was the word of the devil. Non-Muslims together with their book are *nagass*, meaning "filthy" or "dirty." Muslims often whispered the word *nagass* when describing Christian Egyptian Copts, especially after a disagreement with one. So reading or knowing anything from another religion's holy book was a great sin and a threat to the Muslim establishment, and everyone knew it and abided by it. (We knew that some Muslim countries, such as Saudi Arabia, put those who carry Bibles in jail.) As a result of these prohibitions, most Muslims know nothing about other religions or how close Islam is to both Judaism and Christianity. For instance, they never associate the great feast in Islam with the biblical story of Abraham and his son Isaac, but with a Muslim Abraham (Ibrahim) and his son Ishmael. Yet it is the same story, essentially. I remember it was news to my aunt, an upper-middle-class woman, when I told her that Jews also do not eat pork. She said: "Are you serious? They are like us?" She was even more amazed when I told her that their religion preceded ours and that many Muslim religious stories are similar to the Bible stories Judaism and Christianity hold dear. Nor do the masses know that officially Islam recognizes Moses (Mussa) and Jesus (Issa) as prophets, though they are not considered as important as Muhammad, the "final" prophet. We were simply kept in the dark as to the bigger picture. When questions were raised, there was only one answer: Islam is the last religion. It was final and everyone should follow it. The truth is that most Muslims are a part of "political Islam" rather than a religion and a personal relationship with God. Furthermore, the nonpracticing Muslims are often as biased, extreme, and supportive of jihad as the religious extremists.

The values of Muslim society, as it is constituted at the present, cannot survive in a democracy where individuals would have a right to question, debate, change religions, or choose to have no religion at all. As it is, the Muslim faith is assured—even in so-called moderate Muslim countries—through fear, shame, intimidation, imprisonment, and finally by a death sentence. That requires tyranny.

But I had left that all behind. Now I lived in a democracy, one in which religion is neither proscribed nor coerced. I could now choose to worship or not worship, be observant, or not be observant. Now that I was in America, I could practice my religion in an environment of inclusion befitting the great democracy that many of us Arab Americans went through hell to arrive at. I presumed I would be meeting enlightened, educated, Westernized Muslims in American mosques. Being in America, these mosques would of course welcome women. I envisioned that now we could be like Christian and Jewish families who gather together one day a week to worship God in a tolerant community that has respect for all other religions. I was looking forward to thoughtful, moderate sermons more reflective of American religious tolerance instead of calls for the destruction of the infidels by clerics who incited anger, revenge, and intolerance. Those days were behind me. I was in America.

When a close friend of my family from Egypt came to visit us in Los Angeles, my husband and I decided to dress up our children and all go to a mosque. It would be a new experience for me. I had never worshiped in mosques in Egypt. But in America, we Egyptian women were now given the same respect as men and were free to attend a mosque. In retrospect, perhaps I also wanted to please my Egyptian friend and show him how "enlightened" American Muslims were.

I brought a scarf with me and put it on my head as I entered the mosque. It felt strange to cover my head, something I had never done before. Men and women were separated, so our guest and my husband went to the main hall of the mosque where men gathered and I took my children to a children's area (much like a church's Sunday School) where I met a woman who was in charge of the children. I said hello, and without even responding to my friendly greeting, she said, "You should cover your daughter's head." My daughter was only six years old at the time. The woman had an Egyptian accent so I asked her about Egypt. She denied she was from Egypt and claimed she was Kuwaiti. I'm guessing she was an

Egyptian who lived in Kuwait for a while and felt more proud of her links to "rich" Kuwait than to Egypt. As I left the room she told my daughter not to come without a head cover again.

I walked away thinking, "Is this the kind of woman I want to entrust my children's religious education to?" I felt uneasy. I didn't want my children to undergo any of the radicalism and intolerance that I grew up with. I noticed that most of the men in the mosque had beards, and the women were covered from head to toe.

I then entered the women's room, a small room near the men's large hall. All the women were sitting on the floor. (Muslims must show humility before God, and sitting on a chair is considered a sign of disrespect to God.) Many of them were Pakistani, Afghani, and other Arabs who spoke little English. The room was noisy because there were toddlers running around. We could hardly hear the sermon, but I was able to grasp a few words—mostly about Islam in America and how it should grow; how Muslim women in America should be proud to cover up and retain their Islamic identity. Even those women who never covered up in their country of origin, such as Egypt, were encouraged to cover up and proudly show a new Islamic identity here in America. Retaining our identity meant rejecting assimilation into America's permissive society. Even Muslim college girls were encouraged to cover up on U.S. college campuses. We should be proud of who we are and where we came from, we were told. The sermon carried an undertone of anti-Americanism and anti-Semitism. There was no message of tolerance, friendship, and assimilation in the country we had chosen as our new home. The message was that of "us against them." As I continued to listen to the sermon, I wondered, why would anyone move to another country for the purpose of rejecting its culture? I felt very uneasy. The message brought back memories of the intolerance I left behind. It sounded all too familiar.

Ironically, I had left Egypt where no one in my family, not even my deeply religious grandmother, wore a head covering, only to be exhorted to cover up in America! I looked at the women around me and felt very alien. Had I come to America to be segregated, not only in another room but also to separate myself from the rest of America by covering up? Some women around me even covered their faces. This is not why I moved to America.

While these thoughts were churning inside me, I suddenly saw my Egyptian guest with my husband behind him, standing outside the women's door motioning me to come. I got up and went to see what he wanted. My Egyptian friend sternly said, "Let's go."

I went to pick up my children and to my surprise they too were unhappy. My daughter and son pleaded, "We don't want to come here again."

In the car, my moderate Muslim friend complained that the message in the mosque was radical and that the preacher was very uneducated.

When I discussed this later with several of my moderate, non-practicing Muslim friends, they advised me to follow their example, worship at home and not go to mosques, because many mosques in America were likely to be as radical as the ones in the remote parts of the most extreme Muslim countries, such as Saudi Arabia and Afghanistan. The more I learned, the more I understood that the agenda of these radical American mosques, many of them here thanks to the "generosity" of the Saudi Government, was to keep American Muslims in line, Islamize America, and spread a radical Wahabi sect of Islam that even Egyptians find too extreme.

I then began hearing the "good news" from some Arab American Muslims: that more and more mosques would be built by Saudi Arabia, which was also sending its own preachers, and imams from countries such as Pakistan and Afghanistan. These imported radical clerics consider America the Great Satan and believe their mission is to promote jihad and violence against non-Muslims, especially Jews. I asked, "Why don't Muslims in the United States appoint leaders from within our own community rather than bring in the same intolerant, jihadist preachers we left behind?"

The answer from my Muslim friends was that we do not need

some Americanized Muslim religion; we need to bring true Islam to this nation that needs it.

I soon discovered that rabid anti-American feeling is rampant in the majority of U.S. mosques, where Muslims are encouraged to stand out as mujahadeen in America. In these mosques, America's generosity was met with demands for more generosity and concessions from people who never lived a day under democracy in their countries of origin. The messages of most mosques in America can be summed up by the words of Omar Ahmad, cofounder of the Council on American-Islamic Relations (CAIR), who said, as reported by the *San Ramon Valley Herald*, in 1998: "Those who stay in America should be open to society without melting, keeping Mosques open so anyone can come and learn about Islam. If you choose to live here, you have a responsibility to deliver the message of Islam. . . . Islam isn't in America to be equal to any other faiths, but to become dominant. The Koran, the Muslim book of scripture, should be the highest authority in America, and Islam the only accepted religion on earth."

Not all Arab Americans would agree with that. In fact, most Arab American Muslims choose to blend with American society, are happy and proud to be Americans, and do not want to be associated with radical clerics. Many regarded radical clerics imported from Saudi Arabia and Pakistan as a sadistic joke imposed on American mosques by a wealthy Saudi government. In fact, these angry, close-minded, and uneducated preachers, who in our countries of origin would be a laughingstock among the educated Arab classes, have discovered a new status of respectability in America where their freedom of hate speech is protected. Unfortunately, such preachers in the American Muslim community have a silencing effect on moderate Arab Americans, who find themselves unable to escape hate speech even in a democracy. We American Arabs have tended to remain silent around them, afraid to confront them as we are reminded all over again of the power of hate speech and intimidation. We realize that the same preachers who brainwash our children in the Arab world are attempting to do the same to our American children.

My attempt to have a religious life ended. Again I joined the ranks of the nonpracticing Muslims of the Middle East. I never stepped in a mosque in America again. My spiritual life went back to zero. Two prominent, well-respected Muslim American professors advised me that they do not go to mosques in the United States because "they are breeding grounds for hate and intolerance." They told me they prayed at home and advised me to do the same. But to me a religion should be more than just praying by myself at home. I needed the fellowship, the community, and the traditions. I needed to be inspired by a religious experience that elevated my soul and made me a better person, a more tolerant and loving person. I wanted to reach out with understanding and respect to other faiths. Unfortunately I could not find what I needed in American mosques because they had been infiltrated by some of the most radical groups in the Middle East.

A few months passed. One day I was walking in a Southern California mall and saw two Muslim women who were totally covered up. One of them called my name. She was an old friend who moved to the United States almost at the same time I did. We were overjoyed to see one another again, and we reconnected and exchanged phone numbers. But I was surprised to see my old acquaintance covered up from head to toe except for her face. She had always worn Western clothes when she was growing up in Egypt. But I did not question or criticize her. I thought to myself, this is a free country and that it is her choice. I will respect it. She had a nice family and I did not mind befriending her again.

I then began seeing a trend of "looking like a Muslim" among many other Muslim Americans. I was surprised to see many young women at UCLA and other universities cover up too. Muslim men started growing beards. That seemed radical even to Americans of Muslim origin from the Middle East, like myself. I realized that the radical mosques, such as the one I attempted to visit, were having an effect on other Muslim immigrants. Even though they were not particularly religious when they left their home countries in the Middle East, paradoxically, they had discovered radical Islam in American mosques.

The friend I had met at the mall invited me to visit her home. My husband and I went, and to our surprise found it very different from the atmosphere of their previous home in Egypt. Her husband had grown a beard. My friend immediately invited us and the other guests for prayers right there in their home, then she invited me to go with them sometimes to the mosque, and told me I should cover my head like all of her friends did. In the conversations around me that evening, I heard such things as: "Louis Farrakhan is good for the Arab cause." "Israel is gasping in its last breath." "Even if it takes us a hundred years we will destroy Israel." "America needs Islam." "America should teach Arabic in American schools and Muslim holidays should be national holidays."

The hostess was proud that her daughters attended an Islamic school and complained that her older daughter was revolting against Islamic attire. At some point, this daughter came in to say hello and was dressed in what might be considered to be revealing clothes. I heard the mother follow after her daughter, asking her to change. I began feeling very uncomfortable, and my husband and I left early.

It had become clear to me that evening that my old acquaintance did not really want my friendship, but wanted to bring more Muslims to the mosque. Even though I accepted her way of life, she did not accept mine. Needless to say, that was the end of the relationship.

I started wondering why a Muslim family who wants to follow Islamic law to the letter and truly despises Western culture would choose to live in the Judeo-Christian culture of the infidels? Obviously they could better guarantee the upbringing of their children as good Muslims in the Middle East than in the West. If Islam were truly the center of their existence, wouldn't it make sense to live in a Muslim country? Think about it. Why would they risk bringing up their children in a place where after age eighteen they could legally leave home, reject their religion, and even marry an infidel? Why would they subject their children to temptations that could theoretically lead to daughters being beaten—or even killed—for having boyfriends? We have all heard of honor killing of Muslim girls in Europe and America. Given all these temptations and dangers to their families, why would radical Muslims want to live in the land of the infidels?

It did not add up.

The paradox is that many radical Muslims have a condescending view of the West but still love to live under Western freedoms. Why? For one thing, it provides them with freedom of speech. There is no control by anyone, not even the government, over their hate speech and the spreading of their radical agenda—something that even Muslim societies impose restrictions on. (Preachers and religious leaders in the Middle East are employees of the state and often have to adhere to their government's daily agenda. Those who don't are put in jail. Yes, even radical Muslims in the Middle East are tortured and abused if they do not do what they are told by the political leadership.) But in the United States and the West they suddenly enjoy new rights and very quickly begin demanding them from the U.S. government. They consider hate speech and even incitement to violence against America as "freedom of speech." That leaves many Americans bewildered as to how to handle this use of our open society. Muslim radicals are using American democracy to their own advantage and for their own agenda—freedoms they do not have even in the Muslim world to spread their agenda. Remember, many Arab leaders have put the Muslim Brotherhood and other radical organizations in jail when they were out of control. But under the American justice system, if radicals are careful, they can do practically anything—even support terrorism—and be found innocent of any wrongdoing in a court of law. This paradox—Muslims on one hand using our freedoms and on the other hand working to abolish them—seems contradictory. Many Americans cannot understand it.

The Archbishop of Izmir, Giuseppe Germano Bernandini, writing to the Synod of European Bishops, summed up the West's dilemma with Islam by quoting an authoritative Muslim leader he met in a dialogue meeting between Christians and Muslims: "Thanks to your democratic laws we will invade you; thanks to our religious laws we will dominate you."

Westerners in Muslim society are called invaders, but Muslims in Western society have learned to assert their equal rights in the West's open systems and use it to their maximum advantage to promote their ideology and agenda. Standing up to this "legal" invasion to change Western culture is still considered wrong by many Westerners who are not yet prepared to address abuses to their system. The Western concept of "when you're in Rome do as the Romans do" is not a Muslim value. In Muslim culture, if Rome has its door open, that is an invitation to invade and claim it as your own.

The current onslaught against our society is nothing new. Conquering the world for Islam has been going on since the seventh century using pretty much the same tactics. The West, currently struggling with how to preserve its own value system and maintain "political correctness," has been caught unprepared for such an insidious legal invasion and assault on its culture. This is not new either. In the old world there were two superpowers, namely Egypt and Mesopotamia (which today is Iraq). Before the seventh century, Egypt was Christian and did not speak Arabic. The same for Mesopotamia, which had substantial Christian and Jewish populations as well as various other tribal groups and religions. During an era of political confusion and military weakness, the two regional powers were overwhelmed by Arab tribes who swept in from the desert and by force changed their religion to Islam and their language to Arabic. The Egyptian Christian Copts were those who resisted and those who were rich enough to pay the higher taxes imposed on *dhimmis* (an underclass) and remain Christian. In a bold revision of history, which is accepted to this day, the cultural and military superiority of these two great centers of civilization—Egypt and Mesopotamia—were later claimed to be

"Arab and Muslim." The people who today live in Egypt and Iraq, because they have never been taught their own history, are totally unaware that their original heritage is neither Muslim nor Arab.

The raiding Arab armies continued their conquest, claiming all of the Middle East for Islam (including parts of Europe, such as Turkey and Spain) and wiping out advanced civilizations who would never see their glory days again, and whose collective populations would eventually not even remember their original religious or cultural roots.

There is a second reason that many radical Muslims prefer Western freedoms to Islamic tyranny, though they would never admit it: Besides using freedom of speech to spread Islam as they please, they also enjoy the West's economic opportunity. But more than just enjoying it, they covet it and feel it legitimately "belongs" to the Islamic world. To understand this, you will have to follow some twists of logic that may be difficult for Westerners to grasp: Many Muslims think that if Islam conquers the West, they can claim the material wealth of the West for Islam without having to work hard for it, produce it, or invent it. As a matter of fact, a booklet produced by a Muslim organization in California claims that America was actually discovered by Arabs before Christopher Columbus, and that Arabs mixed with the Indians, which gives them claims to America! Some even go as far as to say that the word "California" means the land of "Califa," which in Arabic means "Caliphate" (Islamic state). The old tactics from the seventh century are being used all over again by claiming any superpower is somehow the property of Islam and Muslim culture.

Many Muslims and Arabs are eager to say that the Muslim world is collectively a superpower and can beat America. They are quick to put America and the Judeo-Christian cultural achievements down and claim most of the world's achievements as originally Arab. When they see the high number of Jewish and Christian recipients of Nobel Prizes and the minuscule numbers of Muslim recipients, they feel extremely jealous and often say Arabs invented this or that first. I even heard a Muslim leader once proudly claim

in front of Muslim youth that America was not the true power behind the collapse of the Soviet Union, but it was the Muslim mujahadeen in Afghanistan. America according to them did not win the
Cold War but the Muslim fighters in the caves of Afghanistan did.
Westerners hear these foolish claims and dismiss them as laughable, but to me it is not funny, because the Muslims who believe
these claims feel that the West is taking away their glory. Glory attributed to Islam is very important to Muslims and Arabs.

Furthermore, around many Muslims I have heard the absurd
argument, "Europeans and Americans are the real Muslims because they live as Muslims but don't know it." I was told by a devout Muslim when he met an American Christian neighbor of
mine, "Your neighbor has a great character; he is a true Muslim."
My first cousin, who lives in Egypt and visits Europe regularly, always returns home with great admiration for the European culture
and anger toward Egyptian society. She admires the Europeans for
their honesty, decency, and reliability. She is amazed at their acceptance and welcoming of immigrants. Because of what she sees
as their high moral code, she has told me several times that the
Europeans are the "true Muslims" and that we Egyptians are not.
I wanted to yell, "No, they are Christians, let us not claim their
culture to ourselves." This is a form of piracy and falsifying reality.
My cousin, who is observant and wears a head cover, is disappointed with Egyptian society because she feels Egyptians are not
behaving as good Muslims should.

How could Muslims, with a straight face, claim American or
European success for themselves? That kind of thinking sources
from being taught that all good around the world is Muslim and
evil is non-Muslim. By this thinking, how can good exist *without*
being Muslim? So they truly believe that the "good" Westerners
are actually Muslim, but they just "don't know it." Muslims, therefore, have an obligation to come to America (and the West) and
tell them the "good news" that they are true Muslims. As convo-
luted as this thinking may seem, it is the mind-set of Islamic fundamentalists who wish to convert the West to their "true religion,"

rule them, and change their constitutions to Koranic law and their language to Arabic.

But if we closely examine Muslim culture we may find deeper, embedded motivations beyond the stated "religious" goals. Perhaps the concepts of envy, honor, and shame, which dominate Muslim culture, have something to do with it. The land of the infidels is putting Muslims to shame. Infidel Christians and Jews live in a much more advanced political and economic system in a democracy that provides a much better life for its citizens. Some Muslims dare to ask why Islam has not provided them with a better society than that of the infidels. That puts pressure on the radicals to raise the level of the lies and indoctrination inside Muslim society. There is some evidence that the game is no longer working on the Arab street, which now can see the world through satellite dishes, the Internet, and travel. What they see is beginning to throw the Muslim world into more contradictions and turmoil. In the "proud" Muslim culture, the mere existence of a better society that is *not* Muslim is a source of humiliation, shame, and victimhood. I recall something I heard a young man in Gaza say when I visited that region at age fourteen. He pointed at some European UN personnel and derisively said, "These Westerners are not worth a penny in their homeland!" The way he said it gave an impression of extreme jealousy and perhaps an inferiority complex as a result of a blown-up ego, no doubt given to him by an oppressed mother who will one day celebrate his death in killing the infidels. His description of "not worth a penny in their homeland" was actually describing how Arabs feel about themselves in Arab land. That is indeed how their proud, unbending governments regard these disaffected young men—not worth a penny. I truly believe that Arab men have been spoiled rotten as children by their parents; they were brought up to think of themselves as the best, of their religion as the best, and their lifestyle the best. When they finally grow up and are confronted with the confidence and competence of Western men they simply cannot stand it. Then the culture of pride, envy, and hate kicks in, and they begin to indulge in the blame game. Rather than examining their own system, culture, or religion, they say it must be colonialism, imperialism, past injustice, Israel's existence, or a worldwide Zionist conspiracy that has caused their society to fail. Thus deep-seated feelings of inferiority creates marching jihadists who have nothing else to aspire to than either claim the West for Islam or destroy it.

I do not want to be misunderstood. I am talking about *culture and societal values*, not about all individual Muslims; of course there are many exceptions. I believe that the majority of Muslims who left Muslim countries, even if they don't admit it, have come to live under Judeo-Christian freedoms in America in search of a better future just as I did, a world that encourages personal responsibility and self-discipline and discourages envy, shaming, pride, and anger. Such a society is easier to live in. Nevertheless, once in America, some of them fall under the influence of the radical networks and organizations that dominate the mosques. There are many Arab and Muslim organizations that encourage Arab Americans to vote as a block and not as individuals with different preferences. It is hard to get rid of the bad habits of the old country since these behaviors are often spontaneous and seem normal. Many American mosques show no respect to their host country. They have come with the agenda of changing the culture and not to be part of America. Many of the imams get their salaries directly from oil-wealthy Muslim nations who have sent them to America on religious visas and built their mosques. They don't have to pass the plate in the mosque for donations from worshipers and their salaries are guaranteed. Thus, they continue teaching the only thing they ever knew and are trained to do, and that is hate speech and anti-Semitism. Instead of being a source of comfort and wisdom, these preachers become a source of rage, hate, and subversion right here in America, working the worshipers into a frenzy of anger and paranoia not only against Western values and Israel but also against moderate Muslims who represent the majority of Arab Americans.

Unfortunately, these Muslim radicals within the United States are not here to live in a pluralistic society that has respect for all.

They have come to Islamize America. They have also come to manipulate the new Muslim immigrants to the United States, keep them within their camp, and spread doubt and rejection of America among their ranks. Many of them are easy prey since that was the way they have lived in the old country. These immigrants are then tragically prevented from fully experiencing the American way of life.

Furthermore, to recruit new Muslims in America, radical leaders often go to the most angry and vulnerable population; that is, inside American jails, to turn them against America. And when it comes to converting African Americans, they use the race card. However, they fail to mention that Arabs were among the first cultures to enslave sub-Saharan Africans and promote the slave trade around the world, not to mention that slavery is still practiced by Sudanese Muslims. Radical mosques also work to recruit Middle Eastern immigrants—such as my friend and her husband—to the larger jihadist worldview that has one goal: to overtake and overwhelm America and other Western societies, bring the evil infidels to their knees, and conquer the world for Islam.

Many devout Muslims hold at heart a dream of an Islamic Caliphate, a totalitarian political system encompassing the whole Muslim world—and eventually the entire world—which functions under one constitution (the Koran) and one law, Islamic sharia law. This is not some crazy notion espoused by some lunatic fringe Islamists. Conquering the world for Islam is the stated goal that emanates from powerful, ruling Islamic clerics throughout the Middle East, whether it is the Wahabis of Saudi Arabia, the mullahs of Iran's Islamic revolution, the Muslim Brotherhood of Egypt, the Taliban of Afghanistan, or the followers of Osama bin Laden. This is also the goal of many Islamic organizations operating under false pretences in America and financed and supported by radical Muslim states. Is the Islamic invasion of the seventh century on the superpowers of that time being reincarnated again on the superpowers of today?

These were the questions, fears, and the thoughts that swirled in my mind during the 1980s and '90s as I saw the increasing radicalization within the Muslim community in America. When I gathered my children and walked out of that Los Angeles–area mosque, when I left the house of my newly fundamentalist friend who wished to suck me into it, I turned my back on it. And I closed my eyes to it. But I worried about it. As a mother myself, I wondered how these newly fundamentalist American families could expect their children to live in total isolation and alienation from the larger society. Their only solution was to send their children to Muslim schools. And in these schools in America, the same indoctrination and hate speech against non-Muslims I experienced back in Gaza is now creating a new generation full of alienation and rage, a subculture that rejects the larger society. The indoctrination of these schools here and elsewhere in the West is producing angry young Muslims who cannot relate to the larger community. It is a ticking time bomb waiting to explode.

As I observed my fellow Arabs in America, I was troubled by another thing: The double face of Muslim radicals in the West became clear to me, but unfortunately it was not clear to many fellow Americans. When learned Muslim scholars are questioned about hate speech and Islamic terrorism, they always make the point that Islam teaches love, compassion, and respect for other religions, and they quote supporting portions from the Koran. They purposely deny or ignore other passages of the Koran that encourage killing, jihad, and war against the infidels. Sometimes these respected, educated men will deny, with a straight face on Western TV, that hate is being taught, while in their mosques and on Arab TV one regularly hears hate speech equal to that of Nazi Germany, except that it is now taught as orders from Allah instead of orders from Hitler. Anyone who sees what is daily in Arab newspapers and on television, or looks at the material taught in mosques and schools, knows what is going on. Are some Muslim scholars that disconnected from reality, or do they think the West is too naive to catch them in their lies? Some of these scholars truly believe that Islam is a peaceful religion—that is, after all, a basic function of religion in society. But these same scholars totally ignore the existential reality of the current Muslim society. They are eager to work to change how the West *perceives* Islam, but usually stop short of actually advocating peace to the people who need it the most—Muslims in the Middle East. I truly believe that the Muslim masses around the world are yearning and hungry for new concepts in their life, concepts such as love, respect, responsibility, compassion, forgiveness, and tolerance. Muslims are just human beings like the rest of the world, and deep down, I believe they are fed up with such cruel and archaic teachings, all in the name of Muslim unity against the infidels. However, having not been educated on the devastating psychological effects of such teachings, they are often unaware of how much damage such negative teachings do to their society.

But there is a dilemma for Muslim leaders. If they were to start actually teaching peace and issue fatwas against terrorists instead of critics of Islam, we might begin to see Islamic peace, reformation, and an end to jihad. Ironically, in the current state of things in the Middle East, teaching peace instead of jihad would be rejected by most mosque-goers. You cannot suddenly take away from people what has been their basic religious teachings for generations. An Egyptian friend and writer, Tawfik Hamid, author of *The Real Roots of Islamic Violence*, told me he attempted to preach peace and nonviolence in an Egyptian mosque and was chased into the streets of Cairo with rocks and barely escaped with his life—and that was in Egypt, a place that is not considered a radical Muslim country, at least not yet. Hate speech and intolerance is so deeply rooted that even the average worshipers are sucked into it, thinking this is true Islam. Advocating peace, especially with Israel, would surely get anyone killed.

To some Islamic idealists, what Muslims are doing on earth—terrorism and jihad—is necessary and will be forgiven because they have good intentions to spread Islam to those who don't know they need it. They are sacrificing themselves to die in the hopes of spreading Allah's word. To many, that is a good deed. In their minds, the ideal of peace will be achieved later when Islam dominates the world. They reason that peace can wait until that great achievement, and in the meanwhile, we'll merely "talk about peace" to mollify the West. That is what goes on in the minds of these Islamist defenders. Lying is forbidden in Islam except in certain situations such as war to spread Islam to non-Muslims. The Muslim world considers itself in a constant jihadist war against the infidel non-Muslims, and accordingly lying and deception are permitted. To prove my point, you have only to ask one of these Muslim scholars, "What are you doing to end the lying about the West and the State of Israel in the Arab media and educational system?" You won't get a straight answer to that question. The truth is that very few Muslim leaders even care to end the lies on Arab television—lies as outrageous as saying that Jewish rabbis want to kill Arab children to take their blood for baking cookies. They do nothing when Muslims on Egyptian, Jordanian, and Saudi television call Jews apes and pigs. They merely repeat that Islam is a religion of "peace and tolerance" and count on the decency of Americans to believe them. Muslim leaders say one thing to Americans and another thing to Muslims. We Arabs understand that game—it was once an unconscious part of our own thinking.

Yes, Arabs in America were changing. As I looked around me in the immigrant community, I noticed that some Egyptian Americans even started adopting an Islamic Afghani or Saudi look rather than an Egyptian look. Such changes it seems to me are deliberately intended to make a point to the unsuspecting American community, rather than for their own Muslim community's sake. Indeed, much of what is done was defiance against American culture and values aimed at bringing Islam to the larger community. It is not like Indians wearing the traditional saris to their parties. It has a larger purpose. They have found a new identity in standing out against American culture. It has given them power. This trend has Muslims behaving in a way that boldly states, "I am different" and "I belong to a superior group."

I avoided radical Muslims in America who appeared fake and two-faced to me. But their presence and power was increasing, especially on college campuses, where Muslim student organizations were popping up everywhere. Muslim female students proudly wore the head covering on American university campuses. That was a new movement I have never seen before. I believe that many of these young women welcome the unique identity and defiance this outfit gives them. I have often wondered if these same American-born girls would still cover up if they lived under Islamic regimes that prohibited them from driving or doing many activities without the approval of a male relative. In fact, I believe that these same defiant young Muslim women, if forced to submit to the second-class citizenship their sisters in many Muslim countries endure, might be the first to stand up in defiance and burn their burkas. Most of them were born in America and have never lived under the Taliban or Iranian or Saudi sharia law, and look at their long lost heritage with naive nostalgia and pride. They have never felt the humiliation and oppression that many Muslim women live under. Instead of feeling gratitude to the culture that liberated them, they use their head cover or veil as a form of jihad in defiance to all that America stands for in its pursuit of freedom and equality for women. I was once told by one of them: "My Islamic attire is a political statement." I believed her 100 percent.

Furthermore, I see Arab professors on U.S. campuses who are equally if not even more radical and elusive than any imam in a radical mosque. They are merely more clever in conveying their message of hate and anti-Semitism than the crude preachers are. I heard one Arab professor claim she "just wants to live in peace with Israel," but her speech was full of quotations from anti-Semitic figures who say that Israel is not "worthy" of having a state. Contradictions like that are endless among Muslim leaders and intellectuals. They display a split personality: one side supports and justifies terror and another claims "Islam is a religion of peace," leaving many perplexed as to what their real position is. Whether double-speaking professors or imams, when confronted by the West, such Arabs deny their true intentions regarding Jews and Christians. What they tell one another is different from what they tell non-Muslims. As an Arab speaker I know that. As a child I often saw respectable adults lie to present Islam in a positive light. Even moderate Muslims often find themselves on the defensive to justify this or explain away that.

The same radicalism I watched in this country was, of course, also spreading in the Middle East. My contacts and family in the Middle East reported the same thing: some were afraid of an Islamic coup d'etat in Egypt by the Muslim Brotherhood. Family and friends told me that many Egyptian women were covering up, some of their own choice, and others under pressure from their husbands or other women. As I heard these reports, I realized that what is happening was not just some phenomenon of disaffected Arab immigrants in this country, but a *worldwide* jihadist movement supported and financed by oil money from Saudi Arabia and other rich Gulf states. The movement was taking place not just in moderate Muslim countries like Egypt, but was radicalizing and causing uprisings among Muslim minorities around the world, whether in Chechnya, the Philippines, Africa, Bosnia, or India.

As we moved into the 1990s, Islamic terrorism was also on the rise around the world. Oil wealth—the new Arab governments' openly used weapon—had given Arabs an advantage over the West. The sword as an Islamic weapon cannot officially be used by most Muslim governments, even though some radical ones, such as Iran, are foolish enough to make such threats. Thus the sword is left to the terrorists who are the hidden hands of radical Muslim leadership and governments. Oil money was now buying access for radical Islam in the West. Political and cultural demands were being made daily in Western democracies to accommodate Muslims while at the same time prohibit Western influence within the Muslim world. Think about it. Muslim countries do not give the same accommodation and tolerance to Jews, Christians, and minorities in the Middle East that they demand for themselves in the West. Muslims have been building mosques around the world for decades while prohibiting the building of churches and synagogues on

Muslim land. I was hearing of more and more Christian Egyptians being discriminated against, and violence against churches in Egypt was on the rise. With increased Muslim power and wealth has also come increased intolerance of non-Muslims.

As for me and my family, we chose to assimilate and be part of America. We had friends from all backgrounds and races. I was an independent thinker and simply could not submit blindly to any ideology, especially radical Islam, which was now in control of most of the Muslim world. I was tired of my character being defined simply as either a Muslim or a non-Muslim. Nor did I wish to face the dilemma that involved being filled with pride and superiority for practicing Islam or being filled with shame and guilt for not practicing. I considered religion to be a personal matter, not a matter of warriors preparing to conquer the world. Radical Islam has ruined the beautiful aspects of Muslim culture. Despite my natural inclination to be a moral and religious person, I could not be a practicing Muslim because I could not accept the way Islam was being taught and practiced in today's world. I could not dissect the radical portions of Islamic teachings, such as "kill the infidels," from the religion. That should be the job of Muslim scholars who should reform their religion to rescue it from interpretations that lead to violence and terrorism. Islam, as taught today, says that jihad is not optional for a Muslim; even women and the elderly are ordered to give asylum and aid (Surah 8:74). What jihad means to all Muslims is a religious holy war against the infidels. Some Muslim scholars dispute this interpretation, especially in front of Western media. But if they truly dispute this meaning, they should start reeducating their people as to the correct meaning, because people are being slaughtered around the world due to this supposed misunderstanding.

How can a religion be described as a "religion of peace" while its leaders order fatwas to kill those who criticize it? Islamic clerics are still teaching violence, jihad, and glorifying wars that happened in the seventh century as the example—literally—of what Muslims should do today. I am sure there are some radical views in Christianity and Judaism, but they have been reformed, reinterpreted, and are no longer the centerpiece of their religion. Today's Muslim teachings and preaching is depressing, cruel, ruthless, and oppressive. When news of a woman being stoned to death in Iran reached the United States, my American friends said, "How could that happen?" But my Muslim friends said: "What has she done?"

The American reaction is what I relate to. But sadly, I *know* how it could happen. There is no tolerance in modern-day Islamic society for differing views; you either submit or pretend. I couldn't do either. I could only say to myself, Thank God I am now in America, because if I was back in Cairo, I don't know what my life would become.

Despite my tendency to be outspoken and my freedom here in America to speak my mind, it is not easy for me to say these things. It took me many years to actually know I am *not* a Muslim in today's radical culture of Islam, never have been nor want to be. I do not want to convert, discriminate, hate, or do jihad against non-Muslims. I had to find an almost superhuman inner strength to actually extricate myself from feeling a sense of belonging to the culture of jihad, the culture that my father died for.

My love for America, my chosen country, prevents me from belonging to any group that has an agenda against it, or who would love to see the U.S. Constitution replaced with the Koran and sharia law. I also love my personal freedom in America and never want to be shackled again with political Islam. Nor can I live a split personality—I cannot say one thing among Muslims and the opposite in the presence of Americans. I am one person, wherever I am and whomever I am with. Nor can I submit to the observing eyes of other Muslims who treat one another as police enforcers of Islamic law.

I asked myself how could it be that people like me who escaped radical Islam and oppression of women were now facing the same threat right here in the bastion of freedom?

Besides the turmoil I found myself in with the clash of cultures in the 1980s, between a radicalizing Muslim community and my new-found American values, my personal life was also experiencing some turmoil. In 1987 I filed for divorce because my marriage was falling apart. The responsibility for its failure was fifty-fifty, and I had to deal with my choices as best I could for the sake of my children and also for the sake of retaining a decent relationship with a man I once chose to be my husband. I have kept a good relationship with him and his family. The divorce decision was very difficult for me, but as soon as I made it, I felt a great relief. My main goal now was to be the best possible mother to my two children.

My children and I went to family counseling to talk about our feelings. One day when I was alone with the counselor I began crying. When the counselor asked me what was wrong, I said, "My father died!" The counselor assumed my loss was recent. He said: "I am very sorry, when did he die?" He must have been surprised when I answered, "He died when I was eight years old." The counselor asked me if my family and I had talked about it enough. I answered, "No." I realized then that I had never really had the chance to properly grieve. I began talking about my history to the counselor. He was very understanding and sympathetic to what he described as my "fascinating" history and culture. I had never before considered my life, and all its twists and turns, to be unusual. As a matter of fact, I was hiding my history, afraid for people to know I was the daughter of the head of the fedayeen in Gaza. Now the floodgates opened, and I was able to begin talking about and dealing with my past. I put away the shame and pride.

One year after my divorce, I met a neighbor who often played ball with my two children in front of the house. He asked us to attend a concert with him. We did. Later, he and I developed affection for one another and were married in 1991.

My second husband, Howard, was born and raised in Berkeley, California, and came from a very liberal background. His family was distinguished in the university community. They were not religious, but an intact family—a mother, father, brother, and sisters, a lovely family who has accepted me and my children as part of their family and extended their love to all of us. It was remarkable how similar my husband and I were despite having been brought up in two completely different cultures.

As my mother had done with me and my siblings, I sent my children to a Christian school because I wanted to give them the best education possible. I remembered my wonderful St. Clare College in Cairo, the Catholic nuns who were my teachers, and the peace I felt around them.

When I looked at the neighborhood churches and synagogues in my Southern California community, I loved seeing the tradition of families—husbands, wives, and children—going together to worship and pray to God in the presence of their community of faith. I wished that Muslims in the Middle East and in America could experience this unity—going to mosques together as families—one husband, one wife, and their children, a beautiful picture of family unity in front of God. On Friday nights I saw Jews walking to their synagogues, whole families practicing their faith in peace together. The religious traditions that I saw among my Jewish friends were extremely powerful and full of messages of tolerance and compassion. I saw the same among the Christian families in my neighborhood. I felt a deep need to be around spiritual people who respected the traditions, democracy, and pluralism of this great nation, and who advocated tolerance, compassion, and peace. I yearned for a religion that uplifted my spirits. I didn't want to belong to a religion of mujahadeen on yet another mission in a holy war against America.

One Sunday morning I was watching television and began listening to a preacher. I heard him quote the following scripture: "Love is patient, love is kind. It does not envy, it does not boast, it is not proud. It is not rude, it is not self-seeking, it is not easily angered, it keeps no record of wrongs. Love does not delight in evil but rejoices with the truth. It always protects, always trusts, always hopes, always perseveres" (Corinthians 13:4). I was amazed. My daughter walked by and I told her, "He is great!"

She said, "Oh, Mom, that's Dudley."

I said, "Dudley who?"

"Dudley is our school pastor," she answered casually, as if I was supposed to know. What a privilege to have a pastor like that teach my children, I thought to myself.

That church was three miles from our home. The next week on Sunday morning I woke up the whole house early and announced to my husband, "Honey, let's get dressed, we are going to church." We entered the church and heard the music. They were singing a song with words, something to the effect "and I won't be afraid." People were standing up singing along, clapping and raising their hands up high to praise God. We sat near the front row and listened to a message of compassion, love, acceptance, tolerance, and prayer for all of humanity. That day—this made an indelible impression on me—there was some news of violence in the Middle East and the pastor prayed for everyone in the Middle East—Muslims, Jews, and Christians. It was a very different message from the prayers to "destroy the infidels" that I grew up with. My husband and I could barely hold back our tears. I was hungry to hear more. I wished every Egyptian and Muslim I knew could also hear this message of tolerance, something I had never in my life heard from a Muslim preacher. I learned the most important command in scripture was "Love your neighbor as yourself." The pastor reminded us that as residents of Los Angeles we live in a very diverse community, a community that includes Jews, Arabs, Chinese, Japanese, Latinos, and blacks. He said these are our neighbors and we should love them simply because they are our neighbors. Furthermore, a Christian is even commanded to love his or her enemies and to show them kindness. It is an ideal that every Christian must try to live up to. Again, what a sharp contrast to how Muslims are taught to regard "infidels." I was faced with a challenge, nothing less than the choice between love and hate.

This experience was also a revolution in my American husband's life, since he was not brought up with Christianity.

Ever since that day our lives have been blessed. From that moment on I discovered I was truly free. I now know the true meaning of love and hope.

I am grateful to the good people of America, Christians and Jews, who open their hearts, homes, churches, and synagogues for immigrants like me. I now know why this country is great. I am grateful to belong here in America, protected by a Constitution and Bill of Rights written by wise men who understood that it is the Creator who grants us our human rights, and it is our government's role to protect those rights for everyone. Consequently, the citizens live with relative inner peace and confidence in their government. That is why the system is smooth, predictable, and dependable. This country allows me to practice any religion or no religion, and gives me human rights I could only dream of in my culture of origin. Americans often take these rights for granted. But if you have lived under tyranny as I have, you know how precious those rights are.

I had also found a spiritual home, a community of worshipers where I felt I belonged. I realized what the role of religion should be. It should not be by force, but by convincing, explaining, and by setting an example. Fear, jihad, anger, and terrorism should not be advocated in any house of worship. The human mind, when filled with hate, anger, and envy, becomes paralyzed and cannot function productively. I have lived for thirty years with people who cheered their dictator as their "savior," forgetting who their true savior was. In Islam it should be Allah. But they have surrendered to pride, shame, anger, and envy—all sins by any religion's standards. They have given allegiance to tyrants instead of Allah, and to advocates of hate rather than to advocates of love.

It was the love of God I was desperate for but was unable to find in my culture of origin. I lived half my life trying to practice Islam yet my soul remained empty. But in America I learned from Jews, Christians, blacks, Asians, and all God's people to love humanity regardless of religion, race, or national origin. I am now more in tune with a humanitarian and tolerant outlook on faith. I beg my people to see faith the way it should be, as a source of bringing the world together. I long for the religion and culture of my origin to reject hatred and the jihad obligation to subdue, dominate, and control the world. In our mission to dominate we have suppressed our own humanity and love of life. I do not consider myself an ultra-religious person, but I need to feel the love of God. I truly believe that Islam can and one day will reform and be a partner among the world's monotheistic religions to bring out the best in a person and in world civilization. In this church, that day, my soul was revived and nourished with the love of a tolerant and forgiving God.

Many immigrants come to this great nation in search of material gain, which is fine; however, the biggest prize I gained was my religious freedom and learning to love. For me it was nothing short of cataclysmic. I had turned from a culture of hatred to one of love.

Eight | A Second Look After Twenty Years

My third child, a healthy and beautiful girl, was born in 1994, when I was in my forties. I was blessed and happy. My family life was becoming more stable and settled. But two inescapable family tragedies were to impact me in the 1990s.

The first was in 1993, when my younger sister was diagnosed with lung cancer at age forty-three. I was devastated by the news. She was a physician married to a prominent surgeon in Egypt. She had been a heavy smoker ever since she was a teenager—in Egypt many physicians smoke in spite of all the medical facts and statistics about smoking. She and her husband came to the United States for her treatment and stayed at my home for two months. Despite availing herself of the best medical treatment available, her condition was very serious and getting worse. During those two months, we were together almost all the time and became very close. We talked about our families and our childhood for the first time as adult women, opening up to each other and talking about the pain of our childhood, the loss of our father, our life in Gaza, and even the culture of jihad, hate, and indoctrination that we both experienced as children. I believe her heavy chain-smoking was her way to cope with that pain. We cried together and laughed together.

My sister clearly understood and accepted the fact of her impending death. Leaving her children in the best condition possible was her top priority, and she formulated plans and told her husband what to do after she passed away. I was continually amazed by my sister's courage, her hope, and her steadfast prayers. She became very close to God and drew strength from many hopeful verses in the Koran. She was preparing for everything, even paying back debts to anyone who ever did her a favor. After she left to return to Cairo, she sent me a check for some money she thought she owed me but that I did not even remember! As a physician, she understood her condition and was extremely brave. I, on the other hand, felt totally helpless. But I was grateful I had a chance to spend those two wonderful months with her.

When I said good-bye to her as she left to return to Egypt, I knew it was the last time I would see her. As if mirroring my turmoil, the Northridge earthquake of January 17, 1994, hit a few days after she left my home. The armoire in the guest room she had occupied fell onto the bed where she had been sleeping only days earlier. I was grateful she did not have to experience the terrible earthquake in her condition. But while she had escaped the earthquake, she did not escape her fate with cancer. My beloved sister passed away in January of 1995 and left behind two boys, eleven and sixteen years of age. It was a tragedy.

A few months after my sister's death, my brother, who was forty-three years old, was working in Gaza for a short period of time representing the Egyptian government. It was his first visit to Gaza since he left it as a child at age four. He was very well received in Gaza, and, in fact, Yasser Arafat personally greeted him as the son of a hero of Gaza. My father's name was still well known and appreciated in the Gaza community, and my brother received the same royal treatment I had when I visited Gaza as a teenager on a school trip. My brother told me that many people came to visit him and were very kind to him in honor of our father's memory. Our former maid and the school principal who once punished me for not memorizing poems were among those who welcomed him to Gaza. The school and street in Gaza with my father's name are still there.

It seems that all these memories truly impacted my brother, and he began, perhaps for the first time, to actually think about the past. He had, after all, been with my father when the bomb that killed him exploded and had himself been injured in the blast. He may well have been reliving the trauma of those early experiences. One day he collapsed in his residence, and his maid called the Egyptian consulate in Gaza. My brother had suffered a severe life-threatening stroke. He was given only a 3 percent chance of survival.

Since my brother was in Gaza without his family, the Egyptians around him had to make a quick decision as to where they should take him. The question was: Do we take him to a Cairo hospital or to Hadassah Hospital in Israel? The answer was unanimous. If you want him to live, they said, take him to Hadassah.

I kept in daily contact by phone with his wife and my mother, who had flown to Jerusalem to be with him in the hospital where he lay unconscious for more than two and a half months. The doctors and nurses of Hadassah performed a miracle; my brother's life was not only spared, but eventually he was able to walk and talk and function normally. After many long months of rehabilitation and therapy, he was able to resume a normal life.

My mother told stories about her time in Israel that totally contradicted all that we had ever heard about Israel and Israelis. Both she and all the Egyptians who heard her talk about it were amazed at the dedication and professionalism of the Israeli doctors and nurses in their treatment of my brother. My mother spoke of how kind the Jewish people in Israel were and told of how many went out of their way to help her and my sister-in-law during that difficult time. Some Egyptian Jews who did not know my brother or mother before this incident visited them regularly in the hospital.

They were relatives of Jewish Egyptian friends of my brother's in Paris. My mother said she was amazed at such concern and kindness, especially coming from people who were treated as second-class citizens and expelled from Egypt in the 1950s. What also amazed my mother was that they harbored no anger or vindictiveness toward Egypt and spoke only of the good times and good memories. They remembered the food, the people, the music, and the neighborhoods, and never had a bad word to say.

I myself was amazed at what my mother was telling me. That was totally contrary to what Arabs are told about Israel and the Jewish people. Arab countries spend a lot of energy, time, and money on anti-Israel propaganda. My eyes were opened about Israel and its moral standards. I felt very grateful to the State of Israel and the doctors and nurses of Hadassah for taking the higher moral ground and choosing to do the right thing. They did not make some exception for my brother. They regularly treat Arabs equal to Jews. They had saved my brother's life, an Arab Muslim man and the son of a shahid.

I later learned that Yasser Arafat personally insisted on paying my brother's hospital bills in honor of my father's memory.

When Arabs experience for themselves the kindness, compassion, and competence of Israel, they are not often willing to acknowledge it. A few years after my brother's stroke, the son of a former Egyptian high government official suffered a severe car accident and was also rushed to Israel for treatment. As with my brother, the official's son's life was saved. When the high-ranking Egyptian official was criticized by the media for sending his son to Israel for treatment, his answer was: "If saving my son's life meant that I have to take him to the devil for treatment, then I will." I later asked my brother about his feelings toward Israel. He said he has mixed feelings, but he, like many Egyptians, still regards Israel as the enemy. That is the gratitude Arabs give Israel for its good will and decency.

But that incident marked a big change in my views and feelings toward Israel. I thought deeply about it and discovered the decency, beauty, and grace in Jewish culture. But a wall of separation keeps Arabs from seeing the truth inside Israel. We were prevented from seeing Israel for ourselves in a true and objective light. Many questions went through my mind: Why is the Muslim world threatened by Israel? Why are they obsessed with hating it? Why are they doing everything within their means to spread lies and distortions about that little state? What is the Muslim world afraid of? Is it afraid of Israel, or is it that they are afraid of comparing themselves with it and seeing reality? Is the culture of envy once again envious of another culture that is competent and believes in itself? When Egyptians made the decision to send my brother who was dying to Hadassah Hospital, they proved one startling fact: in times of crisis, Arabs trust Jews.

After my views about Israel began changing, I wanted to speak out for peace and respect for the territorial integrity of Israel. However, within my culture, I felt outnumbered by Israel-haters, and I had very little support in the Arab community. After much thought, I chose to stay quiet about Israel and the whole issue of jihad, especially since by that time there was some hope for peace after the Oslo Agreement.

But I did wish to become politically active in some way to show my appreciation for the freedoms I enjoyed in America. I very much admired the way women in America volunteer and work together to help their communities, and so for the first time I began to do volunteer work. I became involved in the Republican Women's Federation, where I started writing a few articles that were published in the organization's newsletters. We registered voters and helped many community causes. My circle of women friends grew tremendously, and I learned a great deal from these dedicated women.

In the 1990s, my husband and I often traveled to the Bay Area in Northern California, and I started learning more about a part of America that was unknown to me previously. In Berkeley I met people who were not happy with America. In fact, many blamed America for most of the ills around the world. Among them I heard things like: White men committed the worst atrocities to humanity. They criticized American foreign policy and the military and often used words such as colonialism and imperialism. They blamed America for using cheap labor around the globe. They were attacking big business and advocating rent control; a topic that I know quite well since Nasser's rent control policies destroyed the housing market in Egypt. *If they only knew*, I would think to myself. These Bay Area people seemed to dislike Los Angeles and were very excited about such things as unisex public toilets. Their view of America was totally opposite of mine. I saw America as a world superpower that was trying to inspire democracy. Furthermore, instead of using its power to rule the world, America struggled to juggle the many conflicting demands by Third World countries as best it could. As one who had come from that Third World, I was amazed at the views of some of the Northern California "intellectuals" with their somewhat uninformed admiration for the Third World. Third World governments are not so innocent. They are expert at blackmailing, using and abusing the superpowers and other industrialized nations to their advantage, and they do not hesitate to use bribery, boycott, or outright terror to get what they want from them. Before the Soviet Union fell, Third World nations were experts at playing the two superpowers off each other. They would favor one side, and then make demands on the other. It's no longer that easy. Now there is no other side so they just gang up against America. That is why the United States has to look after its best interests while trying to reward democracy around the globe. It is not an easy job. There is much about the West that is hidden or distorted in the Egyptian media, but unfortunately, I also saw there are many dynamics behind the international headlines that Western media does not expose—not because they are prevented from doing so, but because they don't understand these dynamics. Many in America and elsewhere in the West who rush to defend the Third World as a badge of honor do not understand these regions, their needs, the reasons behind their turmoil, or the difficult dynamics of how to treat it.

In Berkeley, California, I saw a car bumper sticker that read "Free Palestine." Even though at that time my perception of Israel was still confused and evolving, I felt that many of these pro-Palestinian American activists did not truly understand the core of the problems in the Middle East. They had good intentions, but good intentions are not enough. They were uninformed and naive.

At first I could not comprehend how any American citizens could fail to appreciate America. When I tried to defend my adopted country, I saw that some appeared offended by it. Once again, my tendency to say what was on my mind was getting me in trouble. So I decided to instead be polite and just listen to their attacks on America and not respond. But what they said often reminded me of the old-fashioned, Soviet Union–inspired slogans I used to hear in the Cairo streets in the 1960s, slogans that no Egyptian dared reject or criticize.

That is when I started fully understanding the divisions in American politics and society. I comforted myself by saying that it is healthy to have a range of different views in a democracy like that of the United States. In this country, people may disagree, but unlike my culture of origin, they don't kill each other over their political differences. Influenced by the Berkeley area where he grew up, my husband had a similar ideology when I first met him in the late 1980s. But he gradually changed over the years. We were both changing—he about America and I about Israel.

By the year 2001, I had been away from Egypt for twenty years. I had not been back since my brief trip in 1980. I missed it and wanted to visit Egypt with my family, in spite of the conflicting feelings I held toward my culture of origin. I believe there is a yearning in the heart of every immigrant for the original home-land, a feeling of missing it, wanting to enjoy it, or perhaps to "save it" from the ills that prompted us to leave it behind. My husband and three children were very eager to see Egypt for the first time. My two older children, age twenty and eighteen, as well as my youngest, who was seven at the time, had all been born in the United States. The whole family was excited about a trip to Egypt.

We left during the summer vacation in August and were scheduled to return on September 10, 2001. My husband and son had to return to the United States earlier, but the girls and I planned to stay until September 10. After a brief visit to my older sister in Paris, we all headed to Cairo. I was very excited—almost as excited as I had been on my first arrival at the United States in 1978. I had not seen Egypt for twenty long years. I was very eager to indulge in the many aspects of Egyptian culture I love—entertainment, cuisine, and the family I missed so much. I was as excited as a little child. In the Cairo airport I felt like hugging everyone I met.

But my euphoric feelings gradually evaporated when my husband and I were given an unfriendly stare from the airport passport official who probably did not like an Egyptian immigrant coming back to visit with an American husband. It made my husband and me uncomfortable from the beginning. It was very hot and humid in Cairo as we waited to clear customs. At customs we were asked several times if we had a video camera. When we said yes, we were asked to register it to assure that we took it back home with us. I said to myself, Welcome back home to senseless regulations.

But our spirits were lifted when we saw a large crowd of excited family and friends waiting impatiently for us. Meeting them was the best part in the trip. We drove to my mother's home in Maadi, Cairo, with several cars following us. There we enjoyed a gathering of friends and family, and a huge Egyptian feast of my favorite foods; moussaka, stuffed grape leaves, stuffed pigeons, lamb, and the famous Middle Eastern pastries. It was everything I love about the Middle East.

Many things had changed over the last twenty years. Some members of my family had passed away—my grandmother, my uncle, an aunt, my sister, and a cousin. In those years, the family had also grown larger with the addition of several beautiful nieces and nephews. The discussions gradually moved in the direction of who does not talk to whom, who is envious of whom, who did not attend someone's wedding, who is now wearing Islamic clothes, and who got himself a second wife behind his wife's back. Ah, all the old familiar gossip. Some things do not change.

We stayed at my mother's large four-bedroom home near the Nile River, where she lived alone. My husband was impressed with how elegantly furnished it was. He and I slept in my old bedroom and were awakened in the morning at 6 A.M. by a call to prayer from the loudspeakers of several mosques in the neighborhood. Both of us were shocked by that unrequested morning wake-up call. It struck me as an imposition on the personal lives, comfort, and freedom of non-Muslims and also of Muslims who do not want to wake up at that hour. It was the first reminder, coming early in the trip, that even our freedom to pick the hour to wake up was not our own; we were not in the USA.

My husband went jogging along the Nile shore, which he thoroughly enjoyed, especially when some Egyptian youths were friendly and told him, "Welcome to Egypt." He told me that what I said about Egyptians was true; they are kind and sweet with a great sense of humor and eager to meet and talk to foreigners.

My mother introduced us to a taxi driver who lived in the area, and we hired him to drive us around whenever we needed. There was no question what our first stop would be: the pyramids, which were so close to my mother's house that on a clear day you could see them on the horizon. As we drove, my husband and children were simply amazed at everything they saw. I was also eager to rediscover the country I had left twenty-three years ago, when I emigrated to the United States. Along the way we enjoyed the beautiful palm trees that lined the streets, the impressive Nile, and a great new Supreme Court building. I saw a lot of new developments, streets, highways, and stores. I was amazed at how many Egyptian women were now wearing Islamic attire. The Muslim Brotherhood, which was dissolved and weakened during Nasser's time, had come back with a vengeance. Nasser's socialism has changed to Islamism. But I also saw a lot of things unchanged or even getting worse—extreme poverty, a lot of garbage, flies, and pollution in many streets and along the Nile branches. The streets were dusty, extremely crowded with pedestrians, and clogged by chaotic traffic. Cairo is probably one of the most difficult cities on earth to live in. Just going from one place to another is a challenge.

As we approached the pyramids, my husband and children were in awe. The sight of the pyramids and the sphinx was chilling and breathtaking; a part of ancient Egyptian history that represented a great culture and civilization that stood the test of time. The sphinx and the pyramids have stood up with pride for thousands of years as Egypt changed drastically and went through many dark and painful periods. Many dynasties, kings, and rulers rose and disappeared. Many changes in its language, culture, religion, and political system occurred. Foreign occupiers came and went, but the pyramids remained. It is both humbling and awe-inspiring. When I looked at the magnificent pyramids I wondered, Will a period of enlightenment ever come again to Egyptian soil? I hoped so.

As my children were running around buying souvenirs from vendors on the pyramid grounds, I noticed my eighteen-year-old daughter was purchasing something from two beautiful nine- or ten-year-old girls who were obviously very poor. She gave them one Egyptian pound and took something in exchange. The two girls came running after us, telling my daughter they owed her some change. My daughter told them it was okay, they could keep it. The girls then gratefully gave her one more little gift and thanked her. I later saw my daughter with tears in her eyes. Other children who were selling stuff were very thirsty, and we gave them a water bottle we were carrying. This is the part of Egypt that I love dearly and that also breaks my heart.

As we were taking family pictures around the pyramids, my daughter started laughing when she saw three Arab women in black burkas standing next to one another taking pictures with the pyramids in the background. "How would they know which is which in the picture?" she exclaimed. I laughed along with my daughter; it was a welcome relief from the tears and sadness she felt over the poor little girls.

Knowing the abject poverty I would see, I had brought with me on the trip approximately five hundred dollars to give away. It was not easy because I was not that wealthy in America, but I felt it was my duty toward my fellow Egyptian poor people. At all times I carried several twenty Egyptian pound bills (each twenty-pound note was equal at that time to approximately three dollars) to give to the Egyptian poor around me wherever I went. I did that because I simply did not trust organizations that might divert my donations to fanatic terror groups in the area.

My two older children, of course, loved going out at night with their cousins. They were amazed at how safe they felt walking the streets of Cairo at night. Their only negative experience was when the police tried to extract money from them. They called me in the middle of the night from their cell phone. I asked them to hand the phone over to the policeman, and then gave him a little lecture over the phone. That took care of it!

A few days later I had the opportunity to sit and speak with a large number of young Egyptians who were mostly middle- and upper-middle-class nonpracticing Muslims. They had many questions. Several of them said they could not get married because of severe shortages in apartments, a consequence of the extreme rent control policies by the Egyptian government since 1960. They were restless, angry, unemployed, and confused. Much of their anger was directed at America and the West. They were ready for attack and not a discussion, eager for a fight to blame America, Israel, and everyone but themselves or their own culture. As I spoke with them, it became clear they had no idea about Muslim-upon-Muslim atrocities in Iraq, Algeria, the Sudan, and other places. All they cared about was Israel's humiliation of Palestinians at checkpoints and America's presence in the Middle East, even if it was to protect countries from Saddam Hussein, as it did for Kuwait in the first Gulf War. Some even said that Kuwait deserved the attacks from Iraq. They stood with the aggressor against the oppressed. It was sad for me to hear them justify terror, hate, and aggression. When I asked them if they were aware that Saddam used gas against

Kurdish villages, killing thousands of citizens, they said no. Arab television never showed the pictures the rest of the world saw of Kurdish Muslim women hugging their dead babies on the ground. Arab media systematically cover up Arab dictators' atrocities toward their citizens and instead turn around and blame Israel, using such incidents to stir up Arab anger and turmoil. Not a bad solution to divert the attention of desperate Arab youth—who easily fall into such a trap—from the real problems.

However, amid all the confusion, hate, and anger, I sensed a need by those young Muslims for an escape. While they are vulnerable to being shamed into accepting certain beliefs, they are also smart enough to sense that things do not add up. They are torn between what they hear and what their common sense tells them. They gathered around me with their questions, wanting to defy and test my support for America as their way to learn the truth. I admit to being a little sensitive about their attacks on my new country, the country I love and am grateful for, but I did my best to be honest and truthful without becoming too defensive.

I was not surprised when at the end of the conversation several of them asked me "How can we get a visa to the USA?"

I came away from this encounter amazed that despite the Internet and satellite dishes, Arabs are still incredibly misinformed.

My conversation with these young Egyptians caused me to wonder about the baggage many Muslim immigrants—who are often torn between their new and old cultures—bring with them to the United States. What kind of citizens will they be in America? Given the misinformation, hate, and anger they have been subjected to in their homeland, many Muslim Arab immigrants find themselves alienated from American society. Some even become terrorist sympathizers and easy prey to radical mosques installed in the United States, ironically by the same governments they left behind. All immigrants contribute something to America; my fervent hope is that the culture of hate, anger, and intolerance will not be the contribution Muslims make in the West.

I knew before visiting Egypt that conditions were still bad, but

I could not have imagined how virulent the anti-American senti-ments had become. One would think the opposite should have happened after the United States began pouring almost $3 billion a year in aid to Egypt to help the nation keep the peace with Israel. It can only be understood by looking through the prism of the Arab culture of envy. There is nothing America or the non-Muslim West can do that will be met with gratitude and appreciation. Not even America's and Europe's attacks on the Serbs to stop the slaughter of the Muslims in Bosnia, or defending Muslim Afghani-stan against the Russians, earned the West any favor or gratitude from Arabs. To the contrary, good deeds of non-Muslims toward Muslims only deepen their sense of dependency and inferiority in the context of the macho and pride-driven Muslim culture. In the end, the culture of envy and shame always dominates Arab senti-ments. The famous Egyptian saying "Beware of the evil from those you show kindness to" is what resonates in the Arab street.

The strong anti-American feelings I encountered during my 2001 visit was a shock to my system because at the time I left Egypt in 1978, feelings about the United States were positive. I remem-bered when Nixon visited Egypt in the early seventies, Egyptians spontaneously went out to meet the president of a "savior coun-try." America gave Egyptians hope. Anti-American sentiment was so strong that one of my brothers-in-law who was a high-ranking government official avoided meeting us during our visit. I under-stood and I felt that it was probably a good policy for him not to meet American family members.

I was also in for a rude awakening when I attempted to get news myself while in Egypt. I watched CNN—no other U.S. me-dia outlets were available—and was amazed that the network failed to adequately correct the rumors and misunderstanding regularly promulgated by Arab media. CNN had a golden opportunity to bring the light of truth about the West, democracy, and the virtues of the Western culture—or at least not pander to the local bias. To my surprise, CNN contributed to Arab hatred and suspicion of America by regularly criticizing America and President Bush. At the time I was there, CNN indulged in blaming America for withdrawing from the summit on racism in Durbin, South Africa. They did not tell Arabs the full story of what happened there. That summit was hijacked by Third World and strong pro-Arab and Muslim countries to accuse Israel and America of racism while rejecting any discussion of anti-Semitism in the Muslim world. There were also one-sided anti-Israel demonstrations on the street. America withdrew from the summit because of the virulent and blatant bias and anti-Semitism. I was terribly disappointed at CNN, which has been in business for more than twenty years, a period during which there has been a steady increase in hatred against America. I could not help but wonder if the American media itself was contributing to this hatred.

As to Egyptian media, it was more of the same. With all that is going on in Egyptian society—unemployment, pollution, extreme poverty, the rise of Muslim Brotherhood radicals, not to mention fraud, mismanagement, and corruption in government and business—all I read and heard in the Egyptian media was blaming the West, propaganda against Israel, and encouragement of jihad and martyrdom. For instance, in a front-page article, an Egyptian newspaper said that Israeli Viagra was flooding all over Egyptian markets in order to sterilize Egyptian men! Arab use of hashish was also blamed on an Israeli conspiracy to spread drugs in Egypt. A foreign girl was being accused of being a spy for Israel. But at the time the really big news story was about a Druze Israeli man who was arrested and convicted of espionage by writing in secret invisible ink on women's underwear! His Egyptian attorney was harassed and ostracized by the law community, and shouting against the Druze man was allowed in court. It was more of what I'd witnessed years earlier. The distraction has to constantly be maintained.

Egyptians newspapers ran many vulgar and tasteless articles against Westerners. For example, I read an article lambasting the American ambassador to Egypt simply because he was Jewish. He was transferred from his post in Egypt, and the article bid him a "good riddance."

Egyptian media had also recently revived my father's memory. My mother proudly showed me what she called "a great article" about my father, entitled: "The assassination of the Egyptian head of the intelligence right before his appointment." The article featured many of our family photos and pictures of my father in his military uniform. I told my mother, "They are trying to use his story to promote the good old days of jihad during Nasser's time." I did not like my father's memory to be used in that way. Those were the days just after the 1948 war; now there is supposedly a peace treaty with Israel.

During my visit, I heard rumors that the Muslim Brotherhood, which was gaining in popularity, wanted to take over power and cancel the peace treaty with Israel. Even though Mubarak was not an ideal leader, he was much better than the Muslim Brotherhood. I wondered, Why don't Egyptians learn from their long history of pain and suffering?

Driving around the terribly crowded streets of Cairo, I saw Saudi Wahabi mosques, "King this" and "Prince that" scattered everywhere, named after their benefactors in Saudi Arabia. These radical mosques represented Saudi money in action to strengthen radical Islam's grip in Egypt and perhaps help bring about the Muslim Caliphate they want to build before the oil dries up.

I heard that Saudi power reached into many unexpected areas of Egyptian society. For instance, they paid millions of dollars to some famous belly dancers to quit belly dancing and renounce this form of entertainment as un-Islamic. Naturally, the belly dancers took the generous offer of an early retirement, embraced their newly found virtue, and I personally saw them on TV covered from head to toe advocating that other women follow their example.

The plight of the Coptic Christians, which had already been bad when I left in 1978, had grown even worse by 2001. I heard rumors of Saudi funds being used against Egyptian Christians. According to complaints to Egyptian police by several Copts as well as audiotaped confessions, radical Muslim students were given monthly salaries to seduce Christian girls—with the help of Muslim girls—and convince them to marry Muslim men. I heard of Christian girls who were even kidnapped and drugged and ended up in forced marriages to Muslim men who were then rewarded by Saudi funds designated for reducing the number of Christians in Egypt. Some of these stories were reported by the Egyptian media when the Coptic leadership and parents of kidnapped girls made formal complaints.

My children immediately noticed how class-conscious Egyptian society was. They witnessed for themselves how badly waiters and maids were treated. While slavery in America was once based on race, in the Arab world it is based on class. And it seemed to my American son and daughter that while slavery of another race was condemned, enslaving someone within the same race was somehow justified by Egyptian society. In restaurants they saw men and women mistreat waiters by yelling at them and sending them out to buy them cigarettes. Poorer classes were called fellaheen, the derogatory expression for peasants. My children asked me: "How can the word 'peasant' be an insult when the majority of Egyptians are peasants?" They also asked me how the lower classes could just accept their inferior status without complaint. I told them, "Welcome to the Third World."

The trip was indeed an eye-opening experience for my kids.

After thoroughly touring Cairo, our family visited other locations there, starting with a city that did not exist when I lived there, the beautiful resort Sharm el-Sheikh. Developed into a world-class resort by the Israelis, it became Egyptian property after the peace with Israel. In fact, Sinai, which was now a demilitarized zone, was booming with lovely resorts and thriving towns on the Red Sea in the south and the Mediterranean coast in the north. We loved the water and all the amenities of the beautiful resorts and hotels, most of which are unfortunately financially out of reach to the average Egyptian. One morning my family and I were having breakfast in the hotel restaurant when I saw a man seated nearby who was obviously Arab but not Egyptian—he was wearing a type of Arab headscarf that Egyptians do not customarily wear. We could not help but notice that he was uncomfortable because the waiter was totally ignoring him. After he left the restaurant, the Egyptian waiter told me "That son of a —— has an Israeli passport, let him get good service there!" I was shocked at how Egyptians view Arab Muslims who live in Israel. In the old days we never met or saw anyone who lived in Israel.

We noticed something curiously unique about Egyptian hotels. Sitting in strategic locations in all areas of the hotels were idle-looking workers situated at doors and in hallways—for what reason I do not know. I suppose there is no need for an electronic security system when you can have eyes everywhere. What bothered me was that these idle workers expected a tip every time you passed one of them.

After Sharm el-Sheikh, we visited a resort west of Alexandria, the Northern Coast Hilton. It was beautiful and my kids loved it. While there, I joined my brother-in-law (my deceased sister's husband) for a dinner that included a large number of Egyptian upperclass elites. It was during the time of the Palestinian intifada and an Egyptian doctor at the table casually mentioned that he had visited Jerusalem and said that the place is simply the holy land of the Jews and Christians, and all Muslims have there is the mosque. That statement did not go down well with a woman who then began defending the intifada against Israel. I chimed in, "But if the Palestinians really want their own state they now have a chance to get it and they are blowing that chance by blowing up old people and children in pizzerias in Israel." The woman's reaction to me was arrogant. She answered, "So?"

Another woman, probably intending to compliment me, said: "Americans are the true Muslims because they are good people." I then asked her: "Who are we 'Egyptians' then?" She said: "We Egyptians have not applied Islam right."

Having heard this absurd argument too many times, I couldn't let it pass. "Neither have the Americans," I replied. "Americans are ninety-five percent Christian and built their country according to their Judeo-Christian heritage and not on Muslim principles. They are Christians and we are Muslims, and we should not confuse the two," I further explained. "To call Americans good Muslims just because they have succeeded in building an orderly society is not giving due respect to their religious heritage."

A third woman then asked me how long I had lived in the United States. When she learned that I had not seen Egypt for twenty years, she immediately said, "How could you do such a thing, don't you have a family here?"

Suddenly I was jolted back into the same old shame game. At the individual level, Egyptians can be very mean and disrespectful, yet at the same time also charming and funny. It is a culture of such contrasts and contradictions.

The next morning I was sitting on the beach in my one-piece conservative bathing suit when the same group of Egyptian doctors joined us. One of the women wore a head cover, and as soon as she saw me she gave me a dirty look and then demonstratively looked the other way. Whenever I talked, I noticed she would turn her head away as if I did not exist. I got the message.

When my children and I went to swim in the beautiful hotel pool, I was the only woman in the pool. The pool was full of kids and surrounded by tables with mothers sitting together. Many of the women were covered from head to toe on this very hot August day. I felt uncomfortable when I saw them looking at me. I remembered the old days when my mother would sit on the beach in Alexandria with other Egyptian women, wishing she could take a dip with her daughters. I felt some of these women were wishing the same thing as they looked at me enjoying myself. I was sad for them and sad for my mother.

A friend took us to visit a famous fishermen's town east of Alexandria called Aboukir, where Egyptians like to go to enjoy a fresh fish restaurant meal. It was the site of a historic battle between the French and English two hundred years ago during Napoleon's time. That once wonderful little village has now been transformed into a torn-down, neglected town—but not because there was a shortage of men to work. Instead, the town's men sat in cafés, sipping their Turkish coffee and smoking their shisha right next to piles of garbage, oblivious to the blight around them. I saw women busily heading to the markets to take care of their children and homes. But men sat doing nothing with the famous Egyptian *wana mali* ("none of my business") attitude. The friend who took us to Aboukir was embarrassed at the deterioration of the village and said that he had not been aware of it.

My husband and son left to go back home to the States, and my two daughters and I stayed until September 10, as planned. However, we were getting bored and wanted to go home earlier. But as the penalty for changing the ticket was so expensive, I decided to just stay.

After my husband left, one of my cousins, who is a physician, chose to visit me. When I opened the door, I did not recognize her because all I saw was a woman covered in black from head to toe. I could not even see her face, eyes, hands, or feet. She had covered every inch of her body. She even wore black gloves despite the heat of an Egyptian summer. When I learned who she was, I was very careful not to show my surprise at the great change in her appearance. I wanted her to be comfortable with her new appearance in front of me. Back in 1978 when I left Egypt, she had worn Western-style clothing—even sleeveless, short dresses—during the hot Egyptian summers. When her dress became the topic of conversation, another woman in the room told my cousin that Islam does not demand covering of the face. My physician cousin assertively answered, "I am following the example of Muhammad's women, who did cover their faces." (She said "women" not "wives," since Muhammad did not marry all of his women; the *malak yamin*, meaning "owned slaves," did not count as wives.) I thought, *They probably did cover their faces because of the sandstorms they suffered from living in the open desert in tents!* Of course, I did not say that out loud.

Women and men in the Arabian Peninsula dressed appropriately for a severe desert environment. There was no privacy at the water well, around which everyone lived. There were no trees or mountains to hide behind, and they were all totally dependent on one another. Women and men both had head covers for protection from the sun as well as to protect the face when the severe desert sandstorms erupted. Women's flowing loose robes also gave them privacy. They could literally squat and relieve themselves while covered from view. This same dress—which existed out of necessity long before the emergence of Islam—is now regarded by Muslims as Allah's divine choice for women. The pre-Islamic clothing of the past, which was simply a product of the Saudi desert physical environment, has now been codified for Muslims around the world, regardless of environment, climate, or geography.

Contrary to popular belief in the West, very few Muslim governments actually force women to wear the burka. When I left Egypt, my cousin was a modern-looking physician. She had chosen to wear this on her own. She was always aloof and unfriendly—that was her personality—and the burka gave her the freedom to live in isolation within an angry restless society that she felt was not Muslim enough. As we women sat around and talked, she had taken the covering off her face, but when my fifteen-year-old nephew came into the room, I saw my fifty-five-year-old cousin quickly cover her face. In that moment, I felt I had landed in Saudi Arabia and not in Egypt. Her husband never asked her to do so. On the contrary, she was *his* inspiration to start praying, fasting, and reading the Koran. Strangely enough, the medical schools of Egypt have produced the most radical of Muslims; famous among them is Ayman al-Zawahiri, the second-in-command in the al-Qaeda organization. Contrary to what many liberal activists believe, it is neither ignorance nor Third World poverty that produces radicalism—the extremists from middle- and upper-class families coming out of Egypt's institutions of higher learning and medical schools prove that.

Covering up has become the new identity of Muslim women around the world. That is not just men's doing, but also women's. Teenage Arab girls are often criticized by older women who want them covered from head to toe. After all, it's a great idea for solving the problem of competition among women! The burka is now the great equalizer in the Muslim women's world.

Women have been taught to view their bodies as nothing more than an object of seduction that causes men to commit sin. Think of it, the message is: *I am a piece of meat tempting all men, and I have to carry and cover my shame all my life.* They have to hide from life and from the cruelty and injustice of Muslim society toward women. By hiding her face, a Muslim woman is telling the world: *My individual identity, my comfort, my personal freedom, my body temperature in hot weather, and my choices come secondary.*

When I was about to leave, my cousin's gift to me was a prayer head cover along with her exhortation to cover up in America with pride.

I felt that all the years of Arab women's hard work for advancement, legal equality, and economic parity with men was eroding. What I saw in Egypt and what I knew was occurring throughout the Arab world was very depressing. Newspaper articles were promoting jihad even for females. Saudi money was pouring into impoverished neighborhoods to build mosques, not to feed the spiritual needs of the flock, but to further radicalize the vulnerable poor and turn them against their moderate governments. Verbal and physical attacks on Christians and Jews were increasing, and hatred speech openly blared from the loudspeakers of mosques. I heard that many Christian churches had been burned to the ground, and Christians were being fired at on the street and killed while their attackers went unpunished. Because of this increased pressure on non-Muslims in Egypt, the Christian Arab population was shrinking even more. I noticed that Egypt now has very few minorities and has become almost all Sunni Muslim.

A man we know told us a story that sheds light on the treatment of the weak and poor minorities. He said that his landlord illegally evicted an eighty-year-old woman after her son, who lived with her, died. She was born in Cyprus but lived all her life in Egypt, most of it in the same apartment and had never missed a payment. But a vacant apartment in Egypt is like a pot of gold because of rent control and shortages. Therefore, the landlord, with the help of the building's Egyptian Muslim tenants, moved the old woman from her apartment to a room on the roof. She was the only non-Arab and non-Muslim in the building. The old woman, who had no other family, was forced to live on the roof of the building until the day she was found dead there. When I asked that man if it would be fair for his wife to be treated like that, he answered: "We kept her on the roof and gave her food; she's just a woman from Cyprus."

I missed the United States and my home, and I no longer cared to pay attention either to the examining eye or the evil eye. This time I was just a visitor in Egypt and no longer felt the pressure to please as I once did. And what a relief it was to not have much concern about the watchful eyes around me. In Egypt's August heat, I openly wore above-the-knee shorts, jeans, and T-shirts much of the time. Because I carried myself with confidence, I did not get in-my-face criticism for my clothes. Some people presumed I was just an American who didn't know better, and they did not bother me. My American husband, of course, had to say he was a Muslim when asked. My own family never put that pressure on him. But a few friends did, and Uncle Abbas introduced my husband several times as a "convert to Islam." My husband was extremely uncomfortable with that, but we let it go, since there is no need for defiance about such a sensitive subject in the Muslim world.

A taxi driver I was with once started cursing Jews and Christians. I told him I was offended and to stop, and amazingly, he did. Moments later during the ride, he pointed out to me several apartment building complexes that were left unfinished for more than eight years because of building violations and corrupt contractors. I asked him, "Were these contractors Jews or Christians?" His answer was, "No, they were Muslim." I told him, "Thank you."

When I visited Uncle Abbas and his family, I heard things like: "Islam is conquering Europe, and *in Shaallah* the rest of the world soon." I was fed up with that rhetoric and finally voiced my opinion. "Why don't you first fix Muslim countries before conquering other countries that don't need fixing?"

I had certainly changed over the last twenty years. I was no longer afraid to speak my mind.

My two daughters and I finally were fed up and wanted to be home in the United States as soon as possible, and we started counting the days. The last three days we spent at Mena House Oberoi, near the pyramids, one of the oldest hotels in Egypt. It had been built to receive European royalty on the occasion of the opening of the Suez Canal. In the hotel we met a lot of American military personnel. We were relieved and happy to see them. They symbolized all that is good in America. I was struck with how many different races were represented among the American military, and yet I saw them all the same, as Americans. I felt instantly that I had more in common with them than with the rest of Egypt, where I was born, raised, and lived until the age of thirty. I prayed for their safety and protection as they served in the Middle East.

I discovered that, contrary to what I learned in college, all cultures are not equal. America's Islamic enemies and critics—even those who love living in the United States—are nothing more than pirates. That's what Islamic terrorists are—pirates. Instead of building their own society as a model of what Islam should be, they leave it in ruins and look to conquer hard-working successful lands. To do to Europe and America what they did to Muslim countries? To ruin them the same way they ruined our own culture? They cannot stand to live in a Muslim culture, and they have their eyes set on beautiful and welcoming democracies, not to blend in, but to rob those democracies of their soul and ruin the value system and culture that made them great. Like thieves and pirates, they have their eyes on the greatest prizes: America and Europe. It is up to the West, if they believe in themselves and their culture, to protect it from the barbaric invasion of radical Islam. The jihadists are waiting to sacrifice their lives to win the West. They call America "the Great Satan," but in their heart of hearts they want to acquire it and claim it for Islam. A bit of Arab marketplace "logic" is at work here: one puts down something as fake, cheap, or of little value in order to bring down the price. In the world of Arab markets where cheating, bargaining, and exaggerating are commonplace, you must play this game in order to buy something. If you take the first price you are a fool. The way Arab wealth is used to conquer the West is very similar. The complicated psychological games are not unlike the group of young men I met who claimed America was a terrible place, and then turned around and asked, "How do we get a visa to the United States?"

We left Egypt on September 10, 2001. In the airport, as my daughters and I handed our passports to the government military official, he gave us the same dirty look we'd been given on the way in, a look of contempt for Egyptian women without head covers leaving to return to the land of the free. I handed him my U.S. passport, which had my American married surname. He very rudely asked, "What is your Egyptian name?" and I gave it to him and happily left to board the airplane.

This time my parting from Egypt was neither difficult nor emotional. I just felt very sorry for the people. Egypt was mired in deep feelings of self-pity combined with anger and radicalism. In the minds of many Egyptians, the outside world is conspiring against them and that is why they are suffering. I could no longer relate to these pathetic excuses. I was happy to go and I didn't ever want to come back. As I boarded my plane, I said to myself: "Like the Israelites, I have made my exodus out of Egypt for good." And like the Israelites I did not want to look back.

My daughters and I spent the long hours of the flight talking. We felt there was something very special about individual Egyptians, their kindness and self-deprecating humor. But there was another side of their character that was difficult to deal with whether at the individual, social, or political level. My older daughter and I were eager to be home. While at very different ages, both my seven-year-old daughter and my eighteen-year-old expressed similar feeling of pessimism about Egypt. My pessimism was even deeper and more alarming. I was pessimistic over the prospects of peace in the region, in an area of the world consumed with defying the West and risking a lot to hurt Western and Israeli interests. We talked a great deal about where the Middle East was heading and wondered where is all this anger going? The trip was an eye-opener to the rapidly accelerating anti-America and anti-Israel propaganda and lies in the Middle East media. Perhaps more than anything, CNN had been the last straw for me to tolerate.

I also had other unanswered questions about Western media who rarely reported on Arab anti-Semitism, anti-Americanism, and Muslim-against-Muslim atrocities. They had offices all around Middle Eastern capitals and should have been seeing the same things I saw. Wasn't it their duty to inform and alert the American public? But reports in Western media were often intertwined with messages of blaming America first. Even worse, they were smearing Americans who wanted to alert the American public to jihad in America by calling them bigots and alarmists. Did the American media think that by not reporting on the culture of jihad it would just go away? Or were they just blind? I wondered what was behind all this.

Egypt and Saudi Arabia were ticking time bombs. Egypt, the most populous Arab country on the borders of Israel, was gradually turning into an Islamic fundamentalist state. I feared that peace was gradually evaporating and that the peace treaty that Anwar Sadat and Menachem Begin risked their lives to forge was going to disappear if the Muslim Brotherhood achieved its aim of commandeering Egypt. I was sad for Egyptians who, like many Arabs, are prisoners of misinformation and propaganda, never allowed to learn from their history, and encouraged to risk everything again and again. I asked myself, Why aren't Egyptians just grateful they got the Sinai back? Their value system was not the pursuit of freedom and happiness, but the pursuit of blame, envy, and anger. I wondered if they would ever free themselves from the slavery they are in.

Before landing, my eighteen-year-old daughter said to me, "Mom, thank you for bringing me into the world in the USA." I was thrilled the trip had such an impact on her. I wished that every American child could have the same experience my daughter just had—the chance to understand how wonderful it is to enjoy the freedoms and privileges of living in America.

We arrived at LAX the night of September 10, 2001. My relief was so great that I wanted to kiss the ground when we landed. I appreciated America even more than the first time I arrived. I was glad to be back in the United States, a country that welcomed me with open arms and treated me equal to the citizens who built it. It was late at night by the time we arrived home, and we went to sleep right away.

The next morning the whole world changed. We all woke up at 6 A.M. Los Angeles time to the horrors of 9/11. When I saw the first tower in flames I knew something was not right. Something in my guts told me this was the anger I left behind. I knew the very instant I saw the second plane hit the twin towers that this was Arab terrorism. To my horror, the country that has given me shelter, protection, and hope was under a monstrous attack from my culture of origin. Jihad had come to America.

Nine | Jihad Comes to America

The unspeakable tragedy of 9/11 has changed America and me forever. In the first year of the new millennium, as the world was turning a new and hopeful page in history, nineteen Muslim men, with the blessings and support of a large Arab Muslim network, committed the most horrific and unprecedented terror attack ever on American soil. The magnitude of this event turned the world into a scary place. And perhaps the scariest part of all was that these terrorists believed they were doing God's work. They were trained to view life on earth as of no value and that no act, no matter how barbaric, was off-limits if in pursuit of jihad. The news of the devastation in New York brought cheering crowds into the streets in various Arab capitals, hailing the terrorists as brave martyrs doing God's work for Islam.

The horror of 9/11 hit me in many ways. On the one hand, I was mourning the horrific deaths of more than three thousand fellow Americans and the destruction and suffering in New York and at the Pentagon. On the other hand, I was also mourning the fact that Arab culture had stooped to such a level of madness. I knew there were many other Muslim men out there who wished to be in the terrorists' shoes for the glory and honor awaiting them in heaven.

It was shameful to see Arabs openly cheering in the streets for the nineteen criminals while at the same time denying that Arabs were behind the attacks. With every new terror act in the past two decades, terrorists and the powerful people behind them have become more emboldened and outrageous. They have grown confident that any retaliation from the West would be minimal since the Western world needed their oil. And so they watched the towers fall and celebrated in the street.

The West, caught unprepared and divided, was stunned.

Americans before September 11, 2001, were totally unaware of the jihad declared against them. But the jihadists made no secret of their intentions—it was all over the Al-Jazeera network, on jihadist Web sites, in speeches, and their literature. We knew of their training camps in Afghanistan. But in the West, the very notion that anyone should take the rhetoric seriously was laughable. However, the seriousness of the jihadist's intentions was no secret to any Arabic-language speaker.

I was not totally surprised to learn that an Egyptian was the head of the 9/11 attacks and that fifteen of his collaborators were Saudis. Ironically, the perpetrators had come from two states— Egypt and Saudi Arabia—that the West considers "moderate." Mohamed Atta, in fact, came from a well-to-do Egyptian family in Cairo. He was educated and well traveled. I remembered the Egyptian youth I had met in Egypt only a couple of weeks earlier—some came from privileged families just as Atta had. I recalled their anger, confusion, and tendency to blame America and Israel for all the Arab world's misery.

In the aftermath of the horrific events of 9/11, as the world learned the details, I needed to call friends and family in Egypt to get a feel for Arab public opinion. I needed comfort and wanted to believe that moderate Egyptians were as appalled as I was by the attack on America. I wanted Egyptians to tell me that they were outraged and that this had crossed the line of sanity. I desperately want to hear them say it was time to look within and review what had gone wrong in Muslim culture to produce such barbaric behavior against a nation that had spread a lot of hope and good around the world; a nation that, no matter how many times it was provoked, had never used its full power in the Middle East against any Muslim nation. On the contrary, America has helped the Afghan rebels against the Soviet Union and the Bosnian Muslims against the brutal attacks of the Serbs. I wanted to hear Egyptians tell me that this unthinkable act is not the proper thank-you we give America for the $3 billion a year in aid it gives Egypt.

It never occurred to me as I placed my phone calls to Egypt that there would be any controversy over who had done this. The picture of Mohamed Atta taken as he went through airport security was being shown on TV. Very quickly the world was learning the names and seeing the faces of the nineteen terrorists. This time, without a doubt, Muslims could not place blame on others. Everything was documented.

I first called my mother. She has always had great respect for America. I remember her remarking that when Africans were starving, America was the first to send food, that whenever a catastrophe happened anywhere in the world, Americans were always the first to help. My mother expressed sorrow for the Americans who died. But she was not very interested in talking about the subject and was surprised that in the West they blamed 9/11 on Muslims. But she was eighty-one years old, after all, and I did not want to pressure her to talk.

My sister expressed the same surprise and doubts, saying, "I doubt that Arabs from the caves of Afghanistan did this action."

Next I talked with a very moderate cousin who told me that many Muslims were celebrating in the streets, and then she remarked that her sister, who wears a burka by choice, was kind of happy this happened to America. "As for me," my cousin said, "I am perplexed, but don't you think this is an Israeli conspiracy?" She added that when she told her neighbor that she felt bad for all the victims, her neighbor asked her, "Aren't you a Muslim?"

The next person I called was a childhood girlfriend. Quite harshly, she told me, "Shame on you for dishonoring Egypt by claiming that an Egyptian did that." Then she contradicted herself by saying, "You have to stand by Islam whether right or wrong. Let America experience the terrorism that is widespread in the Arab world! Why should only we suffer from terrorism?" She seemed to consider terrorism to be like an inevitable natural disaster rather than a deliberate act by homegrown Arab Muslim terrorists. She then became agitated and virtually screamed at me: "The flesh on your shoulders was bred by Arab wealth," meaning that I owe everything—my health, my well-being, and especially my allegiance—to my original culture. She continued to lecture me: "You should have more gratitude as a daughter of Egypt. You are a traitor if you blame this on Arabs."

A very high Egyptian government official I talked with shrugged it all off, saying, "It is time for Americans to suffer like the Palestinians."

Searching for sanity among my Egyptian friends and family, I placed a call to the man who was like a father to me—a man whom I considered to be educated and wise. Baba Abbas, who was eighty-five years old by then, told me, "I cannot believe that a good Muslim like you, who is the daughter of a great shahid, can be so blind to the fact that 9/11 was an Israeli conspiracy. How could you blame Muslims for that? Your father must be rolling over in his grave." His son raged that if America tried to hit Afghanistan in retaliation, that it would become America's next Vietnam. I then called a top journalist at the *Al-Ahram* newspaper who told me that the attitude on the Arab street was "Let America feel the bombing and terror that Palestinians are living with daily."

These were all some of the nicest, kindest people you could ever meet. Yet reaction to me ranged from defensive to hostile. Everyone showed some degree of satisfaction over what happened on 9/11. I was immediately shut up and told that 9/11 was orchestrated by Israel! Without exception, they were all angry with me for stating the simple facts: that the attack was committed by Arabs.

I hung up the phone and wept. I felt all alone. I had no one to relate to from Egypt anymore. I was devastated by all their denials and hateful comments, and especially upset at the attempt to shame me by using my father's memory. Without exception, everyone I called was supposedly a moderate Muslim and most of them were non-practicing. Yet they tacitly supported the radical Muslim line.

I needed to face a new reality. I was now totally disconnected, alienated, and disappointed in Egyptians and the Arab world. Though I hesitate to generalize, from the sample I spoke with, I find that most Egyptians today are blind to reality, and are hateful and arrogant. Even if you hit them over the head with reality, they will continue their denial. I knew that I had run full-force into the Arab protective shield against the outside world. It is a psychological barrier that nothing can penetrate, a barrier behind which a majority of Arabs and Muslims will stand together against the West, denying and defending even the worst atrocities. To them, if reality does not fit into their agenda, then it does not exist. The only reality they respect is Muslims appearing unified in front of the non-Muslim world, united in saving face and protecting the image of Islam and Muslims.

Even the father of the 9/11 terrorist leader, Mohamed Atta, first denied that his son did anything and also claimed that the attack was an Israeli conspiracy. Only in 2005 did he finally admit in public that his son was indeed involved and proclaim that he was proud of what his son, the martyr, did. It took him four years to face the truth in public. Even Egyptians were surprised by his admission.

Since speaking to Egyptians about 9/11 was like talking to a wall, and there was no way I could have an honest discussion with most of them, I began calling Arab Americans living in the United States. I felt it was important that we Arab Americans denounce

9/11 and make a stand in support of the United States. But none of my fellow Arab Americans with whom I spoke wanted to get involved. Some echoed what their relatives in the Arab world were saying. Some told me, "Did you know that three thousand Jews who worked in the World Trade Center did not show up for work that day?"

A few days after 9/11, I went to an Arabic market and found customers busy buying their ethnic food items and planning their regular parties and gatherings on the weekend as if nothing had happened. There was very little mention of 9/11, and if the discussion did turn to it, it was to express fears of a backlash and only from the viewpoint of self-protection. For example, I heard: "I hope there will be no negative publicity about Islam and Muslims." I was disappointed that many Arab Americans, even though I know they were grateful to be in this country, chose to stay silent.

Why? Fear is certainly a factor. Most Arabs and Muslims in the United States have come from brutal dictatorships or radical Muslim countries where voicing an opinion can get you killed. Many feel that even living in America cannot protect them from radical Muslims, and so they continue their silence, even in the face of something as horrifying as 9/11. Sadly, they are still prisoners of the tyranny of the old country.

The silence was not confined to the American Muslim community. Even Christian Arabs and Egyptian Copts were silent, mostly because they were trained to never publicly criticize the Muslim majority in the Arab world. For centuries, they have learned to appease those who discriminated against them in the hope of avoiding their wrath or being accused of collaborating with the enemy. Many Arab Christians have become incapable of speaking out against their Islamist oppressors out of the very real fear of reprisals against the "hostage" Christians still living in the Middle East. Most of the Arab Americans I met—both Muslim and Christian—said *"wana mali"* or "none of my business," an expression they have lived by all their lives in the Middle East. Implied in that expression is the notion that if I speak out, I will not change anything so why should I? So after 9/11, most Arab Americans shrugged their shoulders and went back to the business of living.

I was struck by this lack of condemnation within the American Arab community. Where was the outrage? I felt helpless and angry. I simply could not shrug my shoulders and say *"wana mali."* I could not continue living in America as if nothing had happened. How could I deserve to be an American if I were to stay silent? America is the country that saved my life and gave me a beautiful home, safety, security, equality, and respect equal to that of citizens born in the USA. I knew the moment the suicide bombers flew into the twin towers and the Pentagon that a war was on, a very real war. And winning this war required me to do my duty.

And so I began to speak out and write. I headed to my computer and started writing against terrorism and exposing the culture of jihad behind it. My first article against terrorism appeared in several Republican women's group newsletters. And then my articles were reprinted in other newsletters and posted on the Internet. I was stunned by the response. I started receiving e-mails from around the world. There was a huge need for an Arab's honest, unbiased viewpoint; a nondefensive analytical view that aimed for understanding, reformation, and peace.

It was not long before I began receiving requests to speak. I was reluctant but agreed to speak at a Republican women's group. I was not trained in public speaking, and in fact was terrified of speaking in public. It took prayers and all the courage I could muster before my presentation. I kept reminding myself that it was not about me; it was about standing up for America and informing the American public of the danger and the nature of Islamic terrorism. To overcome my terror of speaking, I imagined a giant machine called peace and visualized myself as one small cog in that machine. I had to move my part in the direction of peace. That is the image that helped me concentrate on my message, forget about myself, and overcome my shyness.

The response from the Republican women's group was overwhelming. A dear friend in the group by the name of Selma asked me if I could speak to her Hadassah group. I agreed and wrote a special speech for that Jewish women's group. The title was "Why I support the State of Israel." The room was packed, with an audience made up mostly of women. I will never forget that day—the first time I spoke before a Jewish group. As I was speaking, deep inside I felt a profound sadness about the tragedy of anti-Semitism in the Muslim world. I was thinking about how the small State of Israel daily lives with the terror of suicide bombers, how at any moment they know their children can be blown up on a bus on the way to school, or when they stop for pizza in a café. I looked into the eyes of these gracious and wonderful women who had dedicated their lives to serving their community, not just the Jewish community, but also the community as a whole. I felt deep respect.

As I spoke, I saw tears in the eyes of two women in front of me. I choked and felt the tears running down my face as I was speaking. I managed to wipe them and continue with my speech. The audience was very gracious, and when I was finished, they gave me a standing ovation. It was I who wanted to give *them* the standing ovation. It then hit me, the injustice these people suffered not only in Europe but then later at the hands of my people who called them "apes and pigs" and "enemies of God." What a shame to treat another religion and another people with such persistent and obsessive hatred. These were people whom I personally was learning a lot from—their compassion, their justice, their civility, their education, their humanitarianism and hard work to make the world a better place.

I firmly believe that there is a strong element of envy of Jewish achievements within the Muslim world. Instead of respecting these achievements, we Muslims want to kill them, condemn them, and smash them. Perhaps it reminds us of Muslim society's failures, shortcomings, and poverty despite being blessed by living in an oil-rich area.

I thanked Selma for giving me the opportunity to speak to her Hadassah group. Until then I had never spoken about my history in Gaza and about my father to anyone. I then wrote another article titled "The Daughter of a Shahid Speaks Out." I showed it to Selma and she wept. She encouraged me to publish it and I did.

Again the response was tremendous, and ready or not, my speaking career was launched. This development in my life was not planned by me. My whole life had suddenly been turned upside down. But I felt that I had found my calling. It was something that I had to do. Selma and I developed a close friendship that I will treasure for life. It has been wonderful American women such as Selma who taught me the value of public service and a sense of my duty toward America.

Why do I speak out, and what do I say? I try to help Americans face the truth about the terror threat they are up against, help them understand the mind-set of the jihadists who wish to destroy America. I realize there is fire in my heart. I do not deny it. I am angry at my culture. What arrogance and ingratitude. Who gave my people the right to destroy the world in the name of Allah? No religion should advocate that. Who gave my people the right to destroy people of other religions, cultures, and beliefs? Who gave them the right to declare a fatwa of death on Muslim critics who speak out against Islamist tyranny? Some say this is a clash of civilization. The truth is that this is an attack on civilization itself by haters of civilization.

Even though I understand it, when I look at it from my new American perspective, I am still amazed that, to many Muslims, all this jihad ideology feels and seems normal, honorable, and righteous. In the Middle East, we were never taught consideration, compassion, and empathy toward non-Muslims or nonbelievers. The stories we learned as Muslims always ended with victory for Islam. Even Arab Muslim immigrants to the West still believe in the nobility of jihad and are torn between their Muslim culture of origin and their new country. Caught in the turmoil and confusion between the two cultures, the "silent" majority cannot make a moral stand. When I speak to fellow Arab Americans, they say they are against terrorism but always have an explanation or a "but" that follows. They claim Islam is a religion of peace but refuse to criticize their homegrown terrorists. They will not even acknowledge the dilemma let alone make an independent moral stand. It does not take a rocket scientist to figure out who is wrong and who is right, but many don't have the courage to say that our Muslim culture has spawned monsters and that our system is flawed.

As for me and a few others like me, I see no confusion, no hesitation as to what is right and what is wrong, what is good and what is evil, and when we may look the other way and when we have to make a stand. I see with total moral clarity that my culture of origin has become a threat to world peace. The problem of jihad, terrorism, conflict, and brutality is no longer a local Middle Eastern problem. Once it was a matter of Middle Eastern Muslim cultures inflicting harm and tyranny on their own minorities, such as Jews and Christians. Now, thanks to oil money, technology, travel, and immigration, jihad has crossed borders and is demanding "dhimmitude" and subjugation of the non-Muslim world in the most outrageous and spectacular way the world has ever seen.

Along with the fire of anger in my heart is a profound sadness for my Arab brothers and sisters. The long-term effect of terror is demoralizing and demeaning to human dignity and spirit. I lived half of my life in the Muslim world, where most of the countries lost their liberty a long time ago. They have no memory of how to live in freedom, how to bring it about, how to preserve it. Now, having never tasted the fruits of freedom, they are trying to take away the liberty of the West through terrorism.

After 9/11, many Americans sincerely asked: "Why do they hate us?" Western logic could not comprehend the magnitude of the problem. They were caught totally off-guard. Personally, I don't understand why they did not see this coming. Just a one-month visit to the Middle East in 2001 scared the hell out of me. Bear in mind, I was not a CNN journalist stationed in Cairo, Riyadh, Baghdad, or Damascus, whose job it is to have ears open and eyes peeled and to report back to the world. I was merely returning to Egypt to enjoy my family and show my children their mother's homeland. How did all the Western reporters and embassies miss the open threats that were all over the Arab media and the Arab streets and on the lips of bin Laden himself? I feel that the U.S. media was not doing its job of informing the American public.

There is another American reaction, a close second behind the why-do-they-hate-us question. My American neighbors and friends often politely asked me: "Why aren't Muslims standing up to extremists and terrorists? Why are they silent?" The perceptions of my American neighbors are right; the majority of Muslims are silent and are doing very little to bring about change. Why do we keep on defending, excusing, and blaming terrorism on other nations or on historical injustice? First of all, Arab culture's normal reaction is to refuse to take responsibility and instead find someone else to blame. Israel, in particular, has always been the great excuse, the handy scapegoat. Any wonder why Arabs don't care to make peace with Israel? If they did, then whom would they blame for their next crisis? The existence of a villain upon which to hang all Arab jihad aspirations, violations, aggression, mistakes, terrorism, and corruption is important in order to camouflage, confuse, and mislead the innocent Western bystander who has no idea what hit him.

Another reason for the silence is that for most Muslims, criticizing jihad, martyrdom, or terrorism seems in their minds—rightly or wrongly—to be equivalent to criticizing Islam itself.

To Muslims who remain silent this is what I say: Are you aware that 9/11 and the last forty years of Islamic terrorism has tainted how history will judge Islam? A religion is not judged by writings in a holy book, but by the behavior of its followers, not by the idealism of the religion, but by its actions. Religion's purpose is to elevate and civilize man. Terrorism and jihad against the infidels does not contribute to world civilization but sends mankind back to the Dark Ages. Terrorism is a behavior of desperate people, and Muslims and Arabs should not be desperate. They should be grateful. Arabs have been blessed with land from the Atlantic to the

Persian Gulf, and Muslims are 1.2 billion strong. They have been blessed with oil and a strategic location on the world map. But they are greedy and want more; and in the process they have forgotten and sacrificed their core self. Terrorism is tearing apart Muslim society and rotting it from the core. But instead of working within to reform, Muslims are spilling their turmoil into the rest of the world, infecting the rest of society. Islam is at a crossroads. It is up to Muslim scholars to save Islam by reforming it or to start World War III.

Other great religions have owned up to barbaric actions perpetrated in the name of God and brought about reform from within. During an earlier era, Christian rulers burned "heretics" at the stake, executed "witches," marched their armies into lands to conquer them for Christianity and in so doing brutally plundered and killed local populations. The excesses of the Crusades are well known. And in fifteenth-century Spain, Jews and Muslims who did not convert were brutally executed in a reign or terror called the Inquisition. But at some point, Christianity acknowledged and repudiated such actions and attempted to return to the message of love and redemption found in the Holy Scriptures. It is time now for another of the world's great religions to move from the Dark Ages and Medieval-era excesses and return to the true meaning of Islam. Reform is possible but not easy. It was not easy for Christianity. It will not be easy for Islam. It will take the courage of the faithful, and the admission that change is necessary.

But instead, most Muslims have chosen to avoid and deny the problem. Instead of looking within, they have chosen to attempt to sway the outside world's impressions. In many ways, radical Muslims were emboldened by 9/11 and continued the momentum of the 9/11 "victory." Soon we saw Bali, Madrid, London—radical Islam on a roll to conquer the world by the sword all over again. While the terrorists flexed their muscles, their oil-rich defenders began an effort to calm down world public opinion by making all kinds of excuses and defenses.

Fearing a backlash, a massive Muslim public relations machine was ramped up after 9/11, with Islamic scholars, distinguished clerics, and Arab intellectuals attempting to explain Islam to American audiences. There is no honorable reason for jihad against the infidels in international law; it is called terrorism by the civilized world. Thus they came up with an honorable slogan for terrorists, calling them "freedom fighters." I regret to say some in the West were fooled. Much of what I was hearing was inaccurate and designed to mislead and confuse. In the face of this, I had to act. Because I possess knowledge both of Middle Eastern and American culture, I felt it was my duty to inform Americans and openly speak the truth.

I began speaking out to expose the Muslim radical groups in the United States who claim to be moderate. Most of these groups are well financed by Muslim countries and are concerned with reforming Islam only in the eyes of Americans. Example: An astounding discussion of the meaning of the word "jihad." After 9/11 many Muslims in the West reinterpreted the meaning of jihad as an inner struggle for self-improvement. This new, mystical interpretation of jihad was designed to be more acceptable to Western culture. This "inner struggle" business is hogwash. In the Arab world there is only one meaning for jihad, and that is: a religious holy war against infidels. It is a fight for Allah's cause. Ask anyone in the Arab street what "Jihad for the sake of Allah" means and he will say it means dying as a shahid for the sake of spreading Islam. I have never heard of any discussion of inner struggle in my thirty years living in the Middle East. Such nonsense is a PR ploy for Western consumption only, concocted to save face and protect the reputation of Islam in the eyes of the infidels whom Muslims want to lure into conversion. It was made up by people who are searching for excuses for terrorism and are not standing up against the forces of extremism and violence in the Middle East. Unfortunately, terrorists are encouraged by the defense of these apologists. When Osama bin Laden speaks of jihad, he is not talking about an inner struggle for self-analysis or self-improvement. In all his tapes, he is very clear about his mission to destroy Western civilization and win the world to Islam. That is why many Muslims danced in the streets after 9/11. The dirty little truth is that the majority of people in Saudi Arabia and the rest of the Muslim world regard bin Laden as a hero of Islam. The reason bin Laden cannot be found is because he is loved by a large number of Muslims who will not give him up for any amount of money.

Saudi Arabia also hired American lobbyists to speak on their behalf to improve their image—without Americans knowing that these individuals were paid lobbyists. In fact, one member of a political group to which I belong was constantly defending Saudi Arabia and the Al-Jazeera television network. At the time, many in the group found it noticeably unusual. We later read an article in which her name was listed among others as being a paid lobbyist for Saudi Arabia. We were all surprised that she had never mentioned this fact in her presentations.

While all these PR campaigns were focused on the West, other types of campaigns were going on in Arabic aimed at citizens of the Middle East. Total lies were told in Arab media. My cousin in Egypt, who keeps me abreast of the views in the Middle East, told me that Arab media claimed that America's food drops to Afghani citizens during the war in Afghanistan contained poisoned food. Arabs were also told that the United States wanted to use weapons of mass destruction on Afghanis and Iraqis. On Egyptian television, a three-year-old Egyptian girl, Basmallah, daughter of a famous Egyptian actor, was encouraged to say she hated Jews, whom she described as "apes and pigs." The show praised her as an example of a good little Muslim girl. The host said, "Don't we all wish to teach our children to be good Muslims like Basmallah?" How sad that in the Middle East, Islam has been reduced to hating Jews and feeling paranoid and victimized by non-Muslims.

These two contradictory campaigns—the Arabic one in the Middle East, fueling hatred and anger against the West, and the English one in the West, proclaiming "Islam as a religion of peace"—can bring only disaster between the two worlds.

Muslim defenders often answer questions about the actions of

Muslims by reciting the ideals of Islam. They insist that Islam is a religion of peace and tolerance while ignoring the daily prayers in Middle Eastern mosques for the violent exploits of great heroes and martyrs. Religious leaders across the Middle East are blessing and approving of suicide bombers and those who kill the infidels. Even Muhammad Sayyed Tantawi, the sheikh of Al-Azhar University in Cairo, who is the highest-ranking cleric in Sunni Islam, has issued fatwas in favor of violent jihad against America and in support of suicide bombings.

The notion that Islam teaches peace and tolerance is ridiculous in light of the record of Islamic countries' treatment of their minorities or the sermons preached in neighborhood mosques. Even in the new, supposedly "democratic" Afghanistan, in the spring of 2006 a Muslim who converted to Christianity was sentenced to death, a punishment mandated by sharia law. His life was spared only after Western governments pressured Afghan authorities, and the man was secretly whisked away to Italy in the midst of death threats from top Muslim clerics. So-called moderate Muslim leaders unfortunately were silent and did nothing to protect or defend that poor Afghani convert. There were no Muslim riots to save his life. The only outrage came from the mob wanting to kill him themselves if the government set him free.

Yet defenders will insist that Islam teaches tolerance. Typical is the headline in a full-page ad in the *New York Times* taken out by a Saudi prince who is donating millions to Harvard to fund an Islamic studies program. The ad reads: "Islam teaches the value of understanding other human cultures and civilizations. This leads to the building of bridges in communication and tolerance that enrich the lives of everyone concerned." If only this were actually taught to children in the Muslim world, we would not be in this crisis.

The defenders cannot reconcile the huge gap between the idealism of Islam and the reality of the actions of many Muslims. If they truly believe Islam is a religion of peace, then why do they tolerate the teaching of hatred, violence, and jihad in Muslim schools? Why do they not teach peace in their schools, mosques, media, and political institutions? If they truly believed in the ideals of Islam and the verses they quote from the Koran, they would have to stand up to terrorists and stop defending their actions. If the majority of Muslims are defending the actions of Osama bin Laden—openly or secretly—then we cannot tell the world Islam is a religion of peace. Then it is a lie. If Islam is a religion of peace, then we must teach peace as a major part of Islamic teachings.

After the prominent role Saudi citizens played in the attacks of 9/11, the West criticized Saudi schools for teaching hate. In response, the Saudi government launched an internal review and revision of their textbooks. After new textbooks were published, the Saudi government took out a full-page ad in *The New Republic* to trumpet the program's success, and an embassy spokesman said, "We have removed materials that are inciteful or intolerant towards people of other faiths." However, a translation of the new textbooks reveals otherwise. An eighth-grade Islamic-studies text reads: "As cited in the Ibn Abbas: the apes are Jews, the people of the Sabbath, while the swine are the Christians, the infidels of the communion of Jesus." This is only one of many such examples and serves as a telling example not only of the gap between idealism and reality, but also the huge gap between what the Arabs tell the West and what is in fact really happening within the Arab world.*

After the United States commenced its war against al-Qaeda in Afghanistan, we began seeing even more elaborate and barbaric beheadings in the name of Islam. The whole world was made to feel captive just as were the innocent hostages being slaughtered in the name of Allah. Videos of men in black wearing martyrdom banners showed them holding the Koran in one hand and swords, bombs, or AK-47s in the other, chanting *"Allahu Akbar!"* as they chopped off the head of an infidel. Their chants in Arabic were powerful, mixed with excitement and euphoria while they be-

*The Washington Post, May 21, 2006.

headed *Wall Street Journal* reporter Daniel Pearl, the unsuspecting American Jew who wanted to extend a hand of friendship and understanding to Muslims. There was no mercy. For them it was like taking the life of a bug or a chicken. That was a dark moment for Islam. The message of radical Islam is *Fear us*. Muslim radicals have indeed perfected fear as a powerful tool that produces instant compliance. The beheading of Daniel Pearl was a clear message to the world: *We are Muslims. We hate you. You are infidels and you will be slaughtered in the name of Allah.*

Witnessing the way Daniel Pearl was killed reminded me of the Daheyah feast in which Muslim families ritualistically sacrifice a lamb in their homes. While the rest of the family, including children, watched, a male family member would do the actual slaughtering accompanied by the invocation *"Allahu Akbar."* Those terrorist gangs killed Daniel Pearl, Paul Johnson, Nicholas Berg, and Kim Sun-il in the same ritualistic way. But the Daheyah of these horrific terror rituals were humans, beheaded as a blessing on Muslim soul, accompanied by the same pious invocation.

Beheading as an execution option remains a part of the criminal legal code in Saudi Arabia, Yemen, Iran, and Qatar. Only Saudi Arabia continues the practice.

After every new barbaric incident, I am stunned all over again at the lack of a moral outrage. No outrage by Arab Americans, no outrage on the Arab street, and no outrage by Arab media over such barbaric acts. Yet these are people who are very easily outraged and offended by a simple word, a cartoon, or a criticism of Islam. Even the brutal murder in November of 2004 of Margaret Hassan, a British woman married to an Iraqi who dedicated thirty years of her life to helping Iraqi women, stirred no debate—where were the outraged Arab women over the shameful murder of a woman who was trying to help them? Decades of hijackings, the killing of Christian missionaries, the Taliban's destruction of the Buddha statues, the Russian school massacre of more than three hundred children, blowing up trains in Spain and underground metros in London—not to mention a half a century of terrorism inside Israel—where was the outrage? The Muslim world has closed its eyes to these atrocities and worse, has actually put these perpetrators on a pedestal.

After Daniel Pearl's beheading, I called a cousin in Egypt to get an indication of the mood on the Arab street. Her answer was that most Arabs don't care about beheadings in the name of Islam. She cited media allegations that many of the Western men who were beheaded were raping Iraqi women, and they further excused it by saying that "infidels should not be on Muslim land anyway!" Lies in Arab media to their own people are the only way to justify Muslim brutality to the ordinary Muslim public, she observed.

After every major terrorist attack, instead of outrage, the Muslim world's energy is directed at saving face before the West and reforming the image of Islam rather than reforming the educational and political systems that encourage such acts. They still attend their mosques and listen to fiery speeches that call for destroying the infidels. They want to have it both ways; glorify their beloved jihadists and martyrs, but to Western media insist that they are against terrorism. The West must not be duped by the insincere presentations of people who claim to be moderate Muslims when in fact they are nothing if not radical. If they were really sincere about not supporting terrorism, these "moderates" would be on Al-Jazeera TV day and night condemning terrorism to the Arab world. They would be standing on the street corners of Riyadh, Cairo, Amman, and Damascus loudly protesting terrorist acts. They would be yelling over mosque loudspeakers that terrorism is against Muslim teachings. The sheikh of Al-Azhar, and for that matter, most Muslim leaders in the Middle East, have never condemned terrorism in all shapes and forms. As a matter of fact, just the opposite: most of them have supported terrorism—even against civilians, women, and children as a form of legitimate jihad. So why should Americans buy the claims that "terrorists do not represent Islam?"

Apologists would have us believe that terrorists are just a "fringe minority." That is another big lie. The truth is, there are many volunteers signing up around the Middle East to be the next one to die with honors and go to heaven. There is no shortage of terrorists in the Muslim world. The Iranian government asked students who want to volunteer for terrorism to sign up and thousands did in reaction to the objections of the West to the development of nuclear weapons in Iran. Unfortunately—and it pains me to admit this—terrorists are not a "fringe minority" but a substantial and growing presence that is a direct result of generations brought up with values of jihad, martyrdom, violence, and the mission to conquer the world for Islam. Their agenda is supported on the Arab street in nearly every Middle Eastern country. The radicals are everywhere in Muslim society—in every country and in every family. They are so common and widespread within Muslim culture that Muslims cannot see them anymore.

Most Americans, unless they have children in college, do not know, and would not believe, the bold attempt on college campuses to indoctrinate American young people with the radical Muslim agenda. After speaking for several years on U.S. college campuses to different groups from all backgrounds—religious, educational, political, and racial—I have learned that American students, even after 9/11, are largely misinformed. There is a huge PR campaign going on now on campuses across the country to reform the image of Islam in America by people who have no intention of reforming the way Islam is being taught in the Middle East. Arab donations to create Islamic studies and Middle East studies departments are pouring into our institutions of higher learning, and American deans and administrators are more than happy to allow it. Complaints about the indoctrination have been coming to me from many students all around the country. The misinformation, anti-Semitism, and hate speech that I left behind in Middle Eastern schools have arrived in America.

I attended a peace rally in Berkeley, California, where the exploded number 9 bus from Israel was displayed and several pro-peace speakers from all backgrounds were speaking against terrorism in all shapes and forms. I was among them. Across the street from us there was a counterdemonstration. I could not comprehend why anyone would object to a group speaking against terrorism. A group of Arabs and some American anti-Israel supporters were wearing green "martyrs" headbands with Koranic jihad verses on them similar to those worn by Hamas in the West Bank and Gaza. These protesters were yelling, "Two, four, six, eight, we are martyrs, we can't wait." This scene brought the West Bank and Gaza anger, rage, and support of terrorism to America's streets and its college campuses. It was a sad day for me. Nearby, a group of American leftists were foolishly cheering them on. I wanted to tell them, "You are on the wrong side! You are supporting the oppressors, not the oppressed. You need to see the new reality in the Middle East. Move beyond the sixties. The old causes you are backing are the very ones standing in the way of peace." I wanted to tell them terrorists are not freedom fighters; they are the oppressors and murderers and the ones who refuse to accept peace.

The true freedom fighters—and there are unfortunately too few of them—are those Arabs who are willing to speak out against terrorism and call for reform within their culture. They do so at peril to their lives. These brave people are the true freedom fighters.

On another occasion in early 2004, I attended a presentation during a two-day conference at California State University, San Bernardino. The topic: "Understanding the Middle East." Present in the audience were some Saudi diplomats. The speaker was Dr. Yvonne Haddad, an Arab Christian woman from the Center for Muslim-Christian Understanding at Georgetown University. She discussed "The Bush Administration and the Credibility Gap." Her memories of when she first moved to the United States were not pleasant. She remembered how an American woman on a bus told her, "Whoever civilized you did a good job." That was supposed to be a typical example of how Americans treat Arabs.

She mentioned 9/11 only once, saying that on that day she worried about what the talking heads on TV would say about Muslims. She was very critical of U.S. foreign policy in the Middle East and said that Mohamed Atta and Osama bin Laden were both justifiably upset with that policy. In her opinion, what really hurt U.S. relations with Arabs and Muslims was the United States walking out of the Durbin Conference on racism in South Africa in 2001. She added that Muslims believe that the first President Bush in 1991 declared a crusade against Islam when he "invaded" Kuwait (something the United States was asked to do by the Kuwaitis who had been invaded by Saddam Hussein). She declared President George W. Bush's invasion of Iraq to be the "Second Crusade," and she criticized the way Americans justified what she called "the war on Islam." She claimed the administration's using the Afghanistan invasion and taking out the Taliban "to liberate Afghan women" was a hollow excuse for invasion. She stressed that Afghan women did not want to be liberated and criticized Mrs. Bush for being proud of the U.S. liberation of women in that country.

Dr. Haddad then complained about the treatment of Arabs in the United States and wondered why the Department of Homeland Security is not monitoring Jews or Christians such as Pat Robertson the way it is monitoring Arabs. She attacked President Bush by saying that Arabs now call him "Mufti Bush" because he is telling us what Islam should be. She criticized the new Arab TV station, El Horrah, because it shows Muslims in the United States saying they are well treated and happy in America. In the mind-set of this woman, we Arab Americans are all suffering in misery and persecution.

As I listened, I was flabbergasted. It was amazing to me to see a Christian Arab trying to promote the Saudi agenda of defending Islam by blaming America. She was closing her eyes to what Muslims are doing to Christians and Copts in the Arab world (even though she is Christian) and defending the indefensible. Her speech never gave any explanation for or analysis of Arabs' beliefs and actions in the Middle East, let alone whether these beliefs are right or wrong. Analysis, judgment, and condemnation were reserved only for the U.S. government. The bottom line of her speech was that terrorism was somehow the fault of America and President Bush, and that Americans must watch their language and do everything they can to understand and be sensitive to Arabs. She was making it clear that the very mention of Arab terrorism or any attempt by American citizens to understand or defend U.S. policy is "racism" and "discrimination." This is the mind-set of the Saudi and Arab PR machine. This is what it wants Arab Americans to believe.

Dr. Haddad was applauded enthusiastically by the group of Saudi diplomats present in the audience that day, and I was one of the few who criticized her message during the question-and-answer period. There were some students and teachers at my table who were very uncomfortable with the entire speech. Some even left before it ended. Not me. I stayed to the very end to listen to what was being said, as outrageous as it was. It was a disturbing example of what the Arab American PR machine is trying to do on U.S. college campuses—to indoctrinate American students into believing what the real racists and purveyors of discrimination in the Middle East want them to believe about American freedoms and democracy.

The university's president was apparently very happy with the speech and promised more such conferences, saying that this one was the third in only six months. I thought to myself about how indoctrination requires constant repetition and reinforcement until lies become regarded as truth.

There is nothing wrong with Arabs wanting to reform their image in the United States or promote understanding of Arab culture, but that should never happen at the expense of the victims of terrorism or by attacking America. By branding the U.S government and its foreign policy as "evil" and against the "peace-loving" Middle Eastern Arab countries, these Arab defenders have done everyone a disservice. That will not resolve the problem of terrorism and ultimately discredits them. While they are trying to deceive the American people, they are emboldening the terrorists back home who hear their defenses and excuses. The PR campaign in the United States on behalf of Saudi Arabia and other despotic Arab regimes is alive, well, and shameless. Listening to this nonsense, I felt again like a minority up against all the radical Muslim power, organization, and finances who are portraying themselves as "moderate." The truth is that the powerful groups inside the United States who sponsor such events on university campuses, while they may be Americans, their true loyalty is to the oil-rich kingdoms of the Middle East and not to America.

After attending this conference, I realized how truly vulnerable America is. The war of words and propaganda could be as vital as the actual military war. My batteries were recharged. I realized how important it was to expose and alert Americans to what is happening on our college campuses. I don't want to see the same propaganda, hatred, misinformation, anti-Semitism, and suppression of freedom of speech that I dealt with growing up in the Middle East invade the institutions of higher learning in America. I cannot let anti-American and terrorist sympathizers be the only speakers for Arab Americans. The American people deserve better.

When I speak, I never condemn the Koran itself and I specifically say, "Books don't commit acts of terrorism, people do." But still my Muslim audiences are always hypersensitive and extremely defensive to any criticism. That defensive posture is the common reaction we all learned from our basic Islamic teaching back home. And too often, instead of condemning those who encourage terrorism, they condemn Muslims who say we have a problem.

Those few Arab Americans like me, who dare to openly stand by America's war on terror, are not backed by any organization. We basically work for free, and we have to look over our shoulders every time we speak just in case there is a terrorist behind us or a fatwa declared against us. Fortunately, there are American people who know us, admire us for speaking out, and encourage us to continue speaking on these campuses to balance the anti-American side that defends and excuses terrorism and dares to somehow blame America and the 3,000 American terrorism victims for "bringing it upon themselves."

After 9/11, my fellow Americans should never be in the dark again. They must understand the brutality and persistence of their enemy. As a loyal and grateful American, I feel I must help the American public understand what is at stake. America must understand that Islam is not just a religion. It is a political system; it is a legal system, both civil and criminal. Penalties under Islamic law can be death, limb amputation, or stoning. It is a system that gives power to the vice police to hold a stick in public and use it on women's ankles if they are uncovered. Everyone's rights and duties are spelled out very clearly in Islam, and, no, there is no equality under Islamic law between Muslims and non-Muslims or between men and women. This is what they want for the whole world.

Radical Islam has lofty plans to conquer the West and won't let go. That is something Americans don't understand and have trouble believing. They may be able to understand why the Islamic world hates them; they may get the dynamics behind why they blame America, Israel, and the West for all the ills in their society. They may even be able to understand how these extremists justify violence. But what Americans still don't understand is that the goal of jihad is to conquer the world, literally, for Islam, and to usher in a Caliphate—that is, a supreme totalitarian Islamic government, a lifestyle by force, one nation, one party, one constitution (the Koran), and one law (sharia Islamic law). Anyone who reads and speaks Arabic and monitors Web sites and listens to speeches and sermons in mosques around the world knows how seriously many Muslims believe in their mission to dominate the world for Islam, the one true religion.

Make no mistake about it: They are sacrificing their men, women, and children for this goal of world domination. They are willing to bring about an Armageddon to conquer the world to Islam. We are already in World War III and many people in the West are still in denial. Unlike during the cold war with communism, the enemy is not a superpower, but a fanatical religious movement equipped with a very powerful weapon of mass destruction called suicide/homicide bombers. For generations, thousands if not millions of suicide bombers have been bred, trained, and nourished to give up their lives in service of jihad. That makes this an unprecedented world war. There is no use pretending: We know where the enemy comes from. We know who is financing terrorism and praying for its success. It is at the highest levels of the Muslim world. Each and every dictator in the Arab world, the Muslim leadership, and Arab media—all have been complicit. The young men and women willing to die for Allah are their leader's source of power in a brutal part of the world. They know they don't have the power, the organization, or the armies to win in conventional warfare. They have to circumvent civilized international law to achieve their goal. Terrorism is not by accident; it is part and parcel of the religion and culture of jihad, of the march to world domination that has been brewing for decades in the Islamic world. Ironically, Arabs who accuse the West of imperialism are themselves using jihad to facilitate Arab imperialism.

These are the plain and simple truths about the war we face.

Furthermore, we must be aware of the insidious way Islamic extremists use our own democracy against us, how they are demanding equal rights in America's open system and immigration for one purpose and one purpose only, and that is to make Islam a reality in America. They have perfected the art of playing games with the West by understanding Western weakness and taboos, effectively using buzzwords such as "racist," "Islamophobia," and "profiling." At the same time that Muslims demand tolerance from the West and decry ethnic profiling, they refuse to show tolerance to Jews or Christians in Muslim countries. Muslims freely build mosques around the world, but prohibit the building of churches and synagogues in Muslim countries. Saudis forbid foreigners from practicing other religions and don't allow them to set foot in Mecca and Medina. Americans need to know that what they treasure the most—their freedom—is very much at stake.

When I started speaking out, of course I was accused of defaming Islam. Some even called me an infidel. It is not me—or those few moderate Muslims who are speaking out—who have given Islam a bad name, rather it is the terrorists, their sympathizers, and the silence of the Muslim majority that defames a great religion and a great people. We cannot continue denying the undeniable that there is a major problem within Muslim and Arab society that has produced terrorism. Now is the time to own up to the dysfunction in the Islamic world and seize the moment to bring about change. Good and loyal Muslims all over the world should demand an end to the violence and terror. They should work to reform their institutions, beginning with the education of young children. They should join the other great religions of the world to advocate peace and tolerance, love and harmony.

Five years after my life was changed by 9/11, I continue to speak and write. My strongest motivation for speaking out is my sense of duty to serve America. After all that America has given me, it was time to give back. My writing and speaking have become stronger with each e-mail of encouragement and word of appreciation from the American public.

Why am I such a vocal supporter of America? For those of us who fled tyranny, if not for America, where else could we run? If it weren't for America, where would I be now? I can only imagine myself, a second or third wife competing with other wives for my husband's love and respect, unable to control the upbringing of my children in a culture of hatred and violence. What would have been the future of my daughters and son? What would I be wearing, and what would I be thinking if I had stayed in Egypt and not moved to America in 1978?

I would have grown to be a totally different person. I look at my mother and sisters, cousins and friends in Egypt, and even though most of them are at the top level of Egyptian society, they are all struggling with how the culture regards and victimizes women. The best example was my mother's tragic life. Her beauty, talent, intelligence, and ability to give was devalued and buried in a society that deprived her from a normal family life; a society that placed our family in the Gaza war zone to die in the process of killing Jews; a society that told my mother that her family came second to the hatred and killing of Israelis. And after her husband was killed as a shahid, that same society told her that her household was not as respected as a home headed by a man. The critical and cruel eye of radical Muslim society prevented her from living a free life or even pursuing the simple pleasures of life after my father's death. Like all Muslim women, she lived to please society more than doing what she really wanted. I feel deep sorrow for my mother, what a waste of talent.

So why didn't I just shut up, breathe a sigh of relief, count my blessings, and enjoy my life. In 2001, that momentous year when my life changed, I knew from the outset that speaking out against terrorism and in support of the United States and peace with Israel was going to bring me trouble from Islamists, radical Muslims, and even from moderate Arabs and Muslims in general. But the time of silence, of being afraid to speak out, was over for me from the day the planes hit the twin towers. After seeing 3,000 fellow Americans killed in an instant, I had to stand up for America.

I choose the culture of life and not the culture of death. I choose the culture of freedom and not the culture of tyranny. I choose America.

Ten

Arabs for Israel

Israel has been the object of constant terrorism—a barrage of 9/11's all through its history. As a percentage of their total population, Israel has lost far more lives to terror than the United States did in 9/11. Arabs have always rejected peace with Israel, using Israel as their excuse for a jihad that has now reached all corners of the globe. The way the Jews have been treated in the Middle East is tragic and a disgrace. And the world—including much of the West, with the exception of the United States—has abandoned Israel in order to appease twenty-two Arab countries with large oil reserves.

My position on Israel is in sharp contrast with the majority of the Muslim world and Arab Americans. It is even more unusual coming from an Arab woman. But the stalemate in the Arab-Israeli crisis will not be solved by Arabs and Muslims clinging to the same old outlook toward Israel. There must be a new paradigm, a fresh perspective by Arab countries if they are serious about peace and ending the stalemate.

As my articles in support of Israel began appearing, I started receiving e-mails from Arabs and Muslims who had begun to circulate my articles inside the Arab world. Some supported my views on Israel; I discovered I was not alone in my wish for peace with Israel. There were Arabs just like me who wanted peace and were ready to move beyond the conflict. But almost all of them told me not to post their names. Some of what they told me was very personal, private, and moving. It was a call for help from inside the Muslim and Arab world. The e-mails streamed in from Egypt, the West Bank, Saudi Arabia, Afghanistan, Syria, Lebanon, Jordan, Iraq, Algeria, Yemen, Malaysia, Tunisia—from all over the Arab world. Many of them told me, "You are right on the money!" or "You have the courage of ten Arab men!" Through the e-mails that flooded in, I heard of the suffering on both sides, the Arab and the Israeli.

In February 2004, I founded the Web site www.ArabsforIsrael. com as my answer to this tragedy, my attempt to bring a voice to all these people who needed to express their views without fear. Thank God for the Internet.

ArabsforIsrael.com now provides a forum for Arabs and Muslims who want to express their support for Israel. Tragically, Israel has few friends at this point in history, and I wish through my actions to convey to every Israeli and Jew around the world, that, yes, there are Arabs and Muslims who support them and wish for their well-being.

Some Arabs asked me, why not call the Web site something like "support Israel and Palestinians." To them I say: there is nothing new about an Arab supporting Palestinians; that will not bring any new perspective to solving the crisis. Palestinian Arabs already enjoy the encouragement and support of all Arab and Muslim countries as well as many non-Muslim countries around the world. What we need now is a revolutionary idea, a new perspective—one that regards Israel as an asset and not as an enemy in the region. This new outlook is necessary if our common goal is peace. I was convinced that "Arabs for Israel" was the right name for the new perspective I was advocating. I want to tell Palestinians that they have a neighbor who could be an honest partner with them. Having a neighbor of a different religion and perhaps a different culture can be an asset and not the handicap that the Arab world has been telling them it is for fifty-eight years.

The so-called support the Arab world gives Palestinians is poisonous. In setting up the Web site, I wanted to distance myself from the kind of support twenty-two Arab countries have been giving to Arabs of the West Bank and Gaza. I have seen it, lived it, been immersed in it for too long. Life has gotten only progressively worse for Palestinians since the days when I lived as a child in Gaza. These twenty-two powerful Arab countries have brought nothing to the Palestinians but defeat after defeat, failed promises, and feelings of despair and victimhood. All sorts of tactics have been used in their quest to bring "justice" for the Palestinians: manipulation, shaming, blaming, and rewarding terror. All of it has been done at the expense of a stable life for the Palestinians. In the process, Palestinians have nothing to show for all these decades of war and terror.

Like most of the Arab world around them, Palestinians are predominantly poor, living under corruption, mismanagement, and chronically high unemployment. Conditions for the majority of poor in Egypt is no better. Instead of Palestinians lining up for work on their borders with Egypt, Jordan, Saudi Arabia, or Syria, they have been lining up for work inside Israel—the very country Arabs expect them to terrorize. Several generations of Palestinians have forgotten what life in a normal setting is and are immersed in self-pity. In the midst of the false pity the Arab world around them dishes out, some Palestinians have begun to feel that the world owes them. They don't remember a society with respect for the rule of law, a society in which citizens produce what they need to live on instead of waiting for handouts from around the world. Geographically, Gaza is untenable. It has too many people crowded into a tiny strip of desert that cannot possibly economically support that size of a population. It is an artificial and unnatural situation allowed by surrounding Arab countries to purposely keep Gaza an overcrowded tinderbox of unrest. The Palestinian family unit has been shattered and ripped apart by jihad and terrorism. Encouraged by Arab countries, jihad has become a greater value than motherhood. Women are urged to become terrorists as much as men are. And mothers are brainwashed to be proud when their children blow themselves up to kill Jews.

Arab "love" and "support" of Palestinians has been extremely self-serving, manipulative, and crippling, and has kept them in constant turmoil, terror, and war. They are literally loving them to death. The two regions—the West Bank and Gaza—have simply been cynically used and abused by Arabs as launching grounds for war and terror against Israel. The Palestinian-Israeli conflict represents the focal point of the larger confrontation of the Muslim world against the non-Muslim world. Israel may be the frontline enemy, but beyond the Mediterranean and the ocean is the non-Muslim world that Muslims believe they need to conquer for Islam. In the process, Palestinians have been sacrificed and kept hostage as the human frontline of Arab jihad.

No, I do not want to give *that kind* of support to Palestinians. They have been used and abused enough by the Arab world. Palestinian children deserve better. They don't need hatred; they need hope. They don't need jihad; they need jobs. I reject such eternal jihad and terrorism. I can no longer wish this on any Arab child. That is why when people disapprovingly ask me, "Don't you support Palestinians?" I say to them, "Yes," but not in the same way as the rest of the Arab world. I no longer want Palestinians to be hostages to Arab dreams of a caliphate.

In the meantime, supporting Israel and the Jewish people who have contributed to the Middle East culture for thousands of years is simply good, right, and the honorable thing to do.

The following are the principles that I and other like-minded Arabs have enumerated for the Web site ArabsforIsrael.com:

We Are Arabs and Muslims Who Believe . . .

- We can support Israel and still support the Palestinian people. Supporting one does not cancel support for the other.
- We can support the State of Israel and the Jewish religion and still treasure our Arab and Islamic culture.
- There are many Jews and Israelis who freely express compassion and support for the Palestinians. It is time that we Arabs express reciprocal compassion and support.
- The existence of the State of Israel is a fact that should be accepted by the Arab world.
- Israel is a legitimate state that is not a threat but an asset in the Middle East.
- Every major world religion has a center of gravity. Islam has Mecca, and Judaism certainly deserves its presence in Israel and Jerusalem.
- Diversity should not be a virtue only in the United States, but should be encouraged around the world. We support a diverse Middle East with protection for human rights and respect and equality under the law to all minorities, including Jews and Christians.
- Arabs must end the boycott of Israel.
- Palestinians have several options but are deprived from exercising them because of their leadership, the Arab League, and surrounding Arab and Muslim countries who do not want to see Palestinians live in harmony with Israel.
- If Palestinians want democracy, they can start practicing it now.
- We stand firmly against suicide/homicide terrorism as a form of jihad.
- We are appalled by the horrific act of terror against the USA on September 11, 2001.
- Arab media should end the incitement and misinformation that result in Arab street rage and violence.

- We are eager to see major reformation in how Islam is taught and channeled in order to bring out the best in Muslims and contribute to the uplifting of the human spirit and advancement of civilization.
- We believe in freedom to choose or change one's religion.
- We cherish and acknowledge the beauty and contributions of the Middle East culture, but recognize that the Arab/Muslim world is in desperate need of constructive self-criticism and reform.

I put the Web site together myself—without the support of any organization—with the part-time help of my husband, who was very supportive and lent his professional Web design skills to the project. My abilities to run a Web site were limited and so were my resources, but I did the best I could. The response to the Web site was phenomenal. I received e-mails from all over the Middle East and from other Muslims around the world. Arab fear of speaking out in support of Israel was understandable, so when they asked me, "Please don't post my name," I honored that request. There were other guidelines I followed. For instance, I did not publish letters from former Muslim converts who were hostile to Islam, because I did not want to dilute the positive message of the Web site.

I also received e-mails from Jews and Christians who were stunned by what they were reading. They could not believe what I and other Muslims wrote. The Jewish response, particularly, would bring tears to the eyes of the hardest heart.

In 2003, before I began the Web site, I had participated in a lecture series at Carnegie Melon University called "Arabs for Israel," which was sponsored by the Young Zionists of America. Several Arabs who supported Israel spoke at this event. An Egyptian female student who attended my presentation told me she was offended when I described Arabs who blew up buses and restaurants inside Israel as terrorists. She believed they had a right to do so, and in her mind they were freedom fighters. She also insisted she was never taught hatred of Jews but only Israelis. However, I was pleasantly surprised when two other Muslim students present at the lecture told me they were grateful that I had opened their eyes to the intense hatred and anti-Semitism they grew up with. I realized the need for this open discussion among Arabs and Muslims. The taboo against supporting Israel must be broken. That taboo is simply evil.

Since 9/11, I have been speaking in support of Israel to various groups—Jewish, Christian, political, and secular. I have spoken on college campuses across the United States and Canada as well as in Europe, Israel, and South Africa. Some Arabs and Muslims who read my writings say, "She cannot be an Arab or a Muslim." They send me e-mails wondering who is behind me, who is funding me. That is the way Arabs regard those who dissent; they assume we cannot think like that on our own or act out of free will. Surely it must be a Zionist conspiracy—in their minds, that is the only possible explanation behind those Muslims or Arabs who hold views favorable to Israel or the West. When they learn more about me, they are often shocked that I lived for thirty years in the Middle East, that I was born to two Muslim parents and four Muslim grandparents, and that I am the daughter of a prominent shahid who died in the struggle with Israel. I explain to them there is no one behind me but my own conscience. Writing articles from home and running a Web site does not exactly require a fortune. I have been able to give of my time because I am semiretired. Certainly, without my husband's moral and financial support, I could not have done what I am doing. He has encouraged me and stood behind my work 100 percent. But essentially it is just me, working for what I believe is right.

Before I began actively appearing and speaking on college campuses in support of Israel, I was of course aware of the activism on U.S. campuses by the Muslim and Arab organizations, but when I actually began experiencing it firsthand I was stunned. Radical Islam is not just powerful in the Middle East but is thriving inside the free world, especially in the institutions of higher learning in America. The rallying point for this insidious effort is to exploit the Palestinian-Israeli issue. In doing so, Jewish students across America are constantly put on the defensive, and they and other American students are fed outrageous misinformation.

In March of 2004 at the University of California, in Santa Barbara, I accompanied guest speaker Sheikh Professor Abdul Hadi Palazzi, Director of the Cultural Institute of the Italian Islamic Community and a vocal critic of militant Islam, who was invited to speak on campus. His speech focused on his opposition to terrorism. He described suicide and the murder of civilians as an aberration to Islam. His speech was simply anti-terrorism and he never mentioned Israel. This remarkable Italian Muslim cleric is a supporter of Israel, but that was not the topic of his speech. On his Web site, he often mentions verses in the Koran on God's Covenant with Israel. For instance, "Children of Israel, remember the favor I [Allah] have bestowed upon you, and that I exalted you above the nations" (Koran, The Cow, Sura 2:47).

One would think that the university's Muslims, who vigorously proclaim Islam as a religion of peace, would have been appreciative of Palazzi's message. However, the Muslim Students Association at the university disrupted the event during the question-and-answer period, criticizing Sheikh Palazzi for not beginning his speech by saying "In the name of Allah and his Prophet Mohammed," totally ignoring the fact that the sheikh was not addressing Muslims in a mosque.

Some of the students were holding Islamic prayer beads and wearing clothing that is usually worn only when attending a mosque. They were loud, rude, and aggressively "in your face." It became obvious that they did not want to ask questions but came only to be disrespectful to Professor Palazzi. Two men who claimed to attend an Afghani mosque used their time at the microphone to give their own speeches against the sheikh. When they were politely asked to state their question, they refused, claiming "freedom of speech." A female Muslim student expressed her support of terrorism by asking, "If not terrorism, what would Palestinians then do against the oppression?" At this point, other Muslim students yelled, "We cannot live with Zionism" and even threateningly told the professor, "You are finished, man!" The Muslim students' leader then called on his group to leave the hall, and as they did they were hurling insults at the sheikh.

In 2004, I participated in a panel with a Jewish professor at a library in California where several Egyptian women were in the audience. As soon as I began speaking, I heard yelling by some of them, and two women left the room. In the question-and-answer portion of the event, an Egyptian woman told us, "The Jewish speaker is justified in being biased about Israel, but you [referring to me] are a traitor!"

My speaking requests increased consistently, and I began going on extended tours. I spoke in London, where Muslims in the audience expressed their belief that 9/11 was perpetrated by the U.S. government itself. In Berlin I spoke with an Arab woman who spoke only French and could not speak a word of Arabic, although she claimed she had lived in Algeria all her life. She accused me and my companions of being CIA or U.S. State Department representatives. She was extremely angry and left the room when I discussed Islamic terrorism and radicalism, and its impact on the culture of Europe.

In Rome I was happy to meet an Egyptian Italian journalist, Magdi Allam, who also speaks against terrorism and in support of peace with Israel. During these tours, despite the interruptions and hate encountered, I was often myself inspired as much as I inspired others.

In early 2006, the University of Guelph in Canada cancelled my presentation after the Muslim student association demanded that I not speak, claiming that I have a hateful message. My speech, which is posted on my Web site, was described as very positive by 99 percent of everyone who heard it at the rest of the thirteen campuses I visited on that particular tour. For every Muslim student who rails against me, there are often several Muslim students who tell me they appreciate my speech. As to the Jewish and American audiences, most are extremely supportive. People often come up in tears afterward, thanking me for what I say.

At York University in Canada, Muslim students shouted, "Shame, shame, shame," and "Racist, Racist," during the question-and-answer period. They falsely accused me of saying that *all* Muslims are terrorists. But at the same time, many of them refused to condemn terrorism or take responsibility for breeding terrorists in Arab culture. Some whispered to me as I was leaving, "How dare you!" An indignant thirty-year-old Muslim student in a wheelchair introduced himself as the head of the student association—I was told he'd been a student there for twelve years. He said he would demand an apology from the Jewish group that sponsored my presentation. There was nothing I said that day that should offend Islam—it is terrorism, not Islam, that I condemn. There were no apologies given to that bully. I often wonder who pays the tuitions for all these Muslim students who are sent from the Arab world to get their education in the United States, often staying within these institutions for years, and who while here spend a lot of time spreading anti-American and anti-Semitic propaganda.

On one college campus, I was approached by an Arab student who called me "a terror apologist," meaning—I suppose—that Arabs and Muslims should not apologize for terrorism! His excuse was that all cultures have terrorists, not just Arabs. Other students denied the existence of hate speech in the Arab world, but when I asked these students how long they had lived in the Arab world, the answer was either just a few years or none at all.

When I spoke at a Brooklyn college, my audience included several Muslim women with headscarves who told me they supported polygamy. During my presentation, one of them got up then returned, apparently to bring in a group of bearded Muslim men who did not appear to be students. The sight of these men was not intimidating to me, but the Jewish students in the audience appeared intimidated. The bearded men were not particularly strong in build or eloquent in speech, but they seemed ready for a confrontation. In my mind they looked almost comical, but I sensed that the Jewish students feared them and overestimated their power. That was precisely the impact they were trying to achieve: intimidation of the Jewish students and silencing of Arab Americans like myself. But I knew them too well to fear them or be silenced by them. They were pathetic, and clearly were not in America to become Americans. Instead, they appeared to be here with an agenda and to exercise control over others. They looked very much like the Muslim Brotherhood in Egypt; a group once squashed like flies by President Gamal Abdel Nasser but now gaining control and influence within Egypt. The men asked questions even though they had come at the end of my speech and so didn't hear most of it. They accused me of misrepresenting the word "jihad." So I asked them to define it for me. They said it should be "inner struggle." I congratulated them on their admirable new peaceful interpretation of jihad and told them that interpretation was not what we Arabs grew up with in the Middle East. I told them Arab kids in the Middle East needed their enlightened expertise in reforming the educational system in the Arab world and not just in the eyes of the American audience. I encouraged them to send a letter to Al-Azhar University and Arab media calling upon them to start teaching jihad in the new peaceful light they were advocating to me in front of an American audience. They were speechless after my words of "encouragement." I thanked them for their presence, and they left the hall scratching their heads.

During an April 2006 tour, I asked my Muslim audiences how many of them did something to save the life of the Afghani man sentenced to death for converting to Christianity. Did any of them demonstrate in front of the Afghani embassy demanding the man be set free? I heard silence—which meant that nothing was done to save that Afghani convert's life by the so-called Muslim moderates who call their religion "the religion of peace." No Muslim group anywhere in the world came to that poor man's rescue, only Christian and Western groups worked to save his life. Under Islamic law, a Muslim who converts to another religion is to be put to death. Does this sound like a religion of peace?

As I spoke on campus after campus, it became clear that Muslim students in America, instead of thinking for themselves, are imprisoned in a collective mentality based on wrong assumptions and worn-out platitudes. Saying that "there are extremists and terrorists in every religion" somehow becomes an excuse for Islamic terrorism. Israel striking back at terrorists makes them somehow responsible for terrorism!

When Muslim students ask me to criticize Israel's action of bulldozing the homes of terrorists, I tell them that when terrorism ends, or even abates for one year, I will be the first one to stand in front of the Israeli embassy demanding an end to any retaliation inside Palestinian areas. But I cannot do that now when Israeli children are being killed while riding buses to school or eating pizza in a café. I often tell my Muslim audience to put themselves in the shoes of the Israeli prime minister. Like any leader, his number one job is to protect his people or else he is out of office. When a terrorist attacks Israeli civilians, what do Arabs expect the Israeli leader to do? I offer a little quiz with four choices: (1) Turn the other cheek and allow them to throw you in the Mediterranean like they continually threaten to do. (2) Blow up the whole West Bank and Gaza. (3) Find an Israeli nut case from a mental hospital, strap him with a dynamite belt, and tell him to blow himself up in a Palestinian restaurant or on a bus. Or, (4) bulldoze the home of the Arab terrorist who just killed your Israeli citizens, giving the residents of the house forty-eight hours to leave and take their valuables. Answer number 4 is perhaps the most humane of all, other than turning the other check and allowing the total destruction of Israel.

Without fail, after every speech, Muslim critics employ all the same tired excuses and arguments that confuse the idealism of Islam with the reality of the actions of Muslims and Muslim society. For example, when I speak about Muslim terrorists, the response is that "Islam is a religion of peace." When I say polygamy is hurting the Muslim family unit, Muslim women become very defensive and totally ignore the tragedies stemming out of polygamy in the Muslim world. Their defense is to say that "polygamy is allowed only under certain conditions; that a Muslim man must to be totally fair with all the wives." Then they add that the Prophet Muhammad was the only one who could be fair equally to all his wives and that ordinary Muslim men could not be fair to all of them equally. Therefore, by this circular thinking and quoting the ideals of the book, in their eyes they have solved the problem. They have constructed a logic, which says polygamy is no longer a problem since men cannot apply it the same way Muhammad did. One Muslim student defended polygamy by saying that no one in her family practiced polygamy. I asked her, "Where does your family live?" She said in the USA. I told her she had U.S. laws to thank for protecting Muslim women in her family from the tragedy and insecurity of polygamy practiced elsewhere in the Muslim world. I advised her to conduct research about polygamy in the Middle East by looking into the tragedies dealt with by sharia family courts across the Muslim world.

When I spoke about the oppression of Saudi women, an attractive, modern-looking, uncovered Saudi girl told me repeatedly in the question-and-answer session, "Look at me, look at me, do I look like an oppressed Saudi?" I told her, "If you can walk like that in Saudi Arabia, then you are not."

One Egyptian student defiantly told me after my speech, "You don't speak for me." I told her I hope not and that I never claimed to speak for her or for any other person. I told her I speak only for myself as an Arab American. I reminded her that in a democracy we do not speak for each other and that I hope to one day see the Arab world with many different political parties and many different views, with everyone respecting those differences of opinions. She also objected to my speaking about the oppression of Egyptian Coptic Christians. She said, "I had many Coptic friends, and they never complained to me that they were discriminated against. You are exaggerating their problems." At the end of that same lecture I was approached by another Egyptian student who told me she was Coptic and was too scared to speak in front of the Muslim student union members because they intimidate her even right here in America. She told me she and her family moved to the United States because of the discrimination they suffered in Egypt.

Simply put, the Muslim student organizations wanted to advocate "Islam as a religion of peace" through intimidation and arguments that made no sense. They are still victimizing Coptic students who are too frightened to speak their views even though they have left Egypt and are living under U.S. freedoms. Is that the way for Muslim students to show the world the compassion, forgiveness, and tolerance of Islam?

Vocal American Muslims in my audience often refuse to condemn Hamas as a terror group. They say Israel is born out of sin and should not exist. I consider such statements by Muslims in the heart of our institutions of higher learning an embarrassment. It is not just the Jewish students who should be offended by such statements, but any decent human being. Defending Hamas is supporting terrorism. What arrogance to say that a group of people has no right to exist. The cruelty of what some people in my culture advocate never ceases to amaze me.

Even by Egyptian standards, I am personally shocked by the degree of radicalism I am encountering on American campuses. I look at the covered-up women and the bearded men who appear to be in an exclusive club with a chip on their shoulder and an us-against-them, holier-than-thou attitude. Though we share the same cultural background, I cannot relate to them. I am stunned to see them choose to revive the worst of Islamic culture in America rather than be part of America and demonstrate the best of Islamic culture. I have met many Egyptian Americans who tell me they also cannot relate to their culture of origin—perhaps half the Muslims in America do indeed reject the extremists and fanatics, but stay silent. Most Egyptians who visit Egypt come back to the United

States depressed over the conditions in Egypt and the rest of the Arab world. Many even say, "We don't want to go visit again."

If the majority of American Muslims reject fanaticism, then how does one explain the presence of radical Islam in the heart of U.S. educational institutions? This is not by mere coincidence. Saudi Arabia and oil-wealthy Arab countries support such student Muslim organizations and fund Islamic and Middle East studies departments to promulgate their radical views. They are very well organized.

A further word about the Muslim young women I have encountered on my speaking tours: On every campus I visit, there are always groups of covered-up female Muslim students, a phenomenon one never saw in America or even the Middle East twenty years ago. When I told one covered-up Egyptian Muslim student that when I lived in Egypt, no one was covered up, she reluctantly agreed and said her mother didn't cover up until the late seventies. Her American friend responded, "I never knew that Islamic attire was a *new* thing." I consider myself a reasonable feminist who wants equality and respect, but I feel that treating one's body like a tempting juicy steak that should be covered up—besides being uncomfortable and impractical—implies an arrogant, holier-than-thou attitude. It also displays a symbol of the oppressive ugly past of the Middle East and an in-your-face defiance of all the achievements women have fought for in the last one hundred years. These young women often openly defend polygamy and sharia laws, but have no clue about what happens in sharia courts around the Middle East and the family tragedies that result from the oppression of women in such courts. Their opinions on polygamy and divorce laws are naive because they judge the issues from their own personal perspective where they live protected by American laws, enjoying privileges Muslim women in the Middle East do not have. These girls, so eager to stand out from the other American college women, are championing an oppressive lifestyle they are not living under. I would doubt that even they would tolerate living under the Saudi or

Iranian system. Over there they would probably burn their burkas and demand their equal rights. But in America they love to show defiance. Unfortunately, these naive young women are contributing to the oppression of women in the Middle East by their hard-line stand against reforming sharia laws.

How ironic that while sharia laws are being challenged by brave Arab and Muslim feminists in the Middle East, we are seeing radical Muslim groups promoting sharia laws to apply to Muslims in Canada! I was glad that the Canadian government rejected the attempts of radical Muslim groups to bring sharia laws into the West. In my mind I wondered whether we might even see the day where sharia is reformed in the Middle East but practiced by Muslims in the West. I hope not.

Women's issues have become a hot-button issue, which sometimes impacts my speaking engagements—perhaps because I am willing to speak my mind and tell the truth rather than follow the latest trends in political correctness. In 2004, when I spoke at University of California Santa Cruz in Northern California, the Women Studies Department refused to sponsor my presentation. Other departments did, but not Women Studies. On the other hand, in April 2006, I spoke on a panel in New York on "Middle East Women's Rights," and the response to my presentation was very positive.

One of my most memorable experiences occurred when I was invited in 2004 to speak to a Jewish group called Jimena.org, which stands for "Jews Indigenous to the Middle East and North Africa." That is a group of Jews who were born and lived in Arab countries. At this event, I met Jews from Egypt, Libya, Yemen, Iraq, Syria, and Morocco. They all spoke Arabic and graciously welcomed me to speak. I saw a woman about my age who spoke to me with an Egyptian accent and who looked familiar. We looked at each other, puzzled. Then in my mind I saw a young woman who was at the American University in Cairo with me. She also recognized me, and we realized that we had studied at the American University at the same time, between 1965 and 1969. When I asked her why she had disappeared before graduation, she told me her story. After the 1967 war, her fiancé and all the male members of his family were arrested by Nasser and placed in the Torrah prison in Cairo. It was a brutal jail, where they had to sleep on concrete floors three to a small cell and were tortured and sexually assaulted. These were educated Jews from good upper-class families in Egypt. She said the jailed Jewish Egyptian men begged the women of their families to leave Egypt, but the women refused to go without their men. Under pressure from Western governments, the men were finally released in 1969 and forced to leave Egypt immediately. That explains why my friend suddenly left Egypt before our graduation at the American University. When we were students together I didn't even realize she was Jewish, and I had no idea what she was going through at the time.

We thought we had left all the oppression behind. But it has followed us right here in America, where Jews, Copts, and Arab and Muslim speakers like myself are being silenced and intimidated by radical Muslims right here in America. We are accused of hate speech if we criticize terrorism and radicalism. Our accusers resort to verbal abuse, satire, character assassination, and outright lies. Anyone from my culture who stands up for the war on terror is called names: Islamophobe, bigot, racist, and traitor. Some have been accused of not being true Muslims. They are called apostates and even infidels.

Now I am called an infidel! In their eyes, I am no longer a good Arab or a good Muslim for supporting the war on terror, advocating peace with Israel, and standing up to the culture of jihad. I get dirty looks from Muslim men as I am speaking. With their eyes they are saying, "How dare you, a woman, speak against what we believe in!" They know that if I were back home, I could have been easily silenced, jailed, or killed.

We often hear that "moderate" Muslims are the majority and that terrorist supporters are a minority fringe group. However, when genuine Islamic moderate leaders stand firm against terrorism, we do not see majority Muslim support for their views. To the contrary, such "moderates" shout the speakers down, condemn, and threaten them.

My speaking style is noncombative and quite respectful of Muslim audiences, whom I challenge to stand against terrorists who give Islam a bad name. I emphasize that Arab and Muslim critics of radical Islam are not the problem; the terrorists are the problem. It does not matter how many times I stress that I am not speaking about Islam, but *radical* Islam. They are offended anyway and say they object to the expression "radical Islam" or "political Islam." My answer to that is: Give me whatever term you want to describe Muslim terrorists and their supporters and those who hold the Koran with one hand and slaughter the innocent with the other, while chanting *"Allahu Akbar."* Give me a term for such people and I will use that term. They cannot come up with any name to describe them.

Coincidences continued to occur as I traveled the country speaking. On a tour in Minnesota, I met an older Israeli gentleman who told me that he was a young Israeli soldier in Israel in the 1950s during the fedayeen operations. He said that he fought them from the Israeli side and confirmed that they did cause a lot of problems inside Israel. He added that some Muslim Druze who lived inside Israel were also fighting against the fedayeen infiltrators. As we spoke, he named my father by name. That gentlemen and I hugged, and we both had tears in our eyes.

My speaking career would finally take me to Israel in November of 2004 when I was invited to speak at the second annual Jerusalem Summit held at the historic King David Hotel overlooking the Old City. Visiting Israel is a major taboo in all Arab countries and part of the boycott of Israel. Israel's neighbors, the twenty-two Arab countries that compose the Arab League, forbid their people to visit or do business with Israel and its citizens. Even Arab Christians have been forbidden to visit their holy sites in Israel. Despite signing a peace treaty with Israel, which encouraged travel and tourism between the two countries, Egypt has kept its ban firmly in place. And apparently some Arab Americans also continue to abide by travel restrictions imposed by faroff tyrants.

Despite my vocal support for Israel, I viewed my upcoming visit with some trepidation. My mother had been graciously welcomed by Israel when she went to be with my brother as he recuperated in the Jerusalem hospital that saved his life. I had been invited to come. Israel knew of my support. Yet somewhere deep inside, I wondered, Will they accept me? Will they look at me and somehow know that my father once organized raids into Israel, killing innocent Israeli civilians? Will I accidentally meet people on the street who are the children of people my father killed? And will I pass in the street someone responsible for killing my father? Will they resent me because I come from a culture where many have sworn to annihilate them? All these mixed emotions swirled in me as I contemplated my upcoming trip.

I flew to Israel on El Al airlines because I wanted to have the total Israel experience from start to finish. El Al has always needed to be very security conscious, and the employees of El Al were very thorough, very polite—and somewhat apologetic—when it came to searching my luggage. I told them to please do their job and that searching my luggage thoroughly did not bother me in the least.

My trip to Israel began on the beautiful Mediterranean coast, at Ben Gurion Airport near Tel Aviv, one of the most beautiful airports I have ever been in. My heart was pounding with excitement after landing in Israel; a land that was so close physically, yet so far mentally from where I lived as a child in Gaza. Here I was, a fifty-six-year-old woman, the daughter of a man who died fighting Israel, now extending my hand to this country in peace and love. I sat in a taxi for the half-hour it took to travel from the east side of Israel to Jerusalem, the ancient holy city. In the taxicab, I looked around me. *This is Israel! The forbidden country*, I said to myself. I lived thirty years of my life on the other side of the southern border with Israel. Gaza was just a few kilometers to the south, and Cairo, less than one hour's flight! I thought about how incredible it was that this country had survived, let alone thrived, with my homeland and the whole Arab world doing all they can to blame, boycott, spread propaganda, attack militarily, and terrorize this small country. It must be God's protective hands over this little state, I thought. The sight of a sign on the road that said JERUSALEM gave me chills of anticipation. As we drove into the city, a sense of awe came over me. I felt a deep sadness for everyone in the region.

When I was growing up I did not know the history of Jerusalem. We were taught that it was a city taken away from the Arabs by Jewish invaders. I was never taught that Jerusalem was the ancient capital of the Jews, that King Solomon built the first temple in 957 B.C., that it was destroyed in 586 B.C. and the Jews taken into exile in Babylon, that the temple was then rebuilt seventy years later, that the city was conquered and reconquered over the many thousands of years, until finally, in A.D. 70, the Romans utterly destroyed the second temple and dispersed the Jews, scattering them to the far-flung edges of the Roman Empire—Spain, Arab lands, and Europe. Jews everywhere, over the ages when they celebrate Passover, have said the words, "Next year in Jerusalem," longing for their homeland. Furthermore, historically, when things did not go well between Jews and Arabs in Arab countries, Jews were often told by Arabs, "Why don't you go to Jerusalem, your holy land"—a fact now conveniently forgotten.

Many Arabs also ignore the fact that the land of Israel is also the birthplace of Christianity, the land where Jesus walked and taught. Jerusalem was the site of his crucifixion and resurrection. Therefore, indeed Jerusalem is the historically pivotal holy city for both Christians and Jews. Then six years after the death of the Prophet Muhammad, in A.D. 638, Jerusalem was captured by the Muslims. Caliph Umar built a small mosque on the site of the ruined Jewish temple, then sixty-some years later, the ruling Caliph built the more elaborate Dome of the Rock Mosque to commemorate the spot where Muhammad is said to have ascended into heaven. While Jerusalem's Dome of the Rock is important to Muslims, Mecca and Medina are the principal holy sites for Islam.

Growing up in Egypt, I knew nothing of this history. I was not taught that the Jews were living in Israel thousands of years before Islam even began. Instead, Arab children are taught that the Jews are the descendents of dogs and pigs, a despicable people who have usurped the Arab land of Palestine, and they must be annihilated and driven into the sea.

When Arab students and Muslim critics at my speaking engagements insist that the Palestinians have the only rightful claim to Jerusalem, I often have asked them to imagine a reverse scenario. What if seven centuries after the Prophet Muhammad and the birth of Islam, Jews lay claim to Mecca and refused to allow Muslims to come worship at their holiest sites? That comparison often leaves my critics speechless.

Now as I was entering this holy city, I could not help but think and long for the day when the Holy Land can be made truly holy by giving the Jews the respect and security they deserve in their homeland. I took a moment to also remember the Christian minorities in Arab countries—people of faith forbidden to visit their Holy Land. Many of these Arab Christians, such as the Egyptian Copts, have a history that goes back more than six hundred years before the birth of Islam.

In Bethlehem, birthplace of Jesus Christ, I visited the Church of the Nativity. I expected to see Christians milling about this holiest of sites, but the city population was predominantly Muslim. Entering the church, I noticed a tiny office off to the side. From where I stood, I could see a picture of Yasser Arafat hanging on the wall.

The Christian population of Bethlehem began leaving in fear after the PLO took over the area starting in 1993 after the Oslo Accords. When I saw Jesus Christ's birthplace surrounded by Muslims, I could not help but wonder how many Christians and Jews are allowed in Mecca and Medina? (The answer, of course, is zero.) Yet, to this day, Israel respects all religions, giving people of all faiths protection and access to their religious sites.

To access Bethlehem from Jerusalem and back, I passed through a checkpoint twice. Each time, the Arab taxi driver and I were treated by Israeli soldiers with professional courtesy. I spoke with Israeli Arabs during my visit, and not one complained to me about any discrimination or expressed a wish to move elsewhere. Within Israel's democracy, Arab women and men can vote and practice their religion freely, something Jews cannot do in twenty-two Arab Muslim countries. In fact, several Muslims told me that their travels to neighboring countries in the Middle East made them appreciate Israel's freedoms. One recounted his experience visiting Egypt, where he was accused of being a Zionist because of his Israeli passport. He wondered aloud, "Can you imagine how they would treat us if we were Jews?"

My last experience before leaving Tel Aviv left a lasting impression with me. I visited a small Arab pastry and falafel shop together with a prominent Israeli journalist, Smadar Perry. She told the Arab owners, who greeted her warmly as one of their valued customers, that I was from Egypt. The owners displayed that wonderful Middle Eastern graciousness and hospitality that I so much love about my culture. They didn't want to take our money and gave us free sahlab drinks. As we enjoyed our wonderful sahlab drink, I looked around me. The place was alive with Muslim and Jewish customers who coexisted cheerfully in the store. It was a wonderful picture of perhaps what could be the future of the area—Arabs and Jews living in harmony and mutual respect.

I know that it is possible. I pray that it will one day come to be.

Israel is not perfect, but it has passed a test of amazing endurance, surviving and thriving in a sea of hatred, violence, and terror. Its people remain optimistic, but they desperately need relief from the fear and violence that dominates daily life. I wish the Arab world could see what I saw in Israel—a harmless state that just wants to live in peace with its neighbors.

As I traveled across the small country of Israel and met its people, I continually asked myself: *What are Arabs afraid of? Why are Arab governments going to such extensive efforts to conceal Israel from being seen for what it is in the eyes of regular Arab folks?*

Furthermore, why does the world stand by and do nothing to stop the terrorism against Israel? Worse, why do they condemn Israel when it attempts to defend itself? Even during the worst of times, Jews never flew airplanes into German buildings; they never terrorized the world even when they were being expelled, tortured, and exterminated. I cannot understand how Israel tolerated all this abuse without completely losing its moral standards, faith, and optimism. After my visit, I am even more committed to supporting Israel, a country that has been terrorized since its existence in 1948 and yet has refused to be dragged into the evil and darkness surrounding it.

In September 2005, I was invited to speak in South Africa. In Johannesburg I was stunned to discover one of the most radical and anti-Semitic Muslim groups I have ever encountered. When I was interviewed by a radio show, I was angrily attacked by Muslim callers who accused me of loving the enemy of Islam, the Jews! I stood firm against a barrage of lies and provocations the callers threw at me, answering each question honestly. I did not flinch from defending Israel. The truth is the world is getting increasingly more anti-Semitic. Decent people should speak out against those who perpetuate these lies. To this day, Arab agitation is reviving anti-Semitism in Europe and around the globe—even in Africa. What are we afraid of? We have elevated a fear of Jews to a level that has never existed before in the history of the Middle East. Why? What is so difficult about accepting the presence of five million Jews in an ocean of a billion and a half Muslims?

I believe that the Arab/Muslim world has lost its moral equilibrium and must travel a long road toward reformation. Their paranoid obsession with Israel as the bogeyman in the neighborhood is becoming increasingly unbelievable, and after the cheering crowds on 9/11, their cause is no longer credible.

As an Arab, I often feel deep sadness and shame over what my people have done and are still doing to Israel. Islam should symbolize generosity and aiding the needy. Jews are not alien to our culture. We are connected through history, language, culture, and religion. Our cousins needed protection after World War II; we were obligated to give it to them. We had a golden opportunity to show the world that Islam is truly a religion of peace, compassion, and tolerance by doing the right and gracious thing in 1948, and that was accepting the UN mandate and welcoming the tiny state of Israel to our region. But instead, my people chose to emulate Hitler's defeated monstrous mission to annihilate the Jews. We rejected Jews and denied them any right to their historical homeland. Even Middle Eastern Jews, whose culture and language are Arabic, and who now compose the largest proportion of the population of Israel, apparently did not deserve our sympathy or kindness.

For more than fifty-eight years, Arabs have been blinded by hatred, arrogance, envy, narcissism, and groundless fear. In the process of destroying Israel, their perceived enemy, they are also destroying themselves. I sincerely want to bend on my knees and apologize to the Jewish people on behalf of my people. I am only one person, but I am encouraged by the many e-mails from Arabs who are also sickened by Arab wickedness toward Israel.

To the people of Israel I want to say: You are an inspiration to people who choose to see the truth. You are my heroes. You are a people of faith who will not submit to the darkness and evil surrounding you. You live by honorable principles and moral standards and struggle even in your darkest hours to maintain them. Your courage, persistence, and faith have been an example to me and many other Arabs. Continue doing what you are doing; never give up; continue riding your buses, continue treating Arabs in your hospitals. Do not be in a rush for a quick peace agreement. The people in the area are not ready yet for peace. Protect yourself from terrorism and, if necessary, keep the fence up high and one day the arrogance, intolerance, and cruelty around you will end when God takes away the oil weapon from the hands of Arabs who have used it against you, the world, and ultimately themselves. The good people of the world must support you and they will. I believe that goodness always wins at the end.

I now fully understand why the United States supports Israel and rightfully so. My love of America now extends to Israel. I support Israel because it is not a threat to Arab nations. No one in his right mind would think that Israel would want to occupy Damascus,

Cairo, or Baghdad. Israel is fighting for its very existence. What are Arabs fighting for? They are not fighting for their existence; they are fighting a religious war that has become a ritual and a goal in and of itself.

In early 2006, I was privileged to go on a "Mothers for Peace" tour with an Israeli woman, Miri Eisin, a former colonel in the Israel Defense Force with a background in intelligence. Like me, she is the mother of three children. Miri's presentation brought to life the everyday dilemma every Israeli mother had to face during the intifada—and continues to face every day—decisions about allowing their children to take buses and go to public places when the terror threat is part of everyday life. Miri Eisin and I toured across the country, from Washington, D.C., to New York, to the Midwest and California, speaking to a variety of audiences as two mothers searching for peace and understanding between our two peoples, exploring ways to abolish terror and fear in our beloved Middle East and make a better world for our children.

A few weeks later, on my London tour, I also had the privilege to speak along with another Israeli woman, Hagit Mendellevich, whose thirteen-year-old son Yuval was killed in a suicide bombing in 2003. Hagit's pain was heartfelt, and her emotionally charged speech calling for peace struck a chord with our listeners. Our presentations did not have a political message as much as a humanitarian message in defense of the innocent children in the Middle East, both Arabs and Jews, whom we believed deserve better than to grow up with violence, war, hatred, and terror.

I wish to see the day when Arab and Israeli women can also take their message of peace to Arab capitals. If our common goal in the Middle East is peace, then each side needs to see the humanity and suffering of the other. But so far my side—the Arab side—is not yet ready to allow its people to see the truth about Israeli suffering.

Eleven | The Challenge for America

M y life has been a journey from hatred to love, from a culture that stifled joy and creativity, to a life of freedom and endless possibilities. Because I love my adopted country, I have a duty to alert my fellow Americans to a real and present danger.

Radical Islam has declared war on America and on the West, and the majority of Muslims either support or make excuses for terrorism. It is a kind of war we've never before fought. Worse than communism and Nazism, global jihad is fueled by radicals who believe their mission to conquer the world is God's command, that it is the obligation of the good Muslims to spread Islam by any means. There is no chance that Americans will abandon their precious hard-fought freedoms to embrace the brutal, totalitarian, medieval lifestyle and belief system that radical Islam advocates. Therefore, the only way to "win" us over is by force, just as they captured Egypt, Mesopotamia, Turkey, and much of the Near East in the seventh century.

Of course, not all Muslims are terrorists, but the fear, defensiveness, and silence of the majority is "heard" loud and clear as agreement by the radicals. Cries to kill the infidels, kill the Americans, kill the Jews and Christians, echo in the holiest of places, in mosques across the Muslim world. But this war is not holy. Make no mistake: religion is the game the radical leadership plays as a camouflage for greed. All the radical Muslim countries combined do not amount to a military superpower, yet terrorism has given them negotiating power and, in their view, a kind of "respect" based on fear. In country after country, radical elements have overcome moderates and seized power, and they do not flinch from stating their intentions. Witness the stunning victory of Hamas in the Palestinian territories and the growing strength of the Muslim Brotherhood in Egypt. American Muslims I speak with increasingly express fear of going back to visit their countries of origin. Iran's president has openly threatened the West with terrorism if the West attacks its nuclear facilities. He has also repeatedly made clear his intention to annihilate Israel. When the president of Iran called on young volunteers for suicide/homicide operations, he had thousands of takers. In their goal of world domination, our enemy has discovered a powerful weapon of mass destruction, the suicide/homicide bomber.

So how do we fight terrorism? What is the West to do? What should America do? Every Arab I know who is honestly against terrorism says the same thing: The West should get tougher. For starters, we need to be specific in defining our enemy by name and location. We need to hold the nations that produce terrorists and the governments that threaten to use them responsible. Furthermore, we must inform these nations that it doesn't matter how often they say they are against terrorism in English, we are beginning to translate what they say in Arabic to their own people and that is what we will judge them by. Terrorism is a weapon that gives its state supporters deniability. They leave the dirty work to the shadowy organizations while giving lip service disapproval. That way countries who produce and promote terrorism can always claim: "We didn't do it." Destruction and carnage in the streets of New

York, London, or Madrid is a weapon that can be blamed on no nation but gets the blessings and support of many Muslims.

The West must also open its eyes to the other factors working in coordination with terrorist activities: oil boycotts, threats to moderate Muslims who speak out, financial rewards for those who defend jihadists and make excuses for terror. Terror has a whole culture of support around it.

Western democracies have a great challenge ahead. Are they ready to fight global jihad? Will they cherish and love their freedom and democracy more than the terrorists love going to heaven and conquering the world for Islam? We are already in World War III, but many in the West are still in denial. Can the West win this war given today's attention to political correctness, our open and free society, and nearly unfettered immigration from radical Muslim countries? Can we fight terrorism without sacrificing our own freedom and ideals of tolerance and equality? These are not easy questions. Nor are the answers easy.

Islamist danger is hard to identify by many in the West who respect freedom of religion and believe immigrants have the right to choose not to assimilate into the larger American community if they so desire. America encourages its citizens to cherish and celebrate their cultural diversity. We love our Cinco de Mayo picnics and St. Patrick's Day parades. We feel good when we see Jews congregate in their synagogues for Rosh Hashanah, or Muslims congregate at their mosques for the end of Ramadan or Christians carry palm fronds on Palm Sunday. We love the fireworks and dragon dances on the Chinese New Year, the pageantry of Greek Orthodox Easter, or the rowdy fun of Oktoberfest. This is the kind of multiculturism America cherishes. It makes our society robust, exciting, and vital. But we assume that all the people who have come from around the world to this great melting pot genuinely value tolerance, freedom of religion, separation of church and state, and the protection of civil liberties. Why else would they have come to America?

But what about those who immigrate to destroy our culture instead of to contribute to it? Can we continue worshipping multiculturalism and cultural relativism even at the expense of our own safety and freedom? Does our immigration policy lend itself to being used and abused by people who want to conquer us? We need to learn from the many examples around the world of Muslim minorities in such places as the Philippines, India, and Russia who are fighting and terrorizing for a separatist movement. Are we going to wait until Muslims congregate in parts of America and demand a separatist movement? How do we handle radicals who immigrate to our shores, teach hatred and anti-Semitism, refuse to assimilate, criticize the American way of life, its government and politics, then claim discrimination, profiling, and even cry "Death to America" as part of their free speech? People like Sami al Aryan, the former professor at the University of Southern Florida who was shouting "Death to America" in one of his speeches right here in America even as he was waiting to become a citizen.

Having lived in the West now for close to thirty years, I see its vulnerabilities. It takes constant and persistent hard work to maintain the values of democracy and freedom. Practical solutions must be adjusted and revised constantly, because what worked for us in the past might not work in our present predicament, and the ideals and values of the present might not work with an enemy with archaic, medieval values of subjugation.

The West is always concerned with trade imbalance, but are we equally concerned with cultural imbalance? By cultural imbalance I mean countries like Saudi Arabia who have access inside American society while giving America no access inside Saudi Arabian society. Radical Muslims regard non-Muslims walking on their land as an insult, a desecration of Muslim land, and some Muslim preachers go as far as to say they should be killed. The radical sheikh Hamza in Britain said non-Muslims walking on Muslim lands are like cows—they can be sold as slaves or killed. Muslim countries enjoy the freedom to build mosques, preach Islam, finance Islamic groups and schools, sponsor Middle East studies departments in our state-run universities, and lobby our politicians in Washington while at the same time refusing Americans access to the same rights inside Muslim countries. American citizens or governments have no right to build synagogues or churches, or preach or establish religious schools in Saudi Arabia or any other Muslim country. In Saudi Arabia no religion other than Islam is allowed to be practiced. After 9/11, the United States was denied access to almost all Arab media and prevented from placing ads to explain the U.S. point of view in its war on terror or clarify misinformation and propaganda widespread among the Arab public. Yet over the last few decades, radical Muslim countries such as Saudi Arabia have had almost total freedom to spread radical Wahabi Islam in American society, universities, and even in prisons. Saudis are helping themselves to our open system to Islamize us, and we are not even charging them for it.

Many Americans and politicians were understandably disturbed when it was learned that a company owned by a Gulf Arab country was going to be in charge of loading and unloading goods in some U.S. ports, yet no one decries the fact that our *whole society* is open to oil-rich Arab countries to influence us as they please. We are giving Saudis and radical Muslims the most precious thing of all, the minds and hearts of our children on our college campuses, allowing them to influence and manipulate vulnerable young Americans with hate speech disguised as "Islamic Studies." Professors in departments funded by oil-rich states are spreading the same hatred, anti-Semitism, and anti-Americanism that I was fed in the Middle East, as well as sponsoring campus organizations that are intimidating patriotic American and Jewish students.

The threat is not just to our ports but also inside American culture, American media, and even Hollywood. The normally highly vocal Hollywood activists, despite threats against Los Angeles high-rise buildings and airports, have been strangely silent as innocent people were murdered by Islamic terrorists in Bali nightclubs, hotels in Amman, shops and restaurants in Turkey and Morocco, underground stations in London, and morning rush-hour trains in

Spain. Throughout its history, Hollywood has shown us that their greatest gift comes when they shine a light into the darkest places, when they give voice to the voiceless or power to the powerless. But in recent years Hollywood has given too much glory and "understanding" to terrorists and too little honor to their victims. Perhaps that will change. Some honest, gutsy Hollywood movies could reflect a mirror back to the decent people in my culture of origin where terrorism and hatred has become part of normal life and has caused unimaginable suffering.

The injustice to Christian and Jews in the Middle East should be exposed. There is too much silence in the West about the persecution of Middle Eastern Christians, especially Copts in Egypt. Saudi Arabia, the country that gave birth to Islam and calls Mecca and Medina the holy land of Muslims, denies Christians and Jews their own holy land. That is the same country that tramples on the human rights and dignity of its own people, particularly its women. Our relationship with Saudi Arabia should be consistent with our values. If we cannot survive without their oil, they cannot survive without our technology and dollars either. Our trade exchange should never be oil for our souls, oil for one-sided access to American culture to manipulate it as they please. We should never forget that fifteen out of the nineteen terrorists on September 11, 2001, were Saudi citizens and not exactly from a poor or oppressed Muslim fringe minority as some claim. Saudi Arabia and many other so-called moderate Muslim countries cannot be considered our friends when their media tells their citizens that we Americans are the enemy and deserve what happened to us on 9/11, or when their mosques tell them that we are the Great Satan and a country with no morals. If that is not a major enemy, then what does enemy mean?

America must protect its democracy, culture, and sovereignty from nations with aspirations of conquering us from within. Perhaps it is time to revise the international laws governing not just our trade imbalance, but also "access imbalance." We should demand nothing less than access for access.

Immigration laws and procedures should be examined and tightened. I remember when I was filling out my immigration papers at the American embassy in Cairo, I answered a question that asked: Do you belong to or have any affiliation to the Communist Party? Now that America has won the cold war, perhaps another question is in order: Are you a member or do you have any affiliation with radical Islamist or terror groups, or do you sympathize with them? Perhaps our immigration documents should ask some pointed, specific questions of new immigrants and require some very specific terms. New immigrants should understand and accept the concepts of separation of church and state, equal rights under the law, the differences between free speech and hate speech, and the understanding that inciting to violence is a crime. Criminals are not allowed to immigrate and spread crime and violence. Radical Muslim clerics with dual citizenship or green cards who preach jihad, hatred, incitement, and violence against America should be sent back home. That is probably the one punishment they would hate the most—having to go back to live under the likes of a Saddam Hussein, and once again experience tyranny and restrictions on speech.

Importation of radical Muslim preachers through the generous "religious visa" policy of the West has placed the Western social, political, and cultural systems and values at great risk. Radical Islam does not have mutual respect for other religions, but vows instead to replace other religions. After their many invasions, it has been a custom of Muslims not to build their own mosques side by side with other religions, but to take over other people's temples, churches, and holy sites, and replace them with mosques. Invading Muslim rulers have done exactly that in Egypt, Turkey, and India to thousands of churches, holy sites of Jews, Hindu temples, and Buddhist monasteries. The history of the Arabs and Muslims is full of outrageous denials of the humanity of those outside of their religion and ethnicity. This Nazi-style narcissism and outright invasion is dressed up and camouflaged in religious garb.

Some Westerners who take multiculturalism and compassion

beyond the bounds of common sense will defend and tolerate radical Islam's intolerance and blame themselves. The Muslim world loves this kind of naïveté because it opens the door for them to freely spread anti-Semitism and hatred against America and the West.

Perhaps we also need to address what may be lacking in our culture that renders our children vulnerable to radical Islam and other hate-mongering philosophies. To preserve the values that have made our democracy strong and just, we need to give the children of America limitations and guidance, and teach them clear-cut differences between right and wrong. We all heard the parents of John Walker Jr., the "American Taliban," proudly say they let him pick his own religion as a child and gave him a ticket to Yemen with their blessings, to go learn his newfound religion at age sixteen or so. Some Arabs jokingly say if you want to visit Yemen you need a bodyguard, but Walker's parents apparently found it appropriate to send their vulnerable sixteen-year-old son there. Is John Walker Jr. a symbol of some elements in the West attracted to the clear-cut right and wrong taught in Muslim culture? There is much to be learned here. Children need guidelines and moral certainties in a confusing world. It is the absolutes in Muslim culture that in fact form the attraction that lures some Western young men and women. For example, the differences between the sexes are clear, acknowledged, and respected in Muslim culture. Acknowledging these differences in the West has become a stigma in many circles. "Differences," by the way, should not be confused with issues of equality. Western men are sometimes lured by the fellowship, devotion, and male bonding in Muslim society. Young Western men, like Walker, might become attracted to Muslim male groups that promise total allegiance to one another under the Prophet Muhammad's example. It offers a sense of belonging and purpose. Young Western men may also be lured by the possibility of having respectful, compliant, ready-to-please covered-up Muslim women who have been brought up to "know their place." That is much less threatening to a young man who may have low self-esteem. Western women who crave acceptance and a sense of belonging may be lured by the macho, over-protective, and blonde-crazy Arab and Muslim men. However, sometimes a hidden agenda lurks behind the open arms of marrying into Muslim culture. Some Muslim men who marry Western women do it for the purpose of conversion and receiving a blessing from Allah for doing such a good deed. Very often these Western women and men are alienated from their families and culture as a result. I have received tons of letters through the years from both Western men and women who wanted to get out of the trap they fell in by marrying radical Muslims and converting to Islam. Many in the process have been abused and have had their children taken away from them.

When I speak with Muslims, I call for reform and for tolerance, and I encourage other like-minded Arabs to work to bring about a revival of the goodness in Islam. In my opinion, the first and most important reform is to change the law that forbids a Muslim from converting to another religion, an infraction that can carry a death penalty. The freedom to leave Islam is key to the reformation of Islam. If this is granted everything else follows. Why? When the free marketplace of ideas forces Islam to compete for its existence, it will reform. Right now, why reform, since followers are held within their religion by fear, just like hostages? What is Islam afraid of? If Muslims are truly confident of their religion, then they should not fear the exposure to the free marketplace for people to pick and choose what they want to believe in.

Second, stop blaming America, the West, and Israel for all the problems in the Middle East. Only when the Arab world has lost its scapegoat can it look within and accept responsibility for the failings of its own society and hold its leaders accountable. Accepting responsibility is the necessary step to righting the wrongs in society and forcing the governments of the Middle East to better serve their people's needs.

Third, American Muslims need to do some housekeeping and take control of their mosques. Some American Muslim mosque-goers have shown gross recklessness and negligence by allowing fanatics to represent them. By depending on Saudi Arabia and Pakistan's generosity, they get the likes of the arrested father-son preachers, Hamid and Umer Hayat, of Lodi, California, and Sheikh Omar Abdul-Rahman, who plotted the first World Trade Center bombing. Such people should never have been teachers of American Muslim young people or spiritual leaders of decent Muslims. These radical clerics, often with ties to al-Qaeda, Hamas, and the Muslim Brotherhood, immigrated to the United States through religious visas that are much easier to obtain than regular visas. Many of them entered before 2001 when America did not yet understand the threat of terrorism.

Most moderate Muslims choose to blend with American society and do not want to be associated with radical clerics or mosques imported from Saudi Arabia and Pakistan, and paid for by a wealthy Saudi government. But they cannot simply look the other way and ignore what is happening in radical mosques across this country. It is time to reject the politicization of Islam, the subverting of the call to prayer into calls for jihad, and changing America's Constitution to the Koran. Having thrived financially in the United States for decades, American Muslims can well afford to pay the salaries of their religious leaders and maintain their own mosques. They need to choose preachers who are more in tune to the value system of this society they have chosen to call home, values such as compassion and tolerance and responsible freedom of speech. We owe it to America to return back its generosity and kindness.

Once they have control of their own mosques, moderate Muslims need to reach out to other religions and build interfaith dialogue based on mutual respect with the Christian and Jewish communities. They need to show the positive side of Islam. Some of this is already happening, but the process needs to be accelerated. I believe American Muslims have a golden opportunity to lead the rest of the Muslim world in rediscovering and restoring the humanitarian values of Islam.

I hope the voice coming out of mosques will change. I pray for a day of reconciliation and reformation. In my mind I always see the eyes—the beautiful, haunting eyes of the Arab children, men, and women who long for a better life. I want the best for them. I love them because they are my people. I pray for peace in the Middle East. I pray that my people will abandon terrorism and work together for democracy, freedom, and equality for all.

Shortly before the Mothers for Peace tour in early 2006, our sponsoring organization was researching my background in order to
write press releases when they discovered a book written by an Israeli historian detailing my father's role in Gaza in the 1950s. *Soldier Spies*, by Israeli military intelligence expert Samuel M. Katz,
described my father as a man of integrity, skill, and "one of the
most brilliant analytical minds found in the Egyptian military."

I had read various Egyptian books that highly praised my father, but then Arabs always praise their martyrs in glowing terms.
I took their lavish praise with a grain of salt. But here were my father's enemies praising him. It was quite breathtaking and caused
a flood of mixed emotions. The book went on to report:

> Mutafa Hafaz was a rarity in the Idarat Muchabarat al-
> Askariya ("The Egyptian Army Intelligence") in that he
> was a firm believer in egalitarian ideals. He cared little for
> the trappings of rank and privilege, and cared for his men's
> welfare and happiness in much the same manner as his Is-
> raeli counterparts had learned to do in the IDF Officers'
> Course. . . . Mutafa Hafaz also understood the Israelis: his
> admiration for the Israeli military refuted the claims of
> Egyptian propaganda. Unlike many of his counterparts in
> military HQ in Cairo who were plotting the destruction of

the Jewish state in an ennobled jihad ("holy war"), Lieu-
tenant Colonel Hafaz respected the Jews—their strengths
as well as their weaknesses.*

The book went on to paint my father as a military tactician
who was not motivated by hate, but by a sense of duty to his country and integrity as a soldier. The book described in detail Israel's
tortured debate on whether assassination of this "brilliant" foe was
justified, and how and why the decision was made to "eliminate"
him. It tells the story of several failed attempts on my father's life,
one of them by Ariel Sharon, until they finally devised a way to get
a package into Gaza that my father and only my father would be
likely to open—that fateful exploding package that would indeed
take his life.

In *Soldier Spies*, the story unfolds in all its spy-versus-spy in-
trigue. I was finally finding out exactly what happened. Some of
their facts were wrong, such as claiming my father opened the
package around midnight. It was in the early evening while there
was still some daylight. My mother and I remember the details all
too well. That day is ingrained into my very being. For all the hurt
it dredged up, the book also gave me a window into what an extraordinary man my father was, and what a great loss his death was
to Egypt and its future.

However, I was soon to learn even further startling truths about
my father. As I was concluding the last two chapters of this book, a
contact I'd made as a result of my Israel trip sent me some documents that shed more light and even contradicted things I had
learned about the fedayeen movement that my father headed in the
1950s. These insights came from official Egyptian military and intelligence records that fell into Israeli hands in the course of the
Israeli-Arab war after my father's death in 1956. They were found
in my father's office in the Palestine Intelligence office in Gaza. I

---

*Samuel M. Katz, *Soldier Spies* (Novato, CA: Presidio Press, 1992), pp. 120–21.

read these documents in awe. (Please note that my writing about Palestinian infiltrations in the first chapter of this book was based on Palestinian and Arab viewpoints combined with my own assessments. These newly discovered documents and the light they shed would now change and add to my perspective.)

The captured documents showed that in the beginning acts of infiltration into Israel were not a result of governmental initiative, but were originally initiated by local "strongmen" to carry out theft and revenge and serve as a shortcut between Arab countries. Perhaps that is why Egyptian authorities in Gaza originally jailed Palestinian infiltrators who were caught crossing the border into Israel. Documents point to Egyptian efforts, beginning in July 1952 and continuing over a long period of time, to stop these acts of infiltration. The one-page report by my father stated: "We have been keeping track of the acts of infiltration and have blocked them. Close to fifty persons have been arrested and these incidents have just about come to an end." The documents demonstrate that the Egyptian authorities' opposition to these incidents was not just one of words alone, but there were attempts of implementation in such a way as to subdue the population of the Gaza Strip to bring it into the realm of general Egyptian policy. It was for this reason that my father, Mustafa Hafez, the chief Egyptian intelligence officer, strongly opposed drafting Palestinian residents of the Strip, for he claimed in the same report: "The principle reason for the presence of forces along the cease-fire lines is to prevent acts of infiltration; attacks carried out from these borders will only result in increased tension."

At the bottom of this report, I found my father's typed signature and position: "Commander of the Palestinians Intelligence." Obviously my father, Colonel Mustafa Hafez, according to the document I now held in my hand, was opposed to infiltrations into Israel, but in the last days of 1955, the Egyptian Chief of Staff Abdel Hakim Amer gave an order to turn the Palestinian Civil Guards into a fedayeen reservoir. This signaled a high-level decision of the

Egyptian regime to turn the fedayeen into a military tool to be used against Israel.

My father, being a good and loyal military officer, followed his orders. However, disenchanted with his role and the dangers it posed for his family, he would put in a request to be transferred back to Cairo, a transfer that was approved but kept being postponed until it was finally scheduled to take place two weeks after the day my father was killed.

After reading these documents I wept. I knew that my father, as he wrote in this document signed by him, did not want to cause tension on the borders as a result of the infiltrations. It was Abdel Hakim Amer and President Nasser who directly gave orders to start the fedayeen activities. My father—and potentially my whole family—was sent to his death in Gaza by Nasser, who was consumed by his desire to destroy Israel. President Nasser, the man who wanted me, my brother, and my sisters to avenge my father's death by killing Jews, this man knowingly created and used the fedayeen to spread terror inside Israel. For all the wars, death, and suffering that resulted from this decision, Nasser blamed Israel and never blamed himself, not even for the 1967 war, which was a strategic blunder on his part.

The 1950s represent a different time and a different political climate. My father was an honorable soldier, and I now know in my heart that if he had lived, he would have been on that plane with President Sadat on his trip to Israel for peace. Perhaps I, his daughter, can carry out what I believe was going to be his natural development and final goal of peace. May God rest his soul.